LEAVING SPAIN

A BIOGRAPHICAL STUDY OF
AN ECONOMIC CRISIS AND NEW BEGINNINGS

LEAVING SPAIN

A BIOGRAPHICAL STUDY OF
AN ECONOMIC CRISIS AND NEW BEGINNINGS

Mê-Linh Riemann

Leuven University Press

The publication of this work was supported by the KU Leuven Fund for Fair Open Access. The study was financed by the Stiftung der Deutschen Wirtschaft (sdw) and the Cambridge Commonwealth European and International Trust.

Published in 2022 by Leuven University Press / Presses Universitaires de Louvain / Universitaire Pers Leuven. Minderbroedersstraat 4, B-3000 Leuven (Belgium).

Selection and editorial matter © Mê-Linh Riemann, 2022

This book is published under a Creative Commons Attribution Non-Commercial Non-Derivative 4.0 International Licence.

The licence allows you to share, copy, distribute, and transmit the work for personal and non-commercial use providing author and publisher attribution is clearly stated.

Attribution should include the following information:

Mê-Linh Riemann. *Leaving Spain: A Biographical Study of an Economic Crisis and New Beginnings.* Leuven: Leuven University Press, 2022. (CC BY-NC-ND 4.0)

ISBN 978 94 6270 328 5 (Paperback)
ISBN 978 94 6166 449 5 (ePDF)
ISBN 978 94 6166 450 1 (ePUB)
https://doi.org/10.11116/9789461664495
D/2022/1869/18
NUR: 756

Layout: Crius Group
Cover design: Daniel Benneworth-Gray
Cover illustration: Carmen José, 'Face with bull mask', 2021
Carmen José (°1991) is a Spanish illustrator and art educator interested in questioning the reproduction of visual stereotypes, with a focus on embodied processes. In her work she aims to facilitate spaces for dialogue and coming together working as a freelancer and as a teacher for Illustration and Social Practices in the WdKA Art University in Rotterdam. She left Spain in 2011 in search of academic and work opportunities after having engaged in the 15-M movement in Madrid. https://carmenjose.com/

For my informants

CONTENTS

Acknowledgements	9
1. Introduction	13
2. Mapping the Field	27
Phases of EU mobility: a timeline	28
Zooming in on the Spanish case	38
Taking on a biographical perspective	49
3. Biographical Case Studies	
Adam Sanchez	57
María Navarro	75
Mateo López	94
Where to go from here?	108
4. Time to go?	111
'Going abroad' in the context of one's academic training	112
Withstanding a collective mood of demoralisation	116
Trying to overcome a prolonged period of dependency and stagnation	119
Trying to cope with or escape from a trajectory of suffering	122
In search of professional recognition and adequate pay	128
Acquiring foreign language skills in order to gain a competitive advantage	131

5. On Studying and Working Abroad — 133
Exchange programmes as pathways into a long-term stay — 133
Alternatives to wage labour — 137
'Unskilled' labour? — 141
Skilled labour — 155
Voluntary work — 161

6. A Web of Social Relationships — 165
On working to maintain personal ties to Spain — 166
The emergence of new social relationships in the receiving society — 170
Spaces of transition — 178
Perceived barriers in everyday interactions — 179

7. Established-Outsider Relations in Times of Brexit — 189
The case of Diego — 191
Looking beyond the single case — 200
A note on the recent political developments — 202

8. An Uneasy Homecoming — 207
Returning as an answer to what? — 208
Moving 'back': expectations vs. reality — 215

9. Conclusion — 227
A brief overview of my findings — 227
Addressing different audiences — 232
Looking back and looking ahead — 241

10. Methodological Appendix — 245
A note on biographical research — 245
The autobiographical narrative interview and procedures of sequential analysis — 249
The history of my field research — 257
Data overview — 272
Consent form — 278

Notes — 279

References — 291

Index — 317

ACKNOWLEDGEMENTS

The study at hand is based on my doctoral thesis in sociology, which I completed at the University of Cambridge in autumn of 2020. This book is the final product of a line of research that already started when I was an undergraduate student at the University College Maastricht. Back then, I had no idea that it would eventually evolve into what it is today. I am glad that I could work in an academic environment, where I was encouraged to deepen my specific research interests, and to engage in exploring the relationship between biographies and collective developments and crises.

I am deeply grateful to many people who have supported me along the way.

First and foremost, I would like to thank my informants for their extraordinary openness. Throughout my fieldwork, I never ceased to be amazed at my interviewees' willingness and interest to share their entire life histories with *me* – a perfect stranger whom they were unlikely to ever see again. I never took this privilege for granted, and I hope to have done justice to what has been confided in me as a researcher. For the sake of anonymity, I cannot use their real names in this book, but they know who they are and what their collaboration has meant to me. I have often thought of them during the present Covid-19 pandemic and do wish them well through this unprecedented crisis.

My PhD supervisor, Dr. Anna Bagnoli, has helped me immensely throughout this whole research process. I consider myself very lucky in having had a PhD supervisor with whom I have so much in common, including our interest in qualitative methods and the experiences of migration. Anna's openness to different forms of interpreting biographical data has been nothing but encouraging and helpful. Her valuable comments on my work have helped me in structuring my findings and refining my analysis. I also appreciated Anna's expertise as an *Italian* researcher on southern European countries, which sensitised me to the role of extended family members in my informants' lives and many other phenomena.

At the Sociology Department in Cambridge, I would also like to thank Dr. Brendan Burchell and Dr. Thomas Jeffrey Miley for their support throughout the years. I have greatly appreciated their expertise on, e.g., the experience of unemployment, precarious work, social movements and (sub-) nationalism, which sensitised me to these issues as they appeared in the data.

I am very grateful to Professor Fritz Schütze (Otto-von-Guericke-Universität Magdeburg). His comments on my exploratory studies (BA, MPhil) guided me in my decision to continue this line of research in form of a PhD. I would also like to thank him for reading and commenting on previous drafts of chapter 7. Daniel Bertaux (Research Director, Emeritus, Centre National de la Recherche Scientifique (Paris) and Université de Strasbourg) and Professor Lena Inowlocki (Goethe-University Frankfurt) have been very supportive in the process of turning my dissertation into a book. Their critical yet encouraging feedback has enabled me to revisit my chapters with a fresh perspective and to refine the text accordingly. This manuscript has, furthermore, benefited from Professor Adrian Favell's (University of Leeds) help in identifying parts of an earlier draft, which could be misunderstood and needed clarification.

Throughout the past years, I was invited to present my research on various occasions and receive valuable feedback. I would like to thank Professor Ursula Apitzsch for inviting me to give a presentation at the Goethe-University in Frankfurt at an early stage of my research project. Professor Roswitha Breckner from the University of Vienna provided detailed feedback on first versions of case studies, some of which appear in chapter 3. I would also like to thank the organisers and participants at the Joint Doctoral Workshop that was held at Sciences Po in Paris in April 2019. I am particularly grateful to Professor Virginie Guiraudon for her encouraging comments on a working paper that served as the basis for chapter 7.

I would like to thank my friends who made the past years a very memorable and important chapter in my life. While it would be impossible to name everyone who has become dear to me since I started the PhD, I would like to express my deepest gratitude to Dr. Tanisha Spratt, Dr. Ali Meghji, Norma Deseke, Josh Ivinson, Olivia le Blanc, Maria Jose Liebers, Karina Jakupsdottir, Omer Friedlander, Sarah Ventura, Renee Meijer, Rhea Flach and Corinna Seeger. Last but not least, I would like to thank my good friends Alba Vasquez for her help in transcribing my data, Dr. Melissa Gatter for thoroughly proofreading my chapters, and Carmen José for providing such a thoughtful cover illustration.

I was very fortunate to receive full funding for my doctoral research. I would like to express my deepest gratitude to the Stiftung der Deutschen Wirtschaft (sdw) for their generous financial support. Their trust in my abilities as a researcher, and their belief in the potential of this study has meant a lot to me. I very much enjoyed the numerous sdw seminars, get-togethers, trips and writing workshops that I got to attend throughout the years. I would also like to thank the Cambridge European Trust for covering my tuition fees for the duration of the degree programme. Without these scholarships, I would not have been able to attend the University of Cambridge, an experience that I would never have wanted to miss, neither on a personal nor academic level.

I am very much indebted to St. Edmund's College for granting me the Duke of Edinburgh Award, which greatly facilitated my fieldwork and several conference attendances. Throughout the years, *Eddies* has indeed become a second home for me, and I will forever be grateful for the memories and friendships I got to form through this community.

At the Catholic University of Leuven, I would like to thank Professor Valeria Pulignano for giving me the opportunity to continue doing research on biographies, precarity, and economic crises in a wider European context (i.e. in the ERC-funded research project 'ResPecTMe: Researching Precariousness across the Paid/Unpaid Work Continuum'). I would also like to thank my colleague Claudia Marà for taking a personal interest in this study, and for pointing out the parallels to other intra-European migration waves, including from Italy to Belgium.

Leuven University Press has been very supportive of my manuscript from the start. Getting such an enthusiastic response from the Editorial Board and my editor Mirjam Truwant on my first draft was a great relief, and our collaboration since then could not have been better. Annemie Vandezande and Daniel Benneworth-Gray were very helpful in the process of coming up with the cover design. Their expertise and willingness to incorporate my own ideas have made this part very enjoyable. I would also like to thank Constance Batterbury for her attention to detail when copy-editing the final manuscript. I am very grateful to the KU Leuven Fund for Fair Open Access for their generous financial support in covering the book processing charges. As an early career researcher, receiving this support has been essential on the road to publication. It is truly a privilege to publish my study in an OA format, as it is my conviction that research findings should be as accessible as possible, independent of one's financial means.

Finally, I would like to thank my parents Lê and Gerhard Riemann, my brother Minh Riemann, and my aunt and uncle Hannegret and Friedrich-Karl Schröder for their unfailing support on every level.

1. INTRODUCTION

Europe is in crisis *again*[1]. Covid-19 has brought about societal changes that would have formerly been deemed unimaginable. Back in mid-2019, the concept of lockdowns, the closing of national borders, so-called 'social distancing', and wearing medical masks must have appeared very abstract. Today, more than two years into this pandemic, such restrictions have become very much part of our everyday life. At the time of writing, the World Health Organization (WHO) reports over 5.4 million coronavirus related deaths worldwide, whilst the number of unreported cases is likely to be much higher (WHO, 2022). The effects of 'long Covid-19' are, furthermore, still widely unknown and understudied.

Covid-19 is currently affecting *all* of Europe and the rest of the world. There are, however, important national differences in how societies have been affected by (and coped with) the virus and its devastating repercussions during different stages of this pandemic. During the first wave in the beginning of 2020, southern European countries struggled to accommodate the unprecedented and sudden increase in intensive care unit (ICU) patients[2]. The images of army trucks transporting piled-up coffins out of Bergamo, or news about Spanish hospitals and elderly homes at the verge of collapse were registered with horror in other parts of Europe.

At the time, commentators were quick to point out how austerity measures, which had been introduced in response to the 2008 financial crisis, had left the healthcare systems across southern Europe ill-equipped to deal with an epidemic of this scale (Hedgecoe, 2020). Not only did hospitals lack the necessary equipment for the high number of (ICU) patients, many also suffered from a severe labour shortage. Throughout the past decade, many healthcare workers had left the region to work elsewhere in the European Union and overseas. These healthcare workers represented a considerable workforce, which has been missing in its home countries' efforts to cope with Covid-19 (Costa-Font et al., 2021). Although southern European societies have – since then – been hailed as exemplary in their willingness and efforts to get vaccinated[3], these types of systemic health inequalities persist across the continent. What the current pandemic has demonstrated quite clearly is the need to take longer time spans into account when reconstructing how different collective crises overlap and exacerbate the structural vulnerabilities in various European societies.

Apart from the devastating cost of human lives, there is widespread worry about the long-term economic repercussions of this on-going pandemic. After the financial crisis of 2008, southern Europe had finally been on the road to a slow economic recovery. The coronavirus has cast a dark shadow on this development. Even the tourism sector, which had formerly been considered comparatively crisis-proof in this region, has completely collapsed in 2020.

Although it is difficult to make exact economic predictions at this point in time, policymakers have expressed concern about the potential emergence of "Covid-19's *lost generation*" (Tamesberger & Bacher, 2020), a term that evokes painful memories of the 2008 economic crisis and its devastating repercussions for young people across the region.[4] Back then, employment "suddenly became uncertain, credit was restricted to a few, consumption was reduced to the essentials, social services were deeply cut, and a dark cloud engulfed on the future of their children, reversing the pattern of higher expectations for the next generation" (Conill et al., 2012, p. 210). Across southern Europe, millions of people lost their jobs, homes and, at times, means of existence.

More than a decade after the financial crash of 2008, finding a stable job in one's field of expertise remains a difficult challenge for recent university graduates, forcing many into a prolonged state of economic dependency on their parents (Ayala-Hurtado, 2021). Applying for jobs in one's country of origin can be extremely demoralising, as the competition for the few jobs available is very fierce. One's chances on the labour market are, furthermore, impeded by other deep structural problems, such as nepotism and corruption, that have beset the region for many decades.

THE ORIGINS OF THIS RESEARCH PROJECT

I first developed an academic interest in the social and biographical consequences of the 2008 economic crisis during my final year as an undergraduate student at the University College Maastricht (UCM) in 2013. Spain in particular caught my interest, as I was impressed by the images of hundreds of thousands of young people taking to the streets of Madrid and other cities to express their outrage about the austerity measures and the lack of future opportunities (cf. 15-M, Indignados movement).[5] It was the height of the economic crisis, as the youth unemployment rate[6] exceeded a staggering 56.1%. As someone with little previous knowledge about Spain, I was curious to learn more about the lived reality behind these high unemployment rates and the heated political discourse. In many ways, I could personally relate to many protestors I saw on the news. We were about the same age, shared a middle-class upbringing, and had gone to university in the hope of eventually gaining financial independence. For many young people, the latter had suddenly become very difficult to achieve in their native Spain. Due to structural forces outside of their control, central biographical projects (such as working in one's field of expertise and gaining economic stability) seemed at high risk – a collective development that was not only demoralising, but had almost a violent component to it. Something very important had been taken away from them through no fault of their own.

Trying to find a job under such adverse conditions can be a depressing prospect, which prompted many graduates to look for work elsewhere. Taking advantage of their right to 'free movement' as EU citizens, many people headed north in search of work and life opportunities. Germany and the United Kingdom (pre-Brexit) have thereby been among the most popular destinations (Gonzalez-Ferrer, 2013; Godenau, 2017).

This 'new' south-north movement[7] was, perhaps, not totally unexpected. In the European Union, the economic repercussions of the financial crisis of 2008 were far from distributed equally in geographic terms (Lafleur & Stanek, 2017). Whilst the south has been deeply affected, other countries – mainly in western and northern Europe – recovered from the initial shock relatively quickly.

MEASURING INTRA-EUROPEAN MOVEMENTS: SOME ESTIMATES AND OBSTACLES

When reconstructing the emergence of this new migration wave, it is important to consider the respective unemployment statistics. According to Eurostat (2022), the total unemployment rate in Spain rose from 7.9% in May 2007 to 26.3% in April 2013 – the period in which many of my informants decided to migrate to Germany and the UK as a way out of unbearable life situations (see chapter 4). Since then, there have been clear signs of economic recovery as the total unemployment rate was measured at 13.6% in February 2020. At the time, youth unemployment was estimated to be 30.9%, which was five times higher than in Germany (5.3%) and more than twice as high as in the UK (13.5%). The situation was exacerbated by the coronavirus pandemic as youth unemployment in Spain rose very rapidly to 39.5% in January 2021. After extended periods of lockdown, the labour market conditions for young people have improved as youth unemployment was estimated to be 29.4% in January 2022. This is, however, still the second highest rate in all of Europe after Greece (31.4%) (Fig. 1).

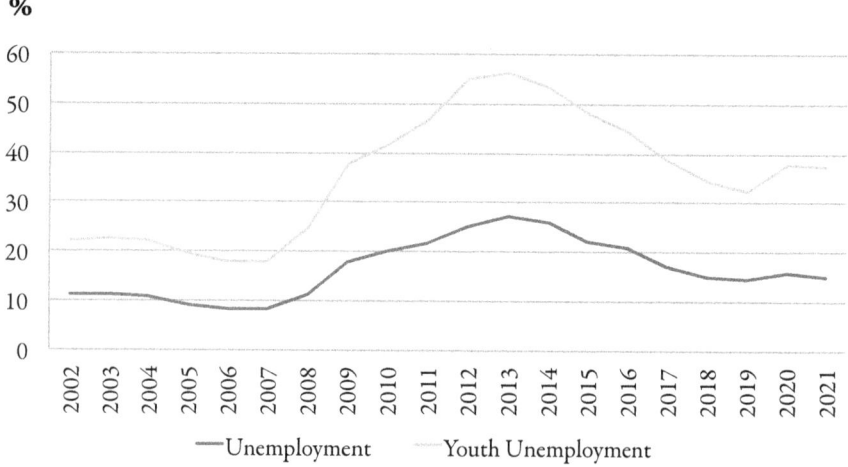

Figure 1: Total and youth unemployment rates in Spain (2002-2021), (Eurostat, 2022)

When bringing up the topic of the new south-north movement in casual conversations, people are quick to point to anecdotal evidence of hearing more Spanish being spoken on the streets of Bristol or Berlin in recent years. Capturing these types of intra-European migration flows statistically has, however, been very challenging (Glorius & Dominguez-Mujica, 2017). When deciding to move from one member state to another, EU citizens are not necessarily required to de-register from the local authorities in their home countries. Many choose not to, as they hope to maintain access to the local healthcare system at home.

In the new country, the procedures are also far from being straightforward. Some migrants plan to stay only for a short period of time and therefore see no point in registering. In some countries, the procedure can be very bureaucratic, time-consuming, and daunting for a non-native speaker. Furthermore, there is little to fear if you fail to register as this negligence is rarely punished. The emigration statistics published by the Spanish government have been criticised as especially flawed, as they refer exclusively to the people who choose to register with the Spanish consulate in the respective receiving society – a step that is by no means obligatory within the European Union (González-Ferrer, 2013; González-Ferrer & Moreno-Fuentes, 2017).

Despite these obstacles, there are certain indicators that help grasp the magnitude of this 'new' migration wave from Spain. In the case of the UK, these estimates are two-fold. Before the UK left the European Union (the so-called 'Brexit'), the most commonly cited statistics regarding EU migration flows were the number of new registrations for a National Insurance Number (NIN) per year, a step that is considered a prerequisite for taking up both formal and informal employment. From 2002 to 2007, circa 10,000 Spanish people registered with the NHS each year, a number that is quite low in comparison to other EU mobility flows during that time (e.g. from Poland). This trend changed with the onset of the economic crisis in 2008, as the number of Spanish nationals registering for a NIN started to rise exponentially and peaked in 2013, when over 50,000 applications were received. Since then, the figures have decreased to circa 7,000 in 2021 (Department of Work and Pensions, 2022) (Fig. 2).

The implementation of Brexit has brought about significant changes for EU citizens living in the UK. Those who want to stay in Britain had to apply for the 'EU Settlement Scheme' until the 30th of June 2021. Whilst the Home Office is still processing these requests, they have published some preliminary figures (Home Office, 2021). By June 2021, over 356,090 Spanish citizens had applied for the EU settlement scheme, making it the fifth most common nationality after Polish (1,107,060), Romanian (1,082,260), Italian (549,510), and Portuguese (418,070).

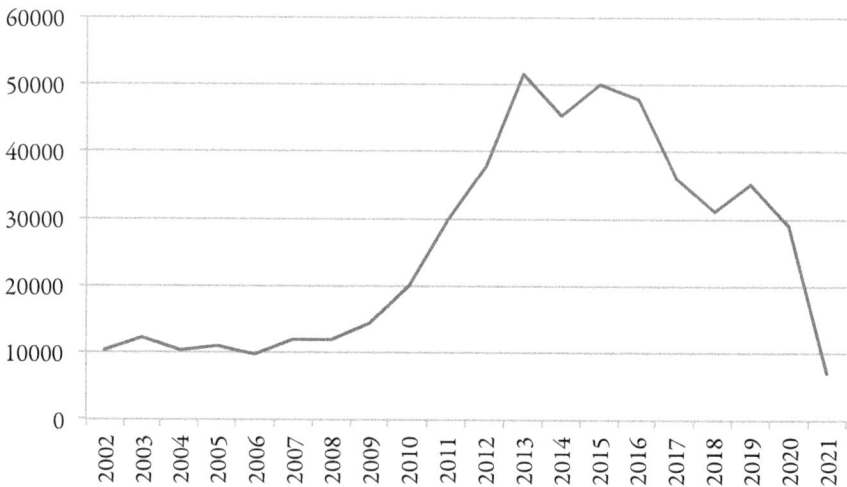

Figure 2: Total number of NIN registrations by Spanish nationals per year (UK) (2002-2021) (Department for Work and Pensions, 2022)

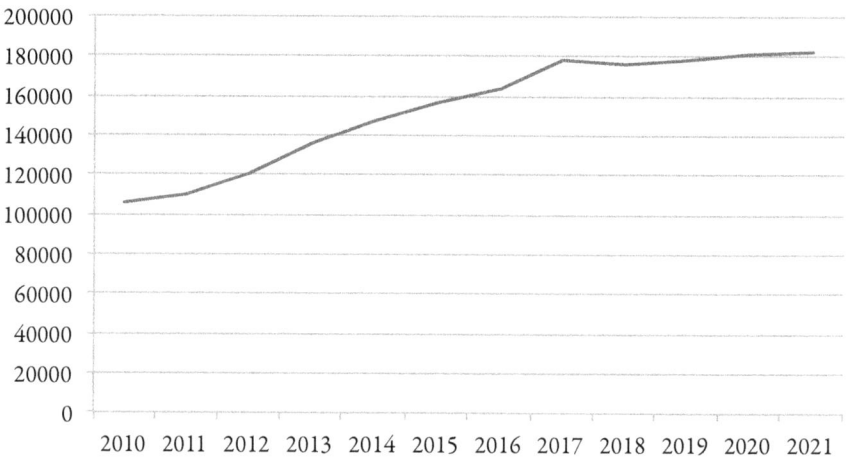

Figure 3: Total number of Spanish citizens registered in Germany (2010-2021) (Bundesagentur für Arbeit, 2022)

In Germany, capturing these migration flows is even more difficult, as Spanish citizens are not required to inform the respective authorities about their move. There are, however, some statistics available with regard to those who did register in their city of arrival. From 2008 to 2021, the Spanish population in Germany officially grew from about 100,000 to circa 180,000 people, a figure that is likely to capture only a fraction of the actual movement during this time period (Bundesagentur für Arbeit, 2022) (Fig. 3).

The cited statistics should be interpreted as an estimate rather than an exact measurement of how many Spanish citizens reside in the respective arrival countries. The difficulties in capturing intra-European migration flows in quantitative terms also have to do with the emergence of phenomena, which have been referred to as 'transnationalism', 'transmigration' and 'circular' migration flows (Vertovec, 2009). Many migrants maintain close ties to their home country and some stay in the receiving society for only a short period of time before either returning home or moving to a third destination. When looking at the high number of NIN registrations per year, it is difficult to estimate how many people actually 'settled' in Britain (at least for a few years) and how many stayed perhaps only for one summer to work, save some money and improve their English.[8] In spite of these drawbacks, the figures give a first impression of the magnitude of this phenomenon. Leaving Spain in the context of the 2008 economic crisis has indeed become a mass phenomenon and a path that thousands of (especially young) people have taken, often in the hope of a better future.

A SOURCE OF POLITICAL CONTENTION

Although Spain is no stranger to mass emigration waves,[9] the mass departure of mostly university graduates was seen as unprecedented. Never before had the education level of Spanish migrants been that high, which incited controversies about the dangers of a potential 'brain drain'. For a long time, the former conservative government under Prime Minister Mariano Rajoy (2011-2018) avoided acknowledging the existence of the phenomenon publicly, as it was seen as a source of potential embarrassment that could even trigger a crisis of legitimacy. In 2012, Marina del Corral, the former Secretary General of Immigration and Emigration, attempted to attenuate the emerging public image of Spain as a country to 'escape from' by claiming that young people had come to the decision to migrate out of a 'spirit of adventure' (Díaz Hernández & Parreño Castellano, 2017). According to her logic, young Spaniards had reached such a high level of education that many doors across Europe and overseas were wide open. The mass departure of university graduates should therefore be regarded as a sign of how international and modern Spain had become since its transition to democracy.

Del Corral's strategy backfired, as Spanish migrants took to Twitter and other social media platforms expressing their anger about her attempt to 'gloss over' the recent development. Under the hashtag #nonosvamosnosechan (translation: "we are not leaving, we are expelled"), thousands of people shared and mutually reaffirmed their frustrating experiences of having felt forced to take that step. Staying in Spain, they argued, was not a viable option due to the pervasive lack of attractive alternatives and governmental support. The online activists also took issue with the image of young Spanish professionals pursuing fulfilling international careers. By sharing their personal stories of working in menial jobs abroad (Serra, 2014), they underlined the difficulties of breaking the cycle of precariousness even after moving to a new country. What they went through was thereby portrayed as not only a Spanish problem, but also a European problem.

The Spanish left was quick to pick up on this widespread frustration, incorporating the plight of those living abroad into their agenda. In April 2013, the anti-austerity organisation 'Juventud sin futuro' organised a campaign specifically for those in self-proclaimed 'economic exile',[10] an initiative that would later evolve into a separate transnational network known as the 'Maroon Wave' (named after the colour of Spanish passports) (López-Sala, 2017, 2019). Since its formation in 2014, the leftist party Podemos has also made efforts to include Spanish emigrants in their electoral programme, such as in the form of proposals to finance social aid for 'those expulsed by the crisis and in need' (Bermudez & Brey, 2017, p. 93).

The differing political stances on the 'new' migration wave are also reflected in its media coverage. Since 2010, the state-owned public broadcaster Televisión Española has been featuring a very popular TV programme titled 'Españoles en el mundo'. Each episode consists of various short portrayals of Spanish people living and working abroad. The show thereby focuses almost exclusively on success stories of so-called 'expats' who 'made it' in a foreign country. The tone of the show is decisively upbeat and optimistic, as its producers seem to carefully edit out anything that does not fit the 'feel-good' narrative (Cobo-Duran & Hernandez-Santaolalla, 2015).

In contrast to that, some left-leaning filmmakers (and newspapers) have made an effort to highlight the difficulties people commonly face when moving to another country. One example is Iciar Bollain's documentary 'En tierra extraña' (2014) on Spanish nationals living in Edinburgh. The film paints a much darker picture on what life abroad entails, as the protagonists openly speak about their struggles with loneliness, their difficulties in getting used to the colder weather, and having to work in low-paid manual jobs that are below their academic qualifications. Their migration projects were thereby framed as a 'sad tale' (Goffman, 1968b, pp. 140-142) of being in 'economic exile' – an impression that was further enhanced by the melancholic background music and the imagery of constant rain and darkness.

Depending on their specific agenda, politicians and activists on each political side seem to frame this 'new' migration wave as either a positive or negative development.[11] These broad public images are very powerful, but rarely capture the multi-layered and sometimes conflicting experiences that individuals associate with their personal migration projects. Migrating from one country to another is a biographically complex undertaking. Understanding it properly requires maintaining some analytical distance from the heated public debates and the pervasive collective images in this arena.

ADOPTING A BIOGRAPHICAL PERSPECTIVE

This book is based on a biographical study about the 'new' Spanish migration to Germany and the United Kingdom. When approaching the topic from a research perspective, I wanted to give Spanish migrants the time and space to share their own story – and their 'whole story'. Keeping a distance to terms such as 'economic exile' is anything but apolitical. It simply means being open for new discoveries (Glaser & Strauss, 1967) instead of presupposing how collective crises and structural conditions have shaped their life histories. The 'how' awaits discovery.

Instead of reducing the participants to the status of 'migrant workers', I wanted to discover how their migration – including experiences of transmigration (Siouti, 2013) or circular migration (Vertovec, 2013) and remigration – fits into the whole of their life-histories. I was, furthermore, intent on reconstructing how my informants' theories about their own lives can be contextualised in their biographical experiences. Studying the country-specific experiences of Spanish migrants, i.e. their experiences at home *or* later in their destination country, would have been limiting in the analysis, as the different phases in their lives are interconnected. The aforementioned controversy in Spanish politics about how to evaluate the phenomenon of the mass exodus of (mostly) young people raises many questions. There is uncertainty not only about how people make the decision to leave ('spirit of adventure' vs. 'economic exile'), but also about what awaits them in the new country ('self-fulfilment' vs. 'exploitation'). By paying close attention to *how* people's lives developed prior to the migration, continue to evolve in the new country and are shaped by processes of transmigration and return migration, one may gain a more nuanced and deeper view of what is actually happening.

Furthermore, the biographies of Spanish migrants reflect different macro-developments in Europe. Their lives were first marked by the economic crisis in Spain (in some cases along with Catalonia's strive for independence). After moving to a new country, people's biographies continued to be shaped by the political developments in the receiving society such as the emergence and implementation of Brexit in the UK. If a researcher were to limit his or her focus on what is happening in one country, it would be difficult to analyse how these different European crises are connected and reflected in the lifelines of individuals.

In the past years, there have been a number of notable social scientific efforts to approach the phenomenon of the 'new' Spanish migration. Researchers from Spain and other countries have collected quantitative and qualitative data about (young) people's motives to leave Spain, their participation in social movements (e.g. Marea Granate) and/or specific communication practices (chapter 2). What has been missing so far, however, is a comprehensive study on the long-term biographical processes in recent Spanish migrants' lives. The study at hand is a response to this gap in research.

For this research project, I collected 58 autobiographical narrative interviews (Schütze, 2008) and four follow-up interviews with Spanish migrants who were either currently based in Germany or the UK or who had been there prior to their return to Spain (cf. methodological appendix). I conducted the vast majority of interviews in Spanish and later translated them (or parts of them) into English. When choosing my informants, I refrained from limiting my focus to a specific age group or people of a certain education level or class background. Instead, I wanted to be open to very different biographies of individuals who left Spain in the past decade and approach the phenomenon from a holistic point of view.

The aim of this study has been to develop a sequential model of different phases of Spanish migrants' biographies and how they are interconnected. In doing so it makes use of a type of methodology and analysis that has turned out to be fruitful and 'fine-grained' for discovering and reconstructing biographical and other social processes (Schütze, 2008; Riemann, 2018). In developing a specific form of biographical research, German sociologist Fritz

Schütze has combined insights from socio-linguistics and Grounded Theory (Glaser & Strauss, 1967). After reviewing the relevant literature on intra-European mobility and the 'new' Spanish migration (chapter 2), I will present three in-depth case studies of interviewees whom I call Adam Sanchez, María Navarro, and Mateo López (chapter 3). The specific research questions guiding the rest of the empirical chapters emerged out of the contrasting comparison of these three biographical case studies. Introducing the foci of this study in conclusion to the case study – rather than in the introduction of this monograph or at the end of the literature review – was a deliberate decision. When writing up my findings, I was intent on making the steps of analysis quite visible and creating a structure that reflected my research journey.

In the five comparative empirical chapters (4-8), I draw on the whole data material in order to reassess and differentiate my findings further from the in-depth case studies. These chapters deal with (a) the biographical conditions and processes in which the decisions to migrate evolved, (b) the experiences and biographical meaning of studying and working abroad, (c) the web of social relationships in the host society and at home, (d) the impact of an unexpected collective crisis – Brexit – on everyday life and its biographical meaning, and (e) the experiences of returning to Spain. I regard each of these stages and aspects as part of larger biographical processes. Rather than separate entities, these chapters comprise a sequential model of different phases of my informants' migration experience – and should be read as such. In chapter 9, I conclude with some reflections on the potential of biographical research in studying contemporary Europe and its overlapping collective crises (mass unemployment in southern Europe, Brexit etc.). At the end of this book, readers will find a comprehensive methodological appendix (chapter 10), where I refer to the history of biographical research and give an overview of fieldwork that I have conducted over the course of five years. This study is a contribution to biographical analysis, migration research and European studies.

For readers unfamiliar with this form of biographical research, the in-depth analysis of single cases – the specificities of the processes of acting and suffering as they are revealed in people's oral narratives – may be irritating. It is my conviction that by studying biographical experiences openly, patiently and in depth, it is possible to gain a deeper understanding of collective crises and disasters, i.e., how such developments impinge on the personal sphere and are taken into account and how people develop creative ways to cope with macro crises but also sometimes lose their agency and are caught in trajectories of suffering (a term which will become important for my analysis). This is not just my personal conviction, but also an assumption that I share with many biographical researchers who work with narratives. It would be misleading to relegate such studies to the field of micro-sociology. Biographical research has always been marked by an intense interest in bridging the micro-macro gap and in discovering the nuances of the relationship between structural conditions and life histories. I thereby keep to the maxim of C. Wright Mills, who concluded his landmark book "The Sociological Imagination" (1959) with the following statement (p. 226).

> Know that the problems of social science, when adequately formulated, must include both troubles and issues, both biography and history, and the range of their intricate relations. Within that range the life of the individual and the making of societies occur; and within that range the sociological imagination has its chance to make a difference in the quality of human life in our time.

When writing up my findings, I decided to discuss my data from Germany and the United Kingdom jointly rather than in separate chapters. This decision was deliberate, as I saw more commonalities between my informants in each field site than differences. Whenever I noticed differences between the two field sites (such as perceived cultural differences, labour market regulations, the impact of a collective crisis), I considered them in my analysis, and drew readers' attention to them.

A NOTE ON THE TERMINOLOGY

Finally, I would like to comment on my use of the term 'migrant'. There are very good reasons why social scientists avoid the application of such terms for 'free movement' within the European Union. A non-reflective application entails the risk of participating in attempts to turn EU citizens into strangers and deprive them of their rights. As William Outhwaite (2019, p. 97) writes in his discussion of the exploitation of the migration issue in the manufacture of 'Brexit': "We should, in any case, not be using the term immigrants to refer to European Union free movers." I thought long and hard about this problem. My final decision to refer to my interviewees as 'migrants' and to their move to other EU member states as 'migration' had to do with the self-conception or the 'first-order constructs' (in the sense of Alfred Schütz) of many of my informants. The biographical narratives I collected revealed that quite a few people took pride in coming from a family of 'migrants', a term they used when referring to their parents' or grandparents' move from Andalusia to other regions such as Madrid.

2. MAPPING THE FIELD

Throughout the past decades, intra-European migration flows have received considerable attention in the social sciences. In order to shed light on how the 'new' Spanish migration fits into this picture, it is useful to map out the wider intra-EU mobility trends as they have developed over the course of the past decades. The following chapter is therefore divided as follows.

The first part provides a literature-based overview of three different but overlapping strands of intra-European mobility, the origins of which can be retraced to different geopolitical events: post-1993 (Maastricht Treaty), post-2004/2007 (EU-Eastward Enlargements), post-2008 (Economic Crisis). This timeline serves as the basis for the second part of this chapter, which 'zooms in' on the literature specifically dealing with the 'new' Spanish migration. The purpose of this section is to provide a first thematic overview of what has been published so far. Social scientists from various disciplines (e.g. sociology, anthropology, human geography) have made very valuable contributions to studying the 'new' Spanish migration.

The question of where I see some shortcomings in the existing literature will subsequently be addressed in the third section. In the fourth and final part of this literature review, I will introduce the research perspective of this study by making the case for taking on a *holistic and biographical view*. Given the scope of this book, it would be impossible to provide an exhaustive literature review on the entire field of EU-mobility. Instead, I present a careful selection of important, mostly qualitative studies that deal with the 'lived reality' of EU movers in different contexts. This literature covers a time period prior to the current coronavirus pandemic. Its long-term repercussions on intra-EU mobility flows are still unknown.

PHASES OF EU MOBILITY: A TIMELINE

The following overview provides a chronological periodisation of different phases of EU mobility (cf. King & Pratsinakis, 2019). The first phase of 'free movement' refers to the time period following the Maastricht Treaty of 1993. Back then, the right to move and work freely within the European Union was reserved for citizens of the original twelve – and from 1995 onwards, fifteen – member states (EU-15). The scale of (mostly labour) migration increased significantly in the second phase of EU mobility after the so-called eastward enlargements of 2004 and 2007. The third phase of 'free movement' can be retraced to the global financial crisis of 2008, which triggered a mass departure of mostly young university graduates from the so-called PIGS states in southern Europe (Portugal, Italy, Greece and Spain). It is important to point out that these different migration flows did not subside after the beginning of a 'new' phase. Instead, the movements of economically successful and less successful citizens from different EU member states continue to co-exist and change along with macro-developments that have shaped our continent in recent years (e.g. Brexit, coronavirus pandemic etc.).

Post-1993

The European Union was officially established after the Maastricht Treaty came into force in November 1993. The pact's objectives were to "create an ever closer union among the peoples of Europe" and to "promote economic and social progress (…) through the creation of an area without internal frontiers" (Treaty on European Union, 1992, p. 7). Firstly, the Maastricht Treaty laid the foundation for what would eventually become a monetary union (cf. introduction of the euro in 2002). Secondly, the agreement introduced 'European citizenship', which entitled passport holders to move to and work freely in other EU member states.

The immediate increase in EU mobility following the Maastricht Treaty was quite modest. According to King and Pratsinakis (2019), the removal of legal barriers was insufficient to incentivise 'the masses' to move to different EU member states. The economic inequalities between the original fifteen member states were not very large, which made a purely economically motivated move (e.g. from Germany to France) quite unlikely. Furthermore, most citizens' personal and work networks were firmly rooted in their country of origin. For many people, leaving their familiar structures behind was a daunting prospect, as language and cultural barriers appeared difficult to overcome. Although the scale of intra-EU mobility grew more slowly than originally expected, an increasing number of Europeans started to explore their new freedom from the mid-1990s onwards. King and Pratsinakis (2019) distinguish between three different strands of mobility, which they consider paradigmatic of that period: student mobility, the movement of highly skilled workers, and lifestyle migration. Whilst none of these forms of movement were entirely novel, the Maastricht Treaty facilitated such migration projects by making them significantly less bureaucratic.

Firstly, there is the movement of university students who take part in exchange programmes within the context of their academic training. The Erasmus programme, which was first introduced in the late 1980s, has been widely celebrated as a success story. Krzaklewska (2013) argues that taking part in an exchange programme enables university students to both enjoy their youth as well as overcome challenges in a foreign environment, which helps the students to become more mature. In the biographical interviews she collected, her participants frequently spoke about their Erasmus experience in a way that resembled a 'coming of age' narrative. This form of storytelling has also found its way into popular culture such as in the critically acclaimed movie 'L'Auberge Espagnole' (2002), which depicts the transformative journey of a French graduate student who spends two semesters in Barcelona (cf. Ousselin, 2009). The positive long-term effects of taking part in an exchange programme at university are well documented in academic literature. King and Ruiz-Gelices (2003) found out that Erasmus students develop a stronger sense of a 'European identity' and are more likely to subsequently move abroad again at a later stage of their lives. This raises questions about the experiences of EU movers, who are no longer students but perhaps share some characteristics with their younger counterparts.

For his book 'Eurostars and Eurocities', Favell (2008) conducted 60 in-depth interviews with highly skilled EU citizens, who had moved to the metropolitan areas of Amsterdam, Brussels and London. The sample of this study includes informants from various EU-15 member states who differ in terms of their age, gender, educational background, current occupation, language skills, family constellations as well as general biographical circumstances. What they shared was a high level of professional success, as most informants had fulfilling and well-paid careers in their fields of expertise. The data material is characterised by the dominance of evaluative commentaries, in which the participants openly reflected about the advantages and disadvantages of living and working in a European society other than their country or origin. Favell (2008) provides readers with insights into the milieu of his informants, whom he refers to as 'Eurostars' to mark them as members of a vanguard of European free movers. He generally adopts an optimistic outlook on EU mobility by highlighting the emancipatory quality of moving to a new country. Examples of the latter include opportunities to advance one's career in a stimulating professional environment, to form biographically significant relationships with fellow Europeans, as well as to learn about new cultures and languages.

Quite a few of his southern European participants expressed a deep sense of frustration about nepotism and arbitrary career paths at home (p. 63) – structural problems that evidently preceded the global financial crisis of 2008 by many years. What makes Favell's (2008) informants stand out is that they were usually trained in occupations that were highly sought after in the receiving societies (e.g. international law, finance, aeronautical engineering). Therefore, they could realistically expect to work in their fields of expertise immediately upon arriving in the new country without having to plan for a transition period working in the informal economy, a characteristic that sets them apart from the majority of participants in my study. The interviewees spoke about their decision to migrate as a 'rational choice' in terms of their career development, whilst at the same time alluding to important biographical costs such as being separated from friends and family at home.

The latter is one example of the challenges and downsides of transnational living, which become visible at different points throughout the book. Some informants spoke about painful processes such as losing friendships in their country of origin, difficulties relating to 'settling down', the dissolution of marriages, as well as financial insecurities concerning retirement, problems that Favell (2008) broadly subsumes under the Durkheimian concept of anomie (chapter 13). Such challenges should not be brushed off as the 'first world problems' of an economically privileged group of expats. A few narratives convey a deep sense of alienation, which sometimes had to do with linguistic and cultural barriers that proved to be very difficult to overcome. Even though the informants were 'white' western Europeans and financially stable, they were not exempt from subtle – and sometimes not so subtle – mechanisms of exclusion that reminded them of their foreigner status (cf. the case of Nina, p. 146/147). This was a source of frustration especially among those who had already spent many years living and working in their 'adopted city' in another European society. In the light of these findings, one can raise critical questions about the appropriateness of the term 'Eurostar'. The expression has a very optimistic, if not celebratory, tone to it, which does not always do justice to the at times depressing day-to-day reality of the informants, which includes their mixed emotions about their decision to live abroad.

The third form of mobility that is commonly associated with the post-Maastricht era is the so-called 'lifestyle migration' to southern European countries, mostly after retirement (cf. Benson & O'Reilly, 2009). The scale of the phenomenon is considerable. In 2020, the composition of the British community in Spain is estimated at between 300,000 and one million full- and part-time residents, many of whom are over the age of 65 (O'Reilly, 2020). Whilst Erasmus students and 'Eurostars' (Favell, 2008) are generally portrayed as especially cosmopolitan and open-minded, the findings on elderly lifestyle movers are more ambiguous. In his chapter on 'sunset migration', King (2012) discusses the emergence of 'expat bubbles' or ethnic enclaves where people recreate the comforts of home in a milder climate. Some of his interviewees reduced personal interactions with locals to a minimum, preferring to socialise with fellow British pensioners. Whilst such secluded enclaves exist, various researchers argue against an overly simplistic view of the British community in Spain, a group that is often stereotyped as being quite close-minded. On the basis of her long-term research, O'Reilly (2020) argues that this community now includes "every kind of diversity that exists in the UK", e.g. in terms of age, employment, family relations, and socio-economic background (cf. Henley, 2020).

One theme that frequently appears in the literature on 'lifestyle migration' is that of health-related problems. In their study on frail elderly British citizens in Spain, Hall and Hardill (2016) found that many recent retirees underestimate the serious complications that can appear later in life as they enter into the 'fourth age' (dependence and decline). The authors found that there are quite a few linguistic, cultural and financial barriers that make it difficult for vulnerable British pensioners to access Spanish healthcare. Some retirees fall through the support gap, whereby they are no longer entitled to UK welfare services whilst not being fully recognised by the receiving society either. Brexit, of course, further complicates the matter. Although Britain has already left the European Union by now, many details concerning citizenship rights, health insurance, and freedom of movement are yet to be finalised. There are ongoing negotiations that add much insecurity to the lives of British retirees in Spain (Giner-Monfort & Huete, 2021).

Post-2004 and 2007

King and Pratsinakis (2019) argue that up until the mid-2000s, intra-EU mobility was regarded as unproblematic. Fewer people than expected were moving, partly because the economic inequalities between the EU-15 member states were not that large. This changed after the 2004 and 2007 accession rounds that incorporated 10 eastern and central European countries into the Union. In contrast to their western European counterparts, these 'new' EU citizens did not hesitate to make use of the right to move and work elsewhere. Taking into account that the average salaries in these post-Communist countries ranged from a tenth to about a quarter of the average EU-15 countries, this development was not surprising (King & Pratsinakis, 2019; Recchi, 2015, p. 93). It is estimated that the number of Polish citizens in the UK rose from 75,000 in 2003 to over one million in 2017 (Clark, 2020).[1] To say that this is a significant increase would be an understatement.

The question of why so many Poles headed to Britain during this time period can partly be retraced to the fact that the UK (along with Ireland and Sweden) opened its borders immediately after the enlargement. This was different in other western European countries, which planned for a two-year transition period during which they only gradually granted the newcomers the full right to 'free movement'. By 2006 and 2007, the mobility restrictions for citizens from the so-called A-10 EU member states had mostly lifted in all other member states except for Austria and Germany, which maintained the measures until April 2009 (Favell & Recchi, 2009). Even prior to 2004, these two countries had hosted quite a significant number of central and eastern European (CEE) citizens, many of whom were employed in the informal sector of the labour market. The formal barriers during the transition period did not mean that the borders were completely closed, as CEE citizens still enjoyed privileges such as visa-free travel and preferential treatment over migrants from non-member states (Favell & Nebe, 2009). What changed after the implementation of the eastward enlargement was that much of the previous movement was legalised and facilitated.

In the UK, the arguably quite sudden arrival of central and eastern Europeans was generally treated with suspicion. Although policymakers had previously lamented the fact that fewer EU-15 citizens made use of their right to free movement, this was seen as something quite different. Unlike Erasmus students, highflying 'Eurostars' (Favell, 2008) or British pensioners, this group of newcomers was the target of intense 'othering' in receiving societies across western Europe. Common stereotypes that emerged during this time were that of a 'Polish plumber' who undercuts local wages or of Romanians moving west solely for the purpose of exploiting the welfare state (cf. Fox et al., 2015). The academic literature on the post-accession movement is vast and covers a wide range of topics (cf. Scholten & van Ostaijen, 2018; Burrell, 2009). Examples include empirical studies on the precarious working conditions of CEE migrants in the meat industry (Lever & Milbourne, 2017; Voivozeanu, 2019), hospitality (Alberti, 2014), agriculture (Rye & Andrzejewska, 2010), as well as in care work (Satola, 2016).

Some authors have focused on relational aspects of the migration experience. This includes studies on the integration processes of second generation CEE migrants who moved to the UK as young children. This group of young people has received renewed attention in the context of Brexit, as many have closer ties to Britain than to their parents' country of origin (Sime et al., 2020). Another interesting area of research is the 'racialisation' of central and eastern Europeans in different contexts.

Morosanu and Fox (2013) discuss how ethnicity informs the ways in which Romanian migrants deal with stigmatisation. For this project, the authors collected in-depth interviews with 89 'white' Romanian citizens in the UK, who were mostly young university graduates. In Britain (along with other western European societies), the image of Romanians is frequently conflated with that of Roma, Europe's most stigmatised and marginalised minority (Bogdal, 2011). Some interviewees in this study gave depressing testimonies about feeling ashamed of their country of origin, reinforcing negative stereotypes involving crime and prostitution ("this is what we're notorious for, and they are right, they're absolutely right.", Morosanu & Fox, 2013, p. 442). The authors identified different strategies to deal with such stigmatisation. The most common reaction involved blaming Romanians' negative reputation on the Roma. The interviewees described situations where they felt urged to 'educate' British people about the difference by referring to statistics (only a small percentage of Romanian migrants are Roma), behavioural and cultural differences, as well as ethnic markers such as their own white skin.

CEE migrants' 'whiteness', however, does not always work as a shield against anti-immigration sentiments and discrimination. Botterill and Burrell (2020) suggest that there is a "hierarchy of 'shades' of whiteness where the relational aspects of identity ensure that some groups are deemed to be whiter than others" (p. 24). The authors analysed testimonies of Polish nationals in the UK who openly spoke about being perceived as poor, 'backward', and uneducated (e.g. due to their accent). Botterill and Burrell (2020) argue that Poles occupy an 'in-between' position on the emerging 'hierarchy of Europeanness' in post-Brexit Britain, where 'old-established' western Europeans like Italians receive preferential treatment over e.g. 'Bulgarians' and 'Turks'. The white skin colour of CEE migrants, furthermore, does not always guarantee 'invisibility'. In her study on Polish women in the wider Manchester area, Rzepnikowska (2019) observed that there are other markers of difference, which include Polish registration plates, Polish satellite dishes, or speaking Polish (or having an accent in English) that make people's alleged 'otherness' visible and audible. Furthermore, some of her informants had also experienced street harassment for supposedly 'looking Polish', which indicates that their ostensible facial features and clothing made them identifiable as non-nationals.

In Germany, the so-called 'refugee' crisis of 2015 somewhat overshadowed other migration flows in the public discourse. Unlike in Britain, Polish migrants are rarely the subjects of intense media coverage, but are instead treated like a relatively unproblematic part of the cheap labour force, such as in construction and care (Satola, 2016). This is different in the case of Romanians and Bulgarians, who are often accused of 'welfare tourism' and criminality. Brücker et al. (2013) argue that these stereotypes are largely unfunded as the overall percentage of those receiving social benefits is lower than among other migrant groups. However, the authors also point to the emergence of problematic 'hotspots' across Germany, where welfare dependency is much higher than the national average. One example is Duisburg-Marxloh in the area of Ruhr. In this neighbourhood, the arrival of mostly Roma families from Romania and Bulgaria has caused many conflicts and inter-group tensions involving locals as well as 'old-established' migrant groups such as former guest workers from Turkey. Policy-makers are still looking for ways to improve the situation, which is a challenging task given that the borough is among the poorest in western Germany (cf. Böckler et al., 2018).

The literature discussed in this section gives a first impression of the multi-layered, complicated nature of the new east-west movement in the post-accession era. Unlike western European Erasmus students and 'Eurostars' (Favell, 2008), these 'new' EU citizens are frequently faced with quite intense prejudice and discrimination. Even though common fears about welfare abuse, a strain on public services and increased criminality have been largely unfounded (Ehata & Seeleib-Kaiser, 2017), the bias against CEE movers continues to be very persistent across different receiving societies. Needless to say, the latter also had a significant impact on the historic EU-referendum of 2016, which will be discussed in chapter eight.

Post-2008 until present

King and Pratsinakis (2019) retrace the beginning of the current phase of EU mobility to the global economic crisis of 2008. As discussed in chapter one, the repercussions of the financial crash were far from distributed equally in geographic terms. Whilst countries such as Germany and the United Kingdom recovered from the shock relatively well, southern Europe has been deeply affected and is still in the process of economic recovery, a recovery that is jeopardised by the current coronavirus pandemic. Since 2008, unemployment rates in Portugal, Italy, Greece and Spain (PIGS) have skyrocketed, especially among young people. Each of the crisis-stricken countries has witnessed a mass departure of mostly university graduates, a movement that has fuelled widespread fears of a 'brain-drain'.

When thinking about how this 'new' south-north mobility compares to the previous migration waves (i.e. post-1993, post-2004/2007), it is useful to revisit an example from my introduction. In 2012, conservative politician Marina del Corral attempted to gloss over the phenomenon and claimed that thousands of young Spaniards were leaving the country out of a 'spirit of adventure'. This statement can be interpreted as an attempt to push the mass departure of university graduates into the familiar narrative of the post-Maastricht era. The public was supposed to associate this new movement with that of Erasmus students and successful, high-skilled professionals who left simply out of curiosity about what Europe had to offer. As mentioned before, del Corral's strategy backfired. Thousands of Spanish migrants took to social media and other online platforms to vent their frustration about having felt forced to leave the country ('no nos vamos, nos echan'). They actively rejected the positive label of 'adventurers', as it undermined the harsh migration experiences they had to cope with. 'Cleaning toilets in London' despite having 'two bachelor degrees and a master', as one activist put it (Serra, 2014), did not constitute living some sort of 'European dream'.

This group of 'new' southern European migrants definitely shared certain characteristics with their predecessors. On paper, many young people still corresponded to the educational profile of – perhaps *potential* – 'Eurostars' (Favell, 2008). Most of them shared a middle-class (sometimes even upper-class) upbringing and had earned high academic qualifications in the form of university degrees. Furthermore, they came from 'old-established' EU-15 member states, which meant that their nationalities did not carry the heavy stigma attached to being Romanian, for example (Morosanu & Fox, 2013). However, after arriving in their new country, many young graduates ended up working in the informal segment of the labour market – an experience that they shared with a significant number of their central and eastern European counterparts.

There are a number of edited volumes that specifically deal with south-north mobility in the context of the economic crisis (cf. Lafleur & Stanek, 2017; Glorius & Dominguez-Mujica, 2017). These books contain important studies about aspects of the exodus from different southern European countries, which focus on various issues, including the shortcomings of a 'brain drain' narrative (Tintori & Romei, 2017), political controversies in the sending nations (Bermudez & Brey, 2017; Lopez-Sala, 2017), recruitment practices by employers in the receiving societies (Godenau, 2017; Meinardus, 2017), as well as migrants' motivations to migrate (Glorius, 2017; Pumares, 2017).

Some publications relevant for this study emerged out of very large Horizon 2020-funded research projects such as 'YMOBILITY' and 'GEMM'. Partial results of these initiatives were presented in the form of thematic issues of journals (King & Pratsinakis, 2019; King & Williams, 2018; Quassoli & Dimitriadis, 2019; Pratsinakis et al., 2019). These types of research projects targeted various intra-European migration flows with a particular focus on youth mobility. The south-north migration was thereby simply one of several EU movements of interest, which is also reflected in the presentation of some findings.

One example is Lulle et al.'s (2018) article on EU-migrants' reactions to the Brexit result. On the basis of in-depth interviews with Irish, Italian and Romanian migrants in the UK, the researchers argue that there are

> embedded national, ethnic, and cultural hierarchies of privilege, value and desirability ascribed to different European migrants. These differences are perpetuated and intensified between the desirable whiteness of 'old' or 'West' Europeans, versus 'Eastern' newcomers, seen as poorer and rougher, coming from more economically backward countries of origin. (p. 9)

The authors came to this conclusion after observing how Italian informants tended to receive preferential treatment by Brexit-supporters over eastern and central European migrants. In light of the literature previously discussed in this chapter (post-1993, post-2004/207), this finding is perhaps not that surprising.

Given the focus of my research project, I have been particularly interested in studies involving participants from Spain. As I explain in the next section, some publications focus exclusively on Spanish migrants in different receiving societies (Himmelstine & King, 2019), whilst several others again bring in a comparative perspective. Examples of the latter include research projects that aim to identify similarities and differences between Spanish and CEE migrants in terms of their motives of migration and long-term objectives (Bygnes & Flipo, 2017; Jendrissek, 2014).

Some studies focus on the migration experiences of specific groups of Spanish citizens, such as 'Catalans in London' (Rubio-Ros, 2013). Special attention has been paid to the case of 'onward migrants' who were born in Latin America. These migrants had often moved to Spain in the early 2000s during the country's economic boom and eventually became naturalised citizens. When the economic crisis unfolded, thousands of migrants returned to their home countries, such as Argentina and Ecuador (Cassain, 2016; Bastia, 2011). Quite a few people, however, made use of their newly acquired Spanish citizenship to move elsewhere in the European Union, including the UK prior to Brexit (McIlwaine, 2020; Bermudez, 2020; Mas Giralt, 2017; Ramos, 2018).

The literature on the 'new' Spanish migration has been rapidly expanding in recent years (cf. Bermudez, 2020; Bermudez & Oso, 2020). In the following section, I offer a thematic overview of a careful selection of important contributions, which will help 'map the field'. While most of the research that I will discuss is qualitative in nature, some authors made use of a mixed-method approach including public data and their own survey research. The most commonly cited form of data collection in these studies was that of 'semi-structured in-depth interviews'. In addition, a few authors also conducted focus groups and ethnographic fieldwork.

The majority of publications focus on one specific period in their informants' lives, including the preparation of their departure, the work experiences in the new country, and different forms of activism such as work in 'interstitial trade unions' (Roca and Martin-Diaz, 2016). In some articles, aspects relating to several stages of the migration experience (e.g. before and after arriving in the new country) become visible in the presentation of the data. Some themes are thereby at the foreground of the discussion, whilst others play a subordinate role and are alluded to in a more indirect manner (Pumares, 2017). For the purpose of clarity, I decided to present the literature in a sequential manner by differentiating between different phases of the migration process. This format also informs the order of the empirical chapters in this monograph.

ZOOMING IN ON THE SPANISH CASE

a) Motives of migration

One dominant interest in the social scientific literature on the phenomenon at hand is that of the 'motives of migration'. Several researchers took the aforementioned political discussion ('spirit of adventure' vs. 'economic exile') as a starting point to take a closer look at why people decided to leave Spain and move abroad. With quantitative surveys, informants were asked to sort their own motivations in a pre-formulated set of possible responses where multiple answers were allowed. Options to choose from included 'wanting to get to know a different culture' and 'the economic situation in Spain' (Navarette-Moreno et al., 2014, p. 120; Montero Lange, 2014, pp. 62-66). Similar studies have also been conducted from the perspective of the receiving societies, which are particularly concerned with what has been referred to as "Fachkräftesicherung" (i.e. the securing of skilled workers). These publications focused on Spanish nationals' motives for foreign language acquisition (Glorius, 2017) and their long-term personal and work objectives behind their decision to migrate (Pfeffer-Hoffmann, 2014; Glorius, 2016).

Apart from primarily statistical enquiries, several researchers have conducted open and semi-structured interviews to find out more about their informants' 'reasons' for leaving Spain (Pumares, 2017; Bygnes, 2017). These authors could gain insights and discover argumentation patterns that could not adequately be captured in survey research. Many informants expressed their deep frustration and anger at Spanish politicians, whom they held responsible for the dire economic situation, a theme that appeared in almost every study of this kind. In the analysis, several authors referred to this as a 'political dimension' to their participants' migration projects. Sometimes these insights emerged out of a comparative discussion with informants from other EU member states, including Romania and Bulgaria (Bygnes & Flipo,

2017). Bygnes (2017) emphasised the sociological significance of 'anomie' (i.e. in the Durkheimian sense) as a motivation for migration. Her informants, who were Spanish nationals working in high-paying jobs in Norway, stressed how they did not migrate because of economic reasons (e.g. threat of unemployment). Instead, they frequently cited the widespread corruption, nepotism, and depressing collective atmosphere in Spain as reasons for their decision to leave.

Bygnes (2017) makes a convincing case for the use of the concept of 'anomie' in analysing the deep structural problems in Spain, which have been exacerbated by the economic crisis. That being said, it is difficult to estimate to what extent her informants' political frustrations actually played into their personal decisions to move to Norway. It seems as if some interviewees also reproduced this type of political discourse in order to distinguish themselves from lower-class Spanish migrants. In the media, the latter are often portrayed as having come solely due to economic reasons. Some members of the Spanish community have reacted very negatively to this ascribed motive, as they associate it with a form of stigma. Bygnes' (2017) informants seemed keen to dissociate themselves from this public image by highlighting more neutral and socially accepted motives for leaving Spain (including the general collective atmosphere). This form of argumentation has a specific function in interview situations, which I will return to at a later point in this chapter (see also Riemann, 2019).

In the literature on Spanish nationals' motives of migration, there is a clear tendency to distinguish between different types of migrants, including 'students', 'unskilled workers' and 'highly successful professionals' (Navarette-Moreno et al., 2014; Pumares, 2017; King & Pratsinakis, 2019). In the presentation of their findings, authors sometimes use small data extracts to illustrate each category. These interview sequences are often argumentative in character and entail quite global statements about the lack of job opportunities for young people and/or the widespread nepotism in Spain. These studies provide readers with an initial insight into the heterogeneity of migration projects in the Spanish diaspora. That being said, it is often difficult for readers to get a deeper sense of the informants' long-term biographical processes leading up to the decision to move abroad. This is something that can – as I hope to show in this book – be more easily reconstructed on the basis of narrative (instead of argumentative) data material.

Two scholars who have criticised the dominant focus on 'economic motivations' in the field of the 'new' Spanish migration are Himmelstine and King. In their paper "Healing Young Hearts" (2019), the authors write: "Very few studies have explored the adaption processes of these migrants, their sense of belonging, and the factors that mediate their well-being" (p. 162). In response to this gap in research, they conducted 20 in-depth interviews with Spanish migrants in the UK. In the analysis, Himmelstine and King (2019) pay close attention to the subjective dimension of the migration experience, such as emancipating oneself from the family of origin, escaping difficult personal situations, dealing with loneliness, and adjusting to a new way of life. A few informants made the decision to leave Spain in the midst of a personal crisis, including after a painful break-up. As indicated in the title of the article, moving to a new country often had an emancipatory quality to it as it allowed movers to gain some distance and recover from their problems at home. Himmelstine and King (2019) share some of the research interests of my study. There are, however, important methodological differences in their work because the authors are primarily concerned with identifying the psychosocial factors underlying people's decision to leave Spain. This is quite different from reconstructing long-term biographical processes, a distinction that will become clearer at the end of this chapter and in the methodological appendix.

b) Preparing for the departure

The second step following the decision to leave Spain is preparing for one's departure. Several authors focused on their informants' collective images of various destination countries and metropolitan magnets like London (Rubio-Ros, 2013), Berlin (Dimitriadis et al., 2019), and Cologne (Vilar Sanchez, 2020). Coletto and Fullin (2019) engaged in a comparative discussion of preparation activities of EU citizens from Italy, Spain, Romania and Bulgaria. Their analysis also included a critical discussion of 'social imaginaries' of the host-societies in Germany and the UK. Quite a few of their Spanish and Italian interviewees seemed to share a common 'dream' of living in Berlin or London. In order to make this vision a reality, some informants were willing to work in jobs unrelated to their academic training. The authors identified important differences between medium/low and high-skilled migrants. The latter informants, who were mostly from southern Europe, had better access to transnational networks than their CEE counterparts. Several Italian and Spanish interviewees had previously taken part in Erasmus programmes at university. This experience served as a source of confidence in their ability to adapt to a new and foreign environment quickly.

A second important theme that has attracted attention is that of social networks in the receiving society. Oso (2020) focuses on the city of Paris, which has been a popular destination for Spanish migrants in different historic and political contexts. The author identifies intergenerational connections between labour migrants who had moved to France in the 1960s and 1970s (sometimes escaping Franco), and the more recent arrivals in the context of the economic crisis. Although the latter had often achieved a higher academic status, quite a few informants tended to work in similar occupations as their predecessors, including domestic service and caretaking. Some informants had acquaintances in Paris who originated from the same hometown but had moved north many decades ago. For these informants, who were mainly from working class backgrounds, these contacts in the 'traditional migratory networks' paved the way out of a precarious situation at home. Oso (2020) reconstructs the family connections of individual informants who moved to Paris to live with (and in some cases work for) their aunts and uncles who had settled there decades earlier.

The author deserves credit for uncovering an interesting political dimension, which marks the intra-generational solidarity networks within Spanish diaspora in Paris. The data suggests that older Spanish migrants who left Spain during the dictatorship are very sympathetic towards their younger counterparts, who often share the same political views and opinions. That being said, Oso (2020) also stresses that the younger and older Spanish migrants mostly lead quite separate lives in the French capital. The author suggests that this may also have to do with having different cultural tastes, as younger migrants may find events organised by traditional Spanish associations (e.g. flamenco shows, traditional food festivals) to be quite old-fashioned and prefer more cosmopolitan alternatives.

Whilst specific family ties can play a role in young people's choice of destination, it seems more of an exception than the rule. A more common scenario involves friends and acquaintances (e.g. from school or university), who 'pave the way' and encourage others to join them abroad once they are more or less 'settled'. Already knowing a few people in the receiving society who can provide a first shelter seems to make the step of leaving Spain a lot less daunting.

c) Living abroad

A large part of the literature on 'new' Spanish migrants deals with topics relating to 'living abroad'. This is a very broad category that encompasses various aspects of life, including the experiences of work, maintaining and developing social relationships, the discourse among co-nationals, and various forms of activism and cultural expression. For the purpose of clarity, I will divide the following overview accordingly.

The experience of work

An important part of 'living abroad' is the experience of work, which has been at the centre of various publications on the 'new' Spanish migration. There appears to be a general divide between studies focusing on quite specific professions (e.g. nursing) and the widespread phenomenon of 'qualification mismatch'.

Kuhlmann and Jensen (2015) studied the integration processes of Spanish nurses in Germany. On the basis of secondary statistical data and three focus group interviews, the authors identified several widespread sources of frustration that commonly led to an early termination of work contracts. In Spain, nursing is a university degree and the profession enjoys a high reputation in society. Students are trained to perform exacting tasks, which serve as a source of pride for graduates. In Germany, however, nurses have much less responsibility. This can partly be traced back to the fact that nursing is an apprenticeship, i.e., vocational training that takes place outside of an academic setting. Most medical tasks are reserved for physicians, whilst nurses are expected to, for example, wash patients. Understandably, many nursing graduates from Spain were therefore frustrated about not being allowed to use the skills they had learned at university. The authors argue that this is a serious problem, which has contributed to the fact that over 30% of Spanish nurses in their study had left their German employers after two years.

In their quantitative study on Spanish engineers in Germany, Vijande Rodríguez and Ruiz Yepes (2018) found that, despite intensive training, it is very difficult to become proficient in German. Although some international firms in their study only required applicants to be fluent in English, German was still used for the majority of daily interactions, which put foreign employees in an outsider position. While the informants mostly had secure and high-paying jobs, there still appeared to be a 'glass ceiling' on the career ladder due to significant language barriers.

Among Spanish migrants, nurses and engineers are commonly regarded as the 'exception to the rule' as they are trained in professions that are highly sought-after in the receiving societies. Many of the healthcare professionals can expect to work in their field of expertise immediately after moving to a new country, a privilege that not all migrants share. Castellani (2018) compared the work experiences of new Spanish and Italian migrants in Berlin and the south-west of Germany. Through semi-structured interviews, he found that many Italian and Spanish people who migrated to Germany during the recession still correspond to the profile of 'cosmopolitan' young adults with high cultural capital and qualifications (Recchi, 2015). However, only a minority succeeds in finding a position in their field of expertise. He observed that quite broad segments of southern European migrants seem to 'slip' into the low-qualified end of the labour market. Many of his interviewees spent prolonged periods of time working in jobs unrelated to their academic training, which made them vulnerable to exploitation and very low pay.

Castellani drew parallels to the experiences of Spanish and Italian guest workers in the 1960s and 1970s. He argued that whilst the latter may have suffered from cultural and political exclusion in Germany (e.g. being regarded as 'backwards'), they were usually in full-time employment and had the same benefits as their German counterparts through work. He believes that the exact opposite is happening for the 'new' migrants from southern Europe who arrived in Germany during the economic crisis. While his interviewees seemed culturally accepted as educated Europeans with equal rights and status, they struggled to break the cycle of precariousness with regard to their employment situation.

Although Castellani's (2018) comparison to the 'guest worker' generation is very interesting, one ought to remember that the latter was far from a homogenous group. Some 'guest workers' had quite stable, but physically exhausting, jobs as coalminers or steelworkers. Others, however, worked under extremely harsh and exploitative working conditions in the meat industry. These workers often spent many years living in isolated mass accommodation facilities with virtually no contact with the outside world (cf. Inowlocki & Lutz, 2000), a problem that still exists today and has attracted renewed attention in the context of the coronavirus pandemic. Migrants' struggles to break the cycle of precariousness are therefore not a completely new phenomenon. What makes the 'new' arrivals in the context of the economic crisis stand out from their predecessors is their level of education.

One publication that gives detailed insights into the lived reality of Spanish university graduates working in low-qualification jobs abroad was written by a young journalist, who migrated to London where he worked as a cleaner (Serra 2014). Although this book may not be officially classified as a social scientific piece of research, it is written in the style of an auto-ethnography and includes rich descriptions of everyday work experiences. In 2013, the author gained widespread attention after a post he published on social media 'went viral'. The post, which translated into, "Hello. My name is Benjamín Serra. I have two bachelor degrees and a master and I clean toilets," resonated with thousands of other Spanish migrants who shared it online. For a short time, Serra became the 'face' of this movement, frequently appearing on Spanish TV. This experience inspired him to write a book about his life, which he hoped could empower others in a similar situation.

Maintaining relationships and developing new ties

Some researchers have focused on EU migrants' personal lives and social networks. This includes forms of maintaining social relationships at home, as well as the emergence of new ties in the host society. In this context, authors frequently draw on the concept of 'transnationalism', which can be defined as "the multiple ties and interactions linking people or institutions across the borders of a nation state" (Vertovec, 2009, p. 1).

Several researchers have studied how 'new' Spanish migrants maintain ties to their country of origin. Such everyday transnational practices (cf. Salamon'ska & Recchi, 2019) can take on very different forms. Gordano-Peile and Ros-Hijar (2016) focused on the mobile phone use (and other communication technologies) of 25 young Spanish informants who had recently arrived in London. For most participants, these digital technologies significantly facilitated their everyday life, both in terms of communicating with loved ones in Spain (family, friends, partners) and also as a way of orientating themselves in the host society.

Another perhaps less obvious example of a transnational practice is learning how to cook traditional dishes. Clara Rubio (2017) reflected on the role of food in the lives of young Catalan migrants in the UK. Drawing on her personal migration experience and 42 in-depth interviews, she discussed how many young people only learn how to cook Spanish and Catalan recipes after moving to a new country, as they had previously been 'taken care of' by their parents. Certain dishes thereby become metaphors for their transition to adulthood. Food from home serves, furthermore, as a powerful tool to maintain close emotional ties to Spain (or Catalonia specifically) and also to build friendships with members of the receiving society (e.g. by inviting British co-workers for dinner).

In the context of building new ties to the receiving society, one recent study deserves attention. For his master's thesis, Gonzalez-Exposito (2020) conducted a small-scale ethnographic study on the role of friendships in the lives of 'new' Spanish migrants in Norway. The author took his own experiences as a university student in Bergen as a starting point to explore how his co-nationals socialised in a foreign environment. His nine informants differed significantly in their ability to befriend Norwegians, which had to do with certain interpersonal barriers including language skills. He paid close attention to the topic of loneliness, which appeared in the context of feeling estranged from friends at home.

The political discourse in Spanish migrant communities

Several studies on the 'new' Spanish migration specifically focus on the political discourse in the diaspora. These publications frequently revolve around Spanish migrants' argumentation patterns and forms of drawing symbolic boundaries between themselves and others. Jendrissek (2014) analysed 22 semi-structured interviews with Spanish and Polish migrants in Southampton and the Isle of Wight for his PhD thesis. He notes that while the Polish narratives put a strong emphasis on the present, arguing that their life in the UK compares favourably to their "abnormal" past in Poland, the Spanish narratives appeared "highly politicised" and displayed a "strong sense of individualisation and political anger". Spain, he observes, was commonly referred to as a place of personal and professional stagnation, while time spent in the UK is seen as a conscious investment in human capital, such as English language skills.

Some publications point to the emergence of communication patterns that are characterised by both anger at politicians and also 'gossip' about certain types of Spanish migrants, 'compatriots' with whom the informants did not want to be associated (cf. section on 'motives of migration'). Examples of such self-distinctions include Catalan migrants avoiding the 'Spanish' community in London (Clua i Fainé & Sánchez García, 2017) as well as highly successful professionals who feel embarrassed about 'uneducated' co-nationals who arrive in Norway seemingly without any preparation and resources (Bygnes, 2017).

Activism and cultural expression

One area that has attracted special attention is Spanish migrants' involvement in activism, including transnational solidarity networks (e.g. 'Marea Granate', 'Oficina Precaria') (Tiburcio Jiménez, 2017) and creative expressions of protest (Castellani & Roca, 2021). In their study on solidarity networks among Spanish migrants in the UK and Germany, Roca and Martin-Diaz (2016) introduced the term 'Interstitial Trade Unionism' to describe activist initiatives aimed at supporting foreign labourers. In the past, some traditional trade unions have been very critical of the principle of 'free movement' in the European Union as an attempt to protect local workers from 'wage dumping'. The authors found that some Spanish migrants preferred finding their own 'grassroots' support structures, offering those in need help in their own language. Interestingly, these projects often originated in the 15-M movement in Spain and later evolved into quite independent entities.

Lopez Sala (2019) focused on migrants' initiatives to participate in Spanish politics from abroad. She paid close attention to activists performing creative 'acts of recovery', such as campaigns in favour of maintaining their right to vote in Spanish elections and/or keeping their access to healthcare. Her research highlights the transnational ties to Spain that many migrants maintain after migrating to another country. The activists still regard themselves very much as part of Spanish society, which is especially visible in their slogan: 'You're not getting rid of us'.

The plight of 'new' Spanish migrants abroad has also given rise to different forms of cultural expression. Feixa and Rubio Ros (2017) critically reflect on widespread cultural narratives that have surrounded the new exodus of (mostly young) Spanish people in recent years and how artists of different genres have incorporated this topic in their work. These types of cultural outputs and self-representation (e.g. in form of videos) often differ significantly from mainstream media accounts on Spanish television (Visa Barbosa et al., 2016).

d) The Brexit crisis

The UK's decision to leave the European Union, also known as Brexit, has overshadowed the lives of millions of EU citizens who had made Britain their home. Social scientists have focused on different aspects of EU citizens' experiences, studying their initial reactions to the outcome of the vote (Botterill et al., 2018; Lulle et al., 2018). Their findings point to a range of widespread feelings, including anger, rejection, and disbelief about Brexit, tendencies of division, and the emergence of ascribed ethnic hierarchies among different EU nationalities (Mazzilli & King, 2019).

There have been a few studies that specifically deal with Spanish nationals' experiences with and responses to Brexit (e.g. Cortes Maisonave et al., 2019).

McCarthy (2018) used an online survey that included 60 questions about her Spanish informants' migration history, family situation, employment status, use of English and future plans. Some of her participants had only spent a short period of time in the UK and perceived Brexit simply as a potential catalyst for their return migration (along with Spain's gradual economic recovery). Others took the vote very personally, which was visible in the short comments section of the survey. The author observed how the informants who were born in Latin America (i.e. naturalised Spanish citizens) felt more accepted in the UK and reported less discrimination than their 'native' (or 'white') co-nationals. This perception may have to do with the fact that the prejudice specifically against Latinos might be less prevalent in Britain than it is in Spain, which hosts a much larger Latino population. The Latin American informants in McCarthy's study were also more willing to take steps towards civic integration (e.g. applying for settled status or British citizenship). Given that they had already gone through a similar naturalisation process in Spain, this step did not seem as foreign or daunting to them as to their 'white' co-nationals. When asked about a possible return migration, the Latin American informants expressed a preference for their original home countries over Spain, which seemed to have lost its initial appeal given its current economic state.

e) (Contemplating) returning

Prior to the current coronavirus pandemic, the Spanish economy had been in the process of gradual recovery since 2014. The statistics available suggest that the numbers of new arrivals from Spain in the UK and Germany (cf. chapter 1) have decreased since then. Furthermore, many people have returned to their home country after working abroad for a prolonged period of time.

Domínguez-Mujica and Díaz-Hernández (2019) discussed 'the dilemma of returning' of (new) Spanish migrants by using concepts such as 'liquid migration', a concept that was coined by Engbersen and Snel (2013) under the influence of Bauman's (1999) work on 'liquid modernity'. The concept describes flexible, unpredictable and hence 'more fluid' forms of movement. Engbersen and Snel (2013) argue that EU movers from Poland and other CEE countries, who were at the centre of their research, had developed a 'habitus of intentional unpredictability', which is one of the characteristics of 'liquid mobility'. In other words, the researchers assume that these migrants consciously choose to 'keep their options open' with regard to where to move next. Domínguez-Mujica and Díaz-Hernández (2019) took the concept of liquid migration as a starting point to see how it applies to the 'new' Spanish migration. On the basis of mostly online material (e.g. blogs, newspapers), the authors identified several themes such as migrants' mixed feelings about longing for a stable home (Spain) and more attractive working conditions abroad. A second theme is that of political discontent with the structural conditions in Spain. The authors also focused on accounts of those who returned 'home' after spending months (and sometimes years) abroad. These returnees often found themselves in a similar situation to the one they were in before migrating, which they found disheartening. This finding resonated with other studies on the phenomenon (cf. Rubio Ros, 2018).

Bygnes and Erdal (2017) studied the 'return considerations' of Spanish and Polish migrants in Norway. The authors took a critical stance towards the concept of 'liquid migration', which is mainly associated with the mobility of *young* people. The majority of the informants in this study were in their thirties and forties. The authors note that very few interviewees "envision a free-moving lifestyle, which would uphold the ideals of open options and intentional unpredictability; rather most are looking for the possibility of settling down and living grounded, secure and stable lives" (p. 114). In this context, *staying* in Norway was generally perceived as a more attractive option over returning to Poland and Spain, which the informants portrayed as economically and politically unstable.

When thinking about the concept of 'liquid migration' critically in the context of the 'new' Spanish migration, it is important to remember that many young graduates reacted very negatively to del Corrall's claim that they had left Spain out of a 'spirit of adventure'. Instead, these young activists underlined the involuntariness of this step (as visible in their slogan: 'no nos vamos, nos echan'). Many of the younger informants in my study had a clear idea of their long-term biographical goals (e.g. becoming an engineer) but found it difficult to realise them at home due to structural conditions outside of their control. In other words, they felt that the option of a normal, 'predictable' career path in Spain had been taken away, which angered them. Furthermore, many of them were very frustrated about their unpredictable and precarious employment situation abroad (Serra, 2014). Against this background, one can raise critical questions about the concept of a 'habitus of *intentional* unpredictability' (Engbersen & Snel, 2013).[2] Whilst the desire to 'settle down' may become stronger over the age of 30 (Bygnes & Erdal, 2017), considerations about where to live and work long-term are not completely absent in young people's minds.

TAKING ON A BIOGRAPHICAL PERSPECTIVE

The previous section provided an overview of the social scientific literature about the 'new' Spanish migration in the context of the economic crisis. Whilst this literature review is not exhaustive, I hope to have given the reader an idea of the valuable contributions that researchers from various disciplines (especially sociology, anthropology and human geography) have made to this field over the years. The aforementioned studies provide important insights into specific phases in – and aspects of – the lives of 'new' Spanish migrants. When reviewing the relevant literature, however, some theoretical and methodological questions remained open. In the following section, I would like to offer a few critical comments and queries that serve as the basis for developing the research questions guiding my study.

a) What about the place of the migration experience(s) in people's biographies?

Many researchers focused on very specific phases in their informants' lives, such as work experiences in the new country. In the presentation of the findings, the biographical background of the informants often remained quite vague and unspecific. This 'narrow' perspective can be a problem, as the participants were not just migrants but individuals with complex life histories.

In some qualitative studies, the authors included data sequences, which revealed that the informants used the interview situation to narrate biographically.[3] In other words, they vividly remembered 'how one thing led to another' in their lives, including many ups and downs. The interviewers deserve credit for creating an atmosphere of trust, which evidently encouraged participants to open up. In the analysis, however, the biography itself was not an object of social scientific research. Instead, the researchers used such quotes to illustrate certain categories, including 'motives of migration'. It seemed to me that the deeper biographical meaning of what the informants shared was sometimes overlooked in the process of sorting such data material into different categories.

Some participants remembered how they had gotten into a deep identity crisis in Spain (e.g. questioning their sexuality, relationships, career choices etc.), which had sometimes developed over the course of several years. These interviewees expressed how they had an intrinsic urge to get away from home to discover 'who' they were and what they wanted to do with the rest of their lives. When speaking about their decision to move to the UK, some of these informants then mentioned some subordinate motives such as wanting to 'learn English' or explore a new cultural environment that was less traditional than their hometowns. In the analysis of the data, authors often focused on the latter as they provided logical explanations for why people decided to leave. Furthermore, these types of motives appeared in many different interviews, which encouraged researchers to generalise and develop certain clusters of common themes. Many researchers clearly sensed that there were complicated personal issues at play that go well beyond 'wanting to learn English'. That being said, the structure of the presentation of their findings did not allow for a detailed reconstruction of their informants' long-term biographical processes. My aim here is not to discredit or delegitimise this form of categorisation. Even though some motives such as 'wanting to experience a new culture' are subordinate in some cases, it does not mean that they are untrue or inauthentic. The problem I see with this form of presentation is that it often overlooks more complicated and possibly elusive experiences, (inner) conflicts and biographical processes that played a decisive role in the development of the migration project. Such biographical processes are, furthermore, a legitimate and important sociological topic in their own right. They are social processes as well.

In the literature discussed in this chapter, there is a general trend towards focusing on very specific phases (and aspects) of the migration experience. Some authors acknowledge this limitation in their self-reflexive comments (Gordano-Peile & Ros-Hijar, 2016). Much like pieces of a jigsaw puzzle, these studies contain interesting insights into specific parts of people's migration experiences but they do not provide a 'whole' image of their biographical processes and contexts. Although some authors allude to their informants' past (Pumares, 2017), the presentation often remains vague and unspecific.

In this study, I am making the case for zooming in on details, which initially appear quite unique to the individual informant. It is my belief that by focusing on such specificities, one can actually gain important general insights into Spanish migrants' experiences and other societal phenomena. Examples include cases where personal tragedies and financial problems, which have appeared in the context of the economic crisis, merge and reinforce each other, biographical processes that make 'staying in Spain' a very unattractive (if not impossible) option. What happened 'at home' furthermore informs people's experiences in the receiving society, as different phases in people's lives are interconnected. When analysing migrants' work experiences in the new country, it is important to consider what they had achieved in Spain (i.e. their academic qualifications, previous professional experiences etc.). By taking on a biographical perspective, one can gain a deeper understanding of what it means for university graduates to work in occupations such as cleaning and how they make sense of their current situation and reflect on their future. I argue in favour of studying such developments as part of long-term biographical processes, irrespective of the country in which people happen to be.

b) A lack of differentiation between schemes of communication

When reviewing the literature on the 'new' Spanish migration, I was often left wondering how exactly researchers went about their data collection and analysis. This was especially prevalent in short journal articles that did not leave much space for authors to describe their methodology and fieldwork. Many authors simply included a short note on their use of 'semi-structured, in-depth interviews', which were subsequently analysed via 'open coding'. Whilst there is nothing wrong with this type of research in general, one can raise further questions about what the analytical procedures used actually entailed. What did the interview situation look like? What kinds of questions were asked? How did the researchers then go about interpreting this data? I find it very important to make such research procedures as transparent as possible in order to enable readers to assess one's findings critically (Cicourel, 1964).

One impression that I had when reading the publications on the topic at hand is that authors generally did not explicitly differentiate between different schemes of communication in the analysis of their interviewees' oral presentations (Kallmeyer & Schütze, 1977; Schütze, 2008) and that it would have been easier to assess their procedures of analysis if they had paid more attention to this issue. What do I mean by that? Almost every in-depth interview consists of distinct parts, where an informant engages either in narration, description or argumentation. These are everyday communicative resources which people learn to use methodically during their socialisation. Narration occurs when a person openly remembers how a story unfolded, or in other words 'how this didn't happen until that happened' etc. A free-flowing narration may involve different actors, coincidences, and unexpected events. Furthermore, a narrator may remember how s/he felt in certain situations, recalling inner dialogues and doubts. The communication scheme of description is applied, e.g., when referring to reoccurring routines such as a 'typical day' at work, features of an organisation, regular patterns in interaction or specific inner states (such as the experience of depression) or elements of a territory. Interviewees argue when expressing an opinion on a topic (such as Brexit) or present theories about themselves and what happened to them. They reflect about their biographical problems, puzzles or achievements or evaluate the advantages and disadvantages of living abroad.

These distinct schemes of communication are activated also in reaction to different types of questions. When reviewing the studies covering the 'new' Spanish migration, it was noticeable that many authors often seemed to focus on 'why' people migrated even though the exact wording of their questions remained opaque. As discussed before, the responses that emerged out of these types of interviews were primarily argumentative in character, often entailing strong views about the lack of trustworthiness of Spanish politicians and institution (Bygnes, 2017). These types of arguments give off the impression that they had emerged in a shared political discourse with others in the same situation. The problem with such 'why' questions is that people may feel pressured to justify their migration by listing the reasonable and logical motives behind their decision to go (cf. Riemann, 2019).

Without denying the authenticity of their frustrations about the widespread corruption in Spain, it is difficult to estimate how far this was really the decisive factor in their decision-making process. There is the possibility that such argumentative sequences draw on a widely shared and socially accepted 'vocabulary of motives' (Mills, 1940, p. 907), which enable informants to present themselves in a positive light. In other words, they emphasise ancillary motives in their argumentation for why they left Spain – whilst more personal (and perhaps painful) experiences remain hidden. As a reader, it is difficult to get a sense of people's long-term biographical processes from quite general political statements. This can be more easily achieved through 'narrative' data material that emerges in response to 'how' questions. The benefits of asking 'how', rather than 'why' questions, are not a secret among qualitative researchers. In his book "Tricks of the Trade" (1998), American sociologist Howard Becker writes:

> Why does "How?" work so much better than "Why?" as an interview question? Even cooperative, nondefensive interviewees gave short answers to "Why?" They understood the question to be asking for a cause, maybe even causes, but in any event for something that could be summarized in a few words. And not just any old cause, but the cause contained in the victim's intentions. If you did it, you did it for a reason. OK what's your reason? Furthermore, "Why?" required a "good" answer, one that made sense and could be defended. The answer should not reveal logical flaws and inconsistencies. It should be socially as well as logically defensible; that is, the answer should express one of the motives conventionally accepted as adequate in that world. (...) "How?" questions, when I asked them, gave people more leeway, were less constraining, invited them to answer in any way that suited them, to tell a story that included whatever they thought the story ought to include in order to make sense. They didn't demand a "right" answer, didn't seem to be trying to place responsibility for bad actions or outcomes anywhere. (...). (Becker, 1998, p. 59)

Although Becker (1998) does not explicitly state this, he presupposes that narrative sequences (prompted by 'how' questions) are better suited than argumentative accounts (prompted by 'why' questions) to reconstruct interviewees' biographical experiences and other processes. The way in which Becker formulates his insight as a rule of thumb could be construed as a condescending devaluation of all argumentative data, and I do not agree with such a position. Sometimes it can make perfect sense to ask 'why' questions and to engage in an analysis of argumentation patterns (see chapter 8 on "Established-Outsider Relations in Times of Brexit" as an example of such an analysis.). That being said, let us reconsider what Becker said in this paragraph and how it relates to the aforementioned schemes of communication.

When reflecting about his fieldwork experiences, Becker (1998, p. 60) states: "I wanted to know the sequence of things, how one thing led to another, how this didn't happen until that happened." The author intuitively distinguishes between different schemes of communication, namely narration and argumentation. Like Becker (1998), I too have a special interest in the long-term biographical processes in informants' lives, the study of which leads to important sociological insights that cannot be gleaned from purely argumentative responses. Both Becker (1998) and C. Wright Mills (1940) draw attention to the fact that 'motives', which informants list in response to 'why' they did something (or were planning to do something), should not be taken at face value. This is not because they are 'false', but because they have a specific function in social interactions and therefore may conceal (to some extent) processes in people's lives that had a more significant impact on their decision to do something.

To illustrate this point, it is useful to take an example from my research project, which I will explicate further in the empirical chapters. Some informants justified their decision to move abroad by emphasising their deep fascination with the German language and culture, a motive for which they received praise in their extended social circles. A close look at the narrative parts of their interviews revealed, however, that the driving force behind their migration projects was their desire not to live with their parents anymore, a wish they could not express openly without causing offense. This example illustrates the benefits of systematically distinguishing between different schemes of communication in interpreting biographical data. In the next chapter I will write more about my preference for initiating and analysing spontaneous narratives about one's own experiences in order to understand my informants' long-term biographical processes.

When reviewing the literature on the 'new' Spanish migration, I noticed that authors did not explicitly differentiate between informants' argumentative, descriptive and narrative sequences in the analysis and presentation of their findings. Instead, such data extracts were cited in a non-distinctive manner to illustrate certain 'motives of migration'. This is not to say that the researchers in question did not intuitively grasp the relevance of their participants' pasts. Instead, the issue seemed to lie in the lack of specific interpretation tools that take textual features of qualitative data into account and provide writers with a specific analytical vocabulary. This vocabulary has emerged in the minute sequential analysis of autobiographical narratives (Riemann, 2018).

The goal of this study is somewhat different from the research questions of the aforementioned studies. I want to take a deeper look at the complexity of Spanish migrants' life histories and biographical circumstances, as well as understand their migration projects against this backdrop. For this purpose, I found it necessary to draw on a specific type of biographical analysis, which is marked by carefully considering formal features of interviewees' oral presentations, including their use of different schemes of communication. This research approach has so far not been applied to the topic of the 'new' Spanish migration.

I am interested in the 'whole picture' of 'new' Spanish migrants' lives, or in other words how the 'puzzle pieces' (i.e. different structural processes such as trajectories of suffering and biographical action schemes, e.g. a migration project) are interconnected. This study makes use of a specific form of biographical research (Schütze, 2008) that is based on the analysis of narrative interviews in which informants are asked to tell their whole life histories and explain 'how one thing led to another' in their lives. This approach is based on the conviction that a researcher can gain general insights into the impact of a macro-phenomenon (e.g. the economic crisis of 2008) on people's lives through the careful analysis of 'off-the-cuff', spontaneous autobiographical narratives. This only becomes possible by taking certain socio-linguistic features into account, as well as by engaging in contrastive comparisons in the style of Grounded Theory (Glaser & Strauss, 1967).

For quantitative researchers, being confronted with long analyses of single narratives can be irritating, as they may question the purpose of interpreting biographical details of individual participants. Furthermore, they might get impatient with this type of 'holistic' approach (i.e. analysing one's whole biography), expecting seemingly more refined research questions or hypotheses that immediately focus on specific aspects of people's lives. The idea that general insights can be derived from the analysis of single cases will also be quite outlandish for some readers. That being said, it is important to remember that the use of single case studies is neither a new nor isolated phenomenon in the social sciences. Instead, they are part of an important sociological and anthropological tradition that traces its roots to the Chicago School of sociology, especially of the 1920s and 1930s, but also to earlier work in cultural anthropology (cf. methodological appendix).[4]

3. BIOGRAPHICAL CASE STUDIES

ADAM SANCHEZ

Adam was one of the few informants who I recruited via snowball sampling. The day before our meeting in August 2017, I interviewed a friend of his who gave me his phone number. I met Adam, 26 years old, at a cafe in the city centre of Madrid. After spending two years in Manchester working in a hotel, he had returned to Spain about one year prior to our interview. His main autobiographical narrative, which lasted about one hour, was very lively and entailed vivid and detailed sequences on various episodes in his life. I did not interrupt him during this time. Adam finished his introductory narrative with a coda (*"And this is my story more or less! I told you I had a lot to share!"* (laughs)).

When I asked Adam to tell me his life story, he started the interview (after mentioning *"I was born and raised in Madrid"*) with a narrative preamble, in which he expressed something that was biographically significant for him: *"I spent all my life without leaving Spain… Since I was born, I had never travelled to another country."* This preamble already indicates how deeply transformative his migration project to the UK would later become. Throughout the interview, he reflected on his younger naïve self and how his experiences abroad helped him grow as a person. His biographical narrative had the character of a 'coming of age' story.[1]

ADAM'S BACKGROUND AND EARLY INTERESTS

Adam grew up in a working-class district, which he described as *"a bit of a rough neighbourhood in Madrid"*. He is the only child of civil servants. Adam remembered his childhood as normal and unexciting. His parents divorced when he was 16 years old, and he continued to live with his mother. In the interview, Adam did not speak much about how he had experienced his parents' separation, but the data suggests that his peers became very important to him during this period, as he started to spend more time outside his home. As an adolescent, Adam developed an intellectual interest in film and media, but he felt somewhat discouraged from considering work in the creative industry as a realistic option. People in his neighbourhood, he recalled, were more occupied with making a living rather than pursuing an education.

EXPERIENCING THE BEGINNING OF THE COLLECTIVE CRISIS

Adam was still enrolled at school when the economic crisis in Spain first started to unfold. Many of his friends, who had dropped out of school and had formerly worked in the construction sector, found themselves unemployed with very few future prospects. For him, this was a first experience with <u>how the collective crisis deeply affected the lives of his peers</u> – as well as his own. The following sequence illustrates how he experienced this phase of his life (cf. Riemann, 2019).

> *This was a time in my life that I remember very well. It was very (pause) very weird because we would always get together, always with the same people, the same spot in my neighbourhood. And the days, the months would go by without any news. Nobody could continue with school, nobody would get a place. What I knew is that they started studying [for a high school degree], but they were so behind with regard to what is normal because they had left school to work... and the rest wouldn't find work, so they turned to things a little... I don't know how to say it... gently... they started to make money in ways that are hardly legitimate.*

> *It was a really desperate stage to be in, I remember it like that because it was very repetitive. Imagine, for many years, sitting in the same spot with the same people and nobody would do anything, do anything with their lives, achieve anything, get anything… and each one would get into big problems because of the way they made money. So the most exciting thing that could happen to us is when the police would stop us (…).*

In this data extract, certain themes of the experience of mass unemployment call to mind Jahoda et al.'s (1933) description of a 'weary community' in their study of Marienthal, an Austrian town severely affected by the Great Recession. These themes include the repetitiveness of Adam's everyday life, which involved "*sitting in the same spot with the same people*"; the lack of purpose and future perspectives, which resulted in a certain emptiness, which some attempted to fill with illegal activities; and the distorted perception of time, as Adam remembered how "*the days, the months would go by without any news.*" Although Adam was still enrolled in high school at the time, he shared the generational experience in his milieu of peers. The collective atmosphere of lethargy and hopelessness had an impact on him, as he felt demotivated to attend and make an effort at school. He apparently had to repeat school years, graduating "*very late*" in 2011, at the age of 20.

Although Adam spent a lot of time with this group of friends in public, it seems as if he nevertheless tried to keep a certain distance from them. His ambivalent feelings towards his peers become visible in the pronouns he uses. Adam is simultaneously talking about "*them*" and "*us*" when referring to his friends. He had a slightly more privileged socio-economic background than his peers, as both of his parents had stable incomes as civil servants. In contrast to his friends who had dropped out of the education system to work in construction, Adam had stayed in school. This fact made him less vulnerable than those who seemed completely 'left behind'.

DEVELOPING A BIOGRAPHICAL PROJECT

For Adam, graduating from high school marked a turning point, as he hoped that it would enable him to break what he described as a "*desperate stage to be in*". Following his interest in media, he had decided to pursue a degree in audio-visual studies as part of his long-term biographical project of working in the film industry. To his surprise he was, however, not admitted to the public university due to a change in admission procedures that year. In my interview with him, Adam was still bitter about this rejection, which became especially visible in a retrospective comment on the Spanish higher education system: "*Yes, really weird, but that's how it works*".

When Adam was faced with the perspective of spending a year "*sitting around with the same people*" with nothing to do, somebody in Adam's extended family decided to intervene by paying the tuition fees at a private institute. While perhaps not very close to Adam (as suggested in his expression "*someone in my family appeared*"), this family member noticed his problems, took his biographical project seriously and tried to support him in developing it. The relative was apparently deeply worried about Adam's situation, as he seemed in danger of biographical stagnation and slipping into a trajectory or losing control.[2]

The programme Adam enrolled in was Audio-Visual Realisation, which trained students to use cameras and recorders specifically for TV productions. He was euphoric about the three-year course, believing that he had finally found his vocation after years of "*doing nothing*" at school. He was well aware that it was not a course at university level, but being a student in this programme intensified his identification with his chosen occupation nevertheless. During his time at the private institute, he developed the dream of finding a way to get paid as a cameraman. This plan, however, turned out to be illusionary as he could only find unpaid internships after graduation (cf. Riemann, 2019).

PARTICIPATING IN THE COLLECTIVE MOVEMENT

Feeling disoriented in this situation, Adam found meaning in becoming an activist in the emerging social movement 15-M. In Madrid, this movement took the form of mass protests and assemblies, which were held in various neighbourhoods. Together with some friends, he started to collect used books and created a small library for protestors to use for free. Adam also got involved by helping immigrants in his neighbourhood who had been (as he described it) unlawfully detained by the police. Whilst being in the movement, he realised that the skills he had acquired during his training could be useful, as there appeared to be a need for what Adam called a "news department". With the vague idea of perhaps being able to sell some of his photographs, Adam started to bring his camera to protests. Earning money this way was, however, not his main motivation, and he emphasised how he had an intrinsic motivation to witness and document what was happening. For Adam, the movement triggered something like a political awakening with which he deeply identified. Being involved in these activist circles also gave him a sense of common purpose, as the group shared this belief in the future they were working towards.

Despite Adam's (and his peers') efforts, his involvement in the collective movement could not provide a lasting source of meaning in his life. He felt despondent because many of the protests became increasingly violent and the confrontations with the police escalated. Adam documented the gradual deterioration of the movement by filming the confrontations and taking photographs. He remembered how there was a time when the movement did not seem to be going anywhere. He again found himself thrown back into a situation of hopelessness and a lack of perspectives (*"No work, nothing else"*) (cf. Riemann, 2019).

AN ACTION SCHEME OF TAKING CONTROL

At this point his mother intervened by suggesting a temporary stay in the United Kingdom in order to learn English. This idea stemmed from the common belief in Spain that speaking English well is a useful skill. She hoped that it would enable her son to find work in the Spanish labour market upon return. Similar to the relative who paid for Adam's tuition fees, his mother took the initiative by trying to give her son a new perspective. His family was worried about Adam's situation, as they sensed how he was at the verge of getting caught up in a trajectory of suffering. That being said, it is clear that this action scheme of taking control was not based on careful planning and entailed unrealistic assumptions about the amount of time this would require. Adam's mother thought that an informal class with a (still to be found) native speaker would be sufficient for the sound acquisition of the English language and that it would take no longer than four weeks.

After multiple failed attempts to give his life a new direction, Adam felt paralysed. He was deeply unhappy about living at home without a job, which took a toll on his self-esteem. Having very little to lose, he reluctantly agreed to spend two weeks in the UK, which he regarded as a *"vacation"* whereas his mother perceived it as an investment in his foreign language skills. When deciding where to travel, Adam picked Manchester; he preferred bigger cities and believed London to be too expensive. In hindsight, it is quite remarkable how this spontaneous and ill-prepared trip evolved into something biographically significant (cf. Riemann, 2019).

ARRIVING IN ENGLAND

Adam's narrative reveals that his arrival in Manchester was overwhelming and has been etched in his memory. At the time of our interview, distance allowed Adam to reflect upon this episode with some amusement (*"Now, the funny story starts!"*). When he spoke about these experiences, his narrative became extremely dense and detailed with a lot of references to dialogues and shifting inner states of wonder, confusion, excitement and pride in being an *"explorer"*. The phase of arrival was obviously still biographically significant for him at the time of our interview, and he enjoyed reliving this time in his narrative.

> *And well, I left the station [Manchester Piccadilly], got a map and started to walk… and I got lost. I didn't have anybody I could call. I didn't have anybody who would take me out of this situation. I was lucky because I have always liked the topic of survival, walking through a forest. I had never done it before, but what I said earlier, it was my curiosity that saved me, my interests. I looked at the map. I found a hotel that wasn't mine on the map and I saw that the other one was in the east. I looked at the sun. I said, "it's getting dark, so the east must be over there, or like the west is over there where the sun sets, so I have to go this way."*

Soon after he left the train station, it started to rain heavily. Having only packed summer clothes, Adam was not prepared for this type of weather. After spending a few hours wandering around Manchester, he finally arrived at the hotel. After some miscommunication with the receptionist (*"I said 'Hola, buenas, tengo una reserva…' in Spanish, because I couldn't speak*

English."), he was able to check in. In the following days, Adam explored his new neighbourhood.

> *What I remember most of these early days was the smell of curry that came from the [Indian] restaurants there, which is really strong. Of course, everything was very exotic, very strange. I felt a bit like an explorer because many of my friends… well, those who can, those who have money and went to university, they spent their Erasmus semester in Germany, the United Kingdom, in South America, wherever. But the people I was closest with, people from my neighbourhood, the ones that had left school, the majority of them had stayed in Spain. Of course, I was some sort of explorer, it was like 'look at this crazy one who went over there!'*

This data extract reveals an important theme in Adam's narrative: the feeling of being an *'explorer'* (positive) versus what he later defines as a *'true immigrant'* (negative). He constantly re-evaluated his migration experience during his stay in Manchester according to this self-theorising spectrum. Adam's descriptions of how different people looked ("*(…) white, so white. They were pink*"), his attempt to orient himself by looking at the sun, and other observations such as the "*smell of curry*" resemble reports of discoverers and perhaps early anthropologists describing their first encounters with foreign cultures. From an outsider's perspective, the analogy appears exaggerated in this context ("*I always liked the topic of survival (…)*") as he was in no real danger. It does, however, authentically capture how Adam felt in the situation. Considering that the whole trip was his mother's idea, which he had only reluctantly agreed to, his new self-identification as an explorer seems somewhat surprising. Although Adam had no strong desire to go, arriving in Manchester seemed like a 'wake-up call' as he was thrown into an environment that was completely new.

DISCOVERING EUROPEAN SPACES

In his first days in Manchester, Adam decided to explore the city. One night, he met a group of Spanish people who had lived in Manchester for a few years. One of them, he recalled, had found a job in his field of expertise while the others were involved in menial work. This encounter, though fleeting, turned out to be important for Adam. Learning that there were jobs that he could realistically attain planted the idea in his mind of perhaps prolonging his stay. Given that he had found himself in a hopeless situation in Madrid, the prospect of finding even a menial job seemed very attractive. Such chance encounters, casual conversations and spontaneous ideas about prolonging his stay could be referred to as 'stumbling into migration'. This process differs from the carefully planned and prepared migration projects of other interviewees in my sample. In Adam's case, his mother's original idea of learning English in two weeks had faded into the background at this point,[3] as the prospect of independence was suddenly within his reach.

Back at the hotel, Adam met a man from Portugal who was working in the cafeteria. Even though his Spanish was quite broken, the two started talking and got along very well. For Adam, this person would become an important mentor during his stay in the UK. A few days after their first encounter, the Portuguese man took the initiative and asked Adam if he was interested in working in the hotel. Adam, who had very little to lose, agreed and gave him his CV. Due to his lack of English skills, the job interview with the manager was a disaster, as Adam recalled. He was hired nevertheless because the Portuguese man previously claimed he had known Adam his entire life (a 'white lie' to improve his chances of getting the job).

After getting the job, Adam found a flat that he shared with two Spanish housemates and was in bad condition. He was, however, relieved about having a place to stay. Adam used his last savings to pay the deposit and rent, which put him in a precarious position. He was getting paid at the end of each month. For the first four weeks at his new job, he therefore had to cope without any money. This included having to eat other people's leftovers and having to endure cold weather (that he was not used to) whilst wearing summer clothes. Despite these hardships, Adam was also deeply fascinated by his new environment.

> *I was working in catering… All day I was moving, I was always tired, I wasn't used to it and then I would have to walk back home. (…) I remember being very tired these first days, and I had to eat. The only food that I tried was the leftovers of the hotel that they would always give to the workers because I didn't have money to buy food. I didn't have money for the bus, I didn't have money for anything… but they would pay me by the end of the month, so I was going to put up with it until then. It was an interesting episode in my life because I met tons of new people. Also types of people I had never encountered before. My neighbours were from Latvia. I had never met people from over there (…). So the first month was (pause), it was cold.*

> *Very cold, I remember. I didn't have warm clothes or clothes that are appropriate for rainy weather. And, of course, in Manchester there's a terrible wind. I think it was the first time that I experienced wind from below. The wind was so strong that it lifted the water from the puddles on the ground. It was hailing too sometimes. It was a time in my life that was very hard, but I enjoyed it too because of all these new experiences that I was making.*

Prior to his departure to Manchester, Adam had never left Spain, which is an important aspect to keep in mind when evaluating his first experiences in the UK. He was deeply curious about meeting people from other countries such as Latvia. Adam was moving within a uniquely *European* space in Manchester, where EU citizens of different nationalities worked and lived together. These were encounters that would not have taken place had it not been for their common migration to Britain.

After a few months working at the hotel, a close friend from Madrid contacted Adam. His friend, he recalled, was in a similar situation as he had been in before: "*without a job, without a degree, without any idea what to do with his life.*" Adam acted like the Portuguese man who had encouraged him to stay and became this friend's mentor and scout. By offering him a place to stay and support in finding a job at the hotel, Adam convinced him to come. The two friends lived and worked together for four months. Adam enjoyed having such a close companion who was in the same situation as him.

THE EXPERIENCE OF WORK

Adam described the hotel as severely understaffed, which made his work environment very stressful. A large part of his job involved setting up tables and chairs for conferences with hundreds of participants. When the conference day ended, he and his co-workers were then in charge of cleaning up, which meant that they often worked until very late at night. His shifts lasted up to 10 hours, which took a toll on his health. The following excerpt reveals something about his experience of work and the tensions between different categories of workers.

> *I was a bit desperate in this situation. I started to feel like a true immigrant… being subordinated to English people and furthermore, they left me a bit on the outside.*

> *The Brits had a life that seemed more normal. My friend, who came from home, his name is Javier, was in the same situation as I was. So, I remember during that time, a lot of people left and they hired only very few new ones. Like nine waiters, nine cleaners, nine workers for events with hundreds of people... 300, 400... I remember one time they had an event with 700 people in the hotel and only nine people to serve them. It was so stressful. There were also a lot of people who "called in sick" (switches to English). That was typical for Brits to do whenever they didn't feel like working and then we were left with the double amount of work. So that's why we started to do the same thing... but with us they weren't as gentle. They threatened to fire us, they were shouting at us why we would do this. This really angered us, so we started a group of people who would complain more – and they were fighting us. It was terrible.*

This narrative sequence illustrates that Adam experienced his working conditions as harsh and unfair. His expression of feeling like a *"true immigrant"* stands out in contrast to his initial euphoria of being an *"explorer."* There is an element of resignation in how he described this situation. Adam was disappointed about the lack of empathy his manager displayed after being informed about his back pain. When he had the impression that British co-workers received a preferential treatment, Adam's feelings of frustration turned into anger, a sentiment that he shared with other European workers. In this extract, one needs to pay attention to the pronouns he used and what they mean in this context. Who are 'we'? Who are 'they'? It seems that, in response to the perceived unequal treatment by the British superiors, new 'we' groups of foreign workers are emerging that are not divided along nationalities. Examples include Adam's first important mentors in Manchester, who were from Portugal and Latvia. Despite some linguistic barriers, they deeply identified with Adam and immediately accepted him as 'one of us'.

FACING THE ONSET OF BREXIT

Adam's observations concerning intergroup tensions at his workplace (i.e. British versus EU workers) were also reflected in the political climate at the time. He had moved to the UK in 2014 and stayed for almost two years. Although he returned to Spain prior to the EU referendum, Adam expressed deep concern about Brexit and shared vivid memories of how he had experienced the onset of this new collective crisis.

> *What I remember more than anything is that during Christmas before Brexit, we would always get newspapers delivered to the hotel every morning in the breakfast area. And I… when I arrived, the first thing that I would do is look at the newspapers before they were laid out for the hotel guests. I would see them when they got delivered. And there was one thing that always caught my attention. It's like they were always saying "immigrants, whatever…"… really sensationalist as if immigrants were the most urgent problem… immigrants, I don't know what. You would see posters of this party everywhere… What is it called? This racist party? [UKIP] You would see the headlines of the newspapers saying that immigration was a problem, but all you would see is that immigrants do the dirty jobs, like it is happening in all countries. (…) We do the jobs that English people don't need to do.*

Adam, who was quite literally 'breaking his back' for a low-paid job, was in charge of laying out tabloid newspapers for hotel guests. These newspapers were media outlets that apparently propagated xenophobic anti-EU messages. He took these anti-immigration headlines personally, as he sensed how his (and his co-workers') contributions were not valued ("*immigrants do the dirty jobs*"). Adam strongly opposed attempts to construct EU migrants as "*the most urgent problem*", as he knew from first-hand experience how hard they worked, even under unfavourable conditions. In this narrative sequence, his use of the personal pronoun 'we' is noteworthy. Adam not only referred to fellow Spanish migrants, but also to his co-workers with other EU nationalities, which points to the emergence of a European identity in response to Brexit.

GOING BACK?

Although the friendships Adam made in the UK were biographically significant, the community of EU migrants could not offer him a lasting foundation. Significant others leaving Manchester had become a recurring theme in his life, as people seemed constantly on the move. Even during times of relative stability, it seems as if the fear of loneliness was always present. Adam was deeply frustrated about this pattern, which took a toll on his wellbeing. After his initial euphoria about experiencing 'something new' had worn off, the negative aspects of his 'immigrant' life appeared to outweigh its benefits. Adam started to wonder whether it was time to move back to Madrid. Some of his co-workers had already returned to Spain and appeared happy about their decision, sometimes more out of personal reasons than because of real job prospects. Adam was also consulting his old friends in Madrid, who encouraged him to come back, claiming, *"the crisis was already disappearing"*.

In terms of the structural processes of his life, there appear to be two competing processes, which he alludes to in his contrasting feelings of being an *"explorer"* versus a *"true immigrant"*. Whilst he enjoyed making new experiences, his life in Manchester was marked by many hardships that included physical stress (e.g. the risk of chronic back pain), bitterness about unfair labour conditions and the disappointment of losing close social relationships. Adam was at the verge of getting caught up in a trajectory of suffering.

A NEW PERSPECTIVE

In this situation, which he described as *"desperate"*, Adam met somebody who would change his outlook on life for some time.

> *In this moment, a few new workers showed up in the hotel. Among them was an Italian girl. I liked her a lot. We fell in love. / Well, I fell in love at least (speaks more quietly). It was an episode in my life that I remember very well. One day, we took a trip to Liverpool and some other places. We took walks. I was with her. I was really happy. The problems at work didn't seem so serious. I believed that in September things would get better. I thought that they would hire more people and raise our wages. Besides, I also had some audio-visual jobs. At last, I could do something that was related to what I had studied. You know, I could use my camera and film conferences. On other occasions I recorded the sound. They showed me how to do it and they were paying me more. So I thought that things would get better.*

Adam's mood lifted significantly after meeting his Italian co-worker. Given that she appeared in his life when he was unhappy, it seems that he projected many hopes onto this new relationship. His softly spoken self-correction, *"Well, I fell in love at least"*, already alludes to a certain self-deception and disillusionment he associated with this experience in retrospect. His positive outlook was also based on the fact that he could occasionally film conferences at his workplace and be paid for it. These sporadic audio-visual assignments provided him with a sense of biographical continuity and pride. Falling in love with his co-worker marked a radical shift in Adam's attitude, as he started to view his environment (including *"problems at work"*) through rose-coloured glasses. He was hopeful about making progress in his life.

SLIDING INTO A TRAJECTORY OF LOSING CONTROL

What happened next exposed the fragility of his newfound optimism. After dating his Italian co-worker for a few months, Adam sensed that *"things were starting to get weird"*. He suppressed his doubts about her fidelity and went to Spain for one week to visit his friends and family. During his stay, Adam felt disconnected from his old peers. Their worldview, he recalled, was very different from his own (*"It just seemed as if time had stood still in Spain"*). At this moment, Adam already sensed that a return migration would not be as easy as he had imagined. In Manchester, his new relationship and his occasional filming assignment had served as a source of cautious optimism. When he returned to the UK, however, Adam experienced a rude awakening.

> *But then when I came back, I found out that the girl that I had been dating and another Spanish guy who she also got along with had had an affair. I found out at a party. I saw them there, kissing and dancing. For me this was a catastrophe. A tremendous catastrophe! I thought this is really bad. I liked her a lot this girl. (Pause) They also started giving me nightshifts again in this place… carrying tables. My back was a little bit better because I had gotten some help. However, if you spend all night working, you work when everybody is sleeping and you sleep during the day. If that's your normal everyday life, you feel exhausted and lonely. Also, I was living next to the Italian girl that I liked and I felt completely devastated. (…) It was an episode in my life when I started to drink a lot and take amphetamines. I hadn't used them before but I started over there. I went to parties and there were drugs and I did them because I needed them. I saw her all the time. Every time I would go out, she was there with this guy.*

For Adam, seeing the woman he was dating with someone else triggered a deep loss of control. He experienced her unfaithfulness as a *"tremendous catastrophe*", which indicates the destabilising effect it had on his life. Aside from his heartache, his working conditions deteriorated, leaving him *"exhausted and lonely"*. Adam was in deep pain, which he tried to numb by turning to alcohol and amphetamines. This was a "trajectory transformation" (Schütze, 1995), as the trajectory of suffering extended to other parts of his life when he ran the risk of developing an addiction (*"I did them because I needed them."*).

On top of these problems, Adam was at risk of losing his accommodation. He had shared his run-down flat (*"The house was horrible"*) with two Spanish housemates who had returned to Spain spontaneously. Adam was unable to pay rent by himself, which put him in a precarious position. Trying to find a room in another flat share turned out to be a frustrating experience. Despite making an effort, Adam received rejection after rejection, which he believed had to do with his status as a male foreigner (*"Don't you have a room for me?"* And they were all like, *"No, it's just that we found an English girl."*).

REGAINING STABILITY

His landlord grew impatient with Adam's inability to pay full rent and threatened him with eviction if he failed to find new housemates within one week. Adam succeeded in this task and found two young women from Pakistan and Germany who moved in with him. He described their presence as a *"radical change"* in his life, as they became close friends within a short amount of time, particularly his German housemate, who he described as *"a bit of a hippie, always happy"*. Her positivity was contagious, and he started to feel optimistic and in control of his life again. Adam expressed pride in regaining both financial and social stability in a situation that he had previously experienced as hopeless (*"What a miracle, I thought. I had lost everything but managed to build up something new"*). Adam expanded his original spectrum of being an 'explorer' versus an 'immigrant' with a new category: being a person who is integrated in society and able to make progress. When thinking about these categories as stages, it seems that he finally arrived at a place where he felt more or less settled in Manchester after overcoming both the initial excitement and hardships.

DECIDING TO RETURN TO SPAIN

Although Adam was content with his life at this point in time, he did not quite trust his newfound stability. While he did manage to get more audio-visual assignments at the hotel, his new friendship with his German housemate had the biggest impact on his emotional wellbeing. Her positivity had a stabilising effect on him, as he no longer depended on drugs and alcohol to ease his pain. After living together for some time, the two friends became romantically involved. This relationship seemed more casual in comparison to what he had felt for the Italian woman. Adam nevertheless regarded his German housemate as an important significant other in his life and feared her departure, as he would "*have to start all over again*". When she revealed that she wanted to move to Spain to learn the language, Adam decided to join her.

When reconstructing Adam's decision to return to Spain, it is worth considering the following biographical conditions: a) the significance of his new relationship and his fear of being alone, b) his critical evaluation of his current work situation, as he was poorly paid and at risk of developing chronic back pain, and c) encouraging messages from his Spanish friends, who claimed that "*the crisis was already disappearing*". Although he did not explicitly mention Brexit as a motive for leaving the UK, it seems that the political atmosphere leading up to the EU referendum exacerbated his feelings of frustration. Adam felt humiliated as someone who was doing the '*dirty work*' whilst at the same time being constructed as a burden for British society.

A DIFFICULT HOMECOMING

After Adam and his German housemate moved to Madrid together, she stayed for only a few weeks before moving to Germany and then to Latin America. Adam did not experience this separation as very dramatic and the two friends remained on very good terms. For Adam, moving back to his old surroundings brought about challenges he had not anticipated.

> *When I first came back, I was so disoriented. All these cafes and shops didn't seem to be in their right spot somehow. There were new shops that had opened since I had*

left. Also the people on the street, they looked different, they dressed differently… I don't know. My old friends, they also had slightly different lives. It was a world that I somehow couldn't enter. None of it made sense to me.

What Adam experienced could be described as an <u>uneasy homecoming</u> (cf. Schütz, 1971), an experience he shared with other participants in my study. His observations that new shops and cafes had opened since he had left may appear insignificant, but they carry a deeper meaning. He recognised the streets where he grew up, yet the streets had changed. Metaphorically speaking, this was also the case with regard to his social relationships. Adam sensed that he could not simply pick up his social life where he had left it, as both he and his old friends had 'moved on' ("*It was a world that somehow I couldn't enter*").

Considering that Adam had left Manchester primarily out of a fear of isolation, this experience was quite disappointing. Although he had already sensed some disconnection with his old peers during an earlier visit to Madrid, he had seemingly repressed these doubts when deciding to return permanently. Adam had hoped to find stability by re-entering social circles that were *not* constantly on the move. This expectation was, however, built on unrealistic expectations as he found himself in an outsider position *again*.

Adam was not only disillusioned about his social life, but also about the labour market situation. His friends' euphoric comments about 'things getting better' had given him the vague hope that the crisis was slowly disappearing. After moving back, however, Adam struggled to find a job that could secure him an independent existence. Eventually, he found a job in road construction. Spending 10 to 12 hours every day lifting heavy materials took a toll on his health, and his back started to hurt again. The money he earned was not sufficient to pay for a room in a flat, which forced him to move back in with his mother, an experience he described as "awful". Together with a few friends, Adam tried to film a documentary, which was an attempt to reconnect with his biographical project and academic training. The project failed, partly because of group dynamics that he described as untrusting and competitive. Lacking the financial resources to complete the film, some of his friends tried to "*find the money illegally*". Adam did not go into details about what these activities entailed but emphasised how his peers' behaviour made him feel uncomfortable.

After the documentary project failed, Adam decided to pursue a degree in cinematography. He applied to the public university but was rejected, which he recalled with visible frustration. Adam did, however, get an offer from a private institute that he accepted. It is important to emphasise that he had not moved back to Madrid with the *intention* of going back to study. Instead the idea developed much like a makeshift solution to avoid the imminent unemployment or underemployment he would otherwise face. In our interview, Adam admitted that the degree was unlikely to increase his chances on the labour market, "*because with that degree you could only aspire to become a movie director and that is very unrealistic*". His main motivation was personal, as he continued to have an intellectual interest in film.

LOOKING TOWARDS AN UNCERTAIN FUTURE

Adam ended his introductory narrative with an evaluation of his life situation, which became visible in a conspicuous argumentative pre-coda sequence[4] beginning with the utterance "*So that's what I am doing now.*" In this pre-coda sequence Adam expressed a sense of disorientation that he attributed both to lacking a clear career path, but also to feeling somewhat *uprooted*. He ended the sequence (and his whole introductory narrative) by stating that he felt he belonged neither in the UK nor in Spain (i.e. "*Over there, they perceive me as a Spaniard and here I see things differently.*"). By weighing up the positive and negative aspects of his stay abroad, Adam revealed certain unsolved problem constellations in his life. It seemed that he needed to work through his experiences abroad.

While he was still enrolled at the private institute, he did not have a clear perspective on how to proceed after graduation. There was an element of resignation in how Adam reflected about his current situation and future prospects. He was not happy about living with his mother again but did not see a clear way out. Adam was pessimistic about finding a job in the film industry but had the vague hope that his English skills might help him find a job as a waiter. His biographical narrative revealed that he took much pride in having overcome many obstacles in Manchester, which was a grand adventure that had a lasting impact on his life. Throughout the interview, Adam enjoyed reliving even difficult episodes of his migration experience. In retrospect, he could see the humour in certain situations and laugh about his former naïve self.

Adam expressed deep gratitude to British society: *"they gave me a job when I had no hope that I would find work, they gave me a life"*. He looked back at his two years in Manchester very fondly despite all the hardships he had to endure during that time. Against this background, he expressed sadness about the possibility of not being welcomed back due to Brexit.

I also had this feeling that if something happens here, if something goes wrong, the same feeling when I first went to the UK, if something goes wrong I could go back to Spain… when I came back I had the feeling that I could go over there again… I have, ehm, I have paid taxes over there, or like, I had the feeling that I could go back and now everything is up in the air.

Adam's comment that he had paid taxes in Britain underlines how he perceived Brexit as a breach of reciprocity. It symbolically devalued his contributions to society and created a barrier to the option of remigration. Europe as a 'mental space' (Schütze & Schröder-Wildhagen, 2012) had become smaller, which he found depressing. The door to the UK, which had previously offered him a way out of a seemingly hopeless situation, was now rapidly closing.

MARÍA NAVARRO

María is an informant I had the opportunity to interview three times in total. The first interview took place in Bristol in April 2014 (in the context of my MPhil project), where she had been working as a kitchen porter for nine months. Two and a half years later (November 2016), I met her again when she was preparing to return to Spain. The third interview took place in a restaurant in Madrid in August 2017, after she had lived there for more than half a year. Being able to follow María's journey throughout the years gave me a unique perspective on her migration experience and personal growth. At the time of our last interview, she was 34 years old.

María had first contacted me after reading a description of my research project that I had posted in one of the Facebook groups for Spanish people in the UK. My interest in people's whole biographies appeared to have struck a chord with her, as it gave her the platform to narrate freely. During our first interview, I sensed that she needed to talk about her difficult experiences with someone outside of her family and social circles. My position as a sympathetic stranger appeared to help in this context, as she felt how she had little to lose in being completely honest with me. Given the long-term nature of this case study, I will proceed by separately focusing on the three interviews and their content. During our first meeting, María told me her entire life history from childhood until the day of the interview. The second and third interviews focused on what had happened since we last saw each other.

FIRST INTERVIEW: APRIL 2014

MARÍA'S CHILDHOOD AND YOUTH

María was born and raised in Madrid. Her parents divorced shortly after the birth of their second daughter, who is 10 years María's junior. After their separation, the children continued to live with their mother. She described her relationship to both of her parents as distant. Her father, who had no academic background, was apparently not very present in his children's lives when they were young (even whilst the parents were still married). They did, however, keep in touch and he supported them financially. María described her mother as moody and emotionally distant, and thereby painted a picture of a rather lonely childhood.[5] Even though she did not mention it explicitly at this point, her biographical narrative suggests that it was during this time that she discovered her love for books as a form of escapism. María also had positive childhood memories that she associated mostly with extended family members on her mother's side. Her grandmother, aunts and cousins played an important role in her upbringing and provided a support network that she could rely on. She always attended private schools and did not mention any financial problems during her youth.

María described her teenage years as *"a difficult time"*, as she was very shy and did not socialise much. She formed one lasting and biographically significant friendship with a classmate who became a single mother as a teenager. From a young age onwards, María sought distance from her parents. She mentioned how she had left home various times during her adolescence to live with a friend.

AN INITIAL BIOGRAPHICAL PROJECT – AND SETTLING FOR AN ALTERNATIVE

After graduating from high school in 2002, María was faced with choosing a university degree. As a teenager, she had developed an initial biographical project of becoming a journalist, as she enjoyed writing. Although she was a good student, María failed to meet the high entrance requirements for the journalism programme at university. She was unwilling to give up on this biographical project completely and looked for an alternative way to achieve it. In the end, María opted for a degree in library science due to her special affinity to books. Her original plan, she remembered, was to study library sciences for three years and then switch to journalism for four semesters. This plan did not materialise in the end, as she took five years to complete her academic training as a librarian. She enjoyed the programme, especially courses in archival work, and spoke highly of the profession.

THE BIOGRAPHICAL RELEVANCE OF WORKING AT A BOOKSTORE

In 2005, María started to work at a large bookstore. She was 21 years old and in her third year at university. She was one of the few informants who reached financial independence at quite a young age. In Spain, it is quite uncommon for children to move out of their parental home for university if they remain in the same city. Since María chose this path deliberately, she was in charge of paying rent. At the bookstore, she received much recognition for being a knowledgeable salesperson. She also enjoyed being part of a team that shared her intellectual interest in books and literature. She enjoyed a positive work environment that differed from her difficult childhood and adolescence.

After graduating from university, María worked at the same bookshop full-time for three years. In total she spent eight years with this company (2005-2013), which made it a biographically significant chapter in her life. María would have preferred to work as a librarian and continued to identify with this long-term profession.[6] In retrospect, María described this period of her life as quite happy, as she had a stable job that she enjoyed and a comfortable rent-controlled apartment. Furthermore, she was in a close long-term relationship with a man she had met through mutual friends.

LOSING CONTROL IN THE CONTEXT OF A FAMILY TRAGEDY

María's life, however, changed abruptly due to a dramatic event (cf. Riemann, 2019). Her younger sister had an accident and as a result suffered from severe and lasting mental impairments. When I asked her about how the plan to migrate emerged, she started to cry and responded:

Oh I knew this would happen (laughs, wipes tears away). (…) Well, then we had a lot of family problems, because my parents don't get along. My father blamed my mother, arguing that she didn't take care of my sister. He did not understand it… (…) Well, we don't know who is to blame. It's not my mother's fault… but well, since they weren't getting along, they started a war. And well, I was in the middle of course… my sister was gone, so I was in the middle. I began having a lot of problems because I didn't know how to deal with all that. It was like a slap in the face. From one day to the next your little sister is crazy. She is crazy. Really crazy. She throws food around, yells, beats us… she is very strong as well. Apart from that my father is blaming my mother, my mother is blaming my father.

Well, I did not know how to… I did not know how to deal with all that. Well, then I fell into a form of depression. I couldn't leave the house. I couldn't go to work. That's when I lost all my friends except for this one girl… and I lost my partner as well, because he… he didn't know what to do either. It's complicated. (…) At work, I used to work 40 hours a week… they reduced it to 20 hours, because I wasn't able to work full-time. I wasn't the same person like before, so that's why they reduced my workload. (…) I couldn't pay rent anymore because I was only working part-time.

This narrative sequence sheds light on how different biographical problem constellations merged in this situation. The depth of her pain was visible not only in her emotional reaction (i.e. the fact that she started to cry), but also in textual features of this excerpt. In contrast to earlier parts about her childhood, her biographical narrative suddenly became very detailed and personal at this point. For María, the memory of her plan to migrate and the family catastrophe were intrinsically linked.

Her sister's accident and its dramatic repercussions destabilised every part of María's life. Apparently, there was much uncertainty about her sister's diagnosis, as psychiatrists differed in their interpretation of this case (e.g.

'schizophrenia', 'bi-polar disorder' etc.), and healthcare professionals were very pessimistic about her prospects of recovery, which made this situation threatening for everyone involved. María's parents, who had been divorced for a long time, dealt with their sense of helplessness by blaming each other. In the interview, María used the metaphor of a *'war'* to describe the intensity of their conflict. She was not only expected to mediate between the estranged parties, but also to take care of her disabled sister. She felt ill-equipped for the task as she had no professional training in caring for people with mental impairments (cf. Riemann, 2019).

Her parents confronted María with institutional expectation patterns of the life-course (Schütze 1981; 2008) that were overwhelming and unrealistic. The idea that it was their daughter's moral duty to take care of her younger sibling evolved into a family trap. It did not take long until María collapsed under the emotional pressure. She got caught up in a deep trajectory of suffering and was quickly losing control over her life. María felt extremely paralysed in this situation (*"I couldn't leave the house"*) and sought professional help. She was prescribed anti-depressants to cope with her feelings. Her boyfriend's decision to end the relationship exacerbated the situation, as she felt abandoned and increasingly helpless. María's biographical narrative suggests that she associated this break-up with the stigma of mental illness. She showed weakness in front of her partner, which she believed had prompted him to leave.

What is striking about María's case is that her personal and financial problems merged in the context of the economic crisis – and serves as an example of how economic crises can *exacerbate* the situation of vulnerable individuals, who are already trapped in trajectories of suffering (e.g. due to personal losses). In her view, her employers showed little understanding in this situation, as they reduced her position by 50% after noticing a drop in her productivity. At this point in time (2012/2013), her chances of finding another job in Madrid to supplement this loss in income were extremely low. Her parents could not offer any moral or financial support. They were fully occupied with her sister. The medical treatments she had received at various private hospitals had ruined the family financially (*"It was like €500 a day"*), yet there were no signs of improvement. Since her salary had been cut in half, she struggled to pay rent. In order to make ends meet, she started to share her flat with a young woman. María began to feel uncomfortable in her own home, as she described her housemate as loud and disrespectful.

THE EMERGENCE OF AN ACTION SCHEME OF ESCAPE

Whilst María felt overlooked by her nuclear family, one of her aunts took notice of her despair. In order to give her niece a break, she offered her a holiday to England. This spontaneous trip would eventually evolve into a biographically significant chapter in her life.

> *But well, one of my aunts… well, I have a cousin here in Bristol who studies at the University of Bristol. Well, one day, one of my aunts decided to buy me a ticket and to send me here for two weeks for a holiday, because she saw that I was miserable. And then… well, I came here… and I met a guy here. A friend of my cousin… (…) He is Italian actually.*
>
> *But yeah, I went back to Madrid after my holiday. I went on with my work and I was living alone again. Well, I couldn't pay rent and at work I also had problems, because I wasn't as efficient as before. In my view it wasn't really fair that they reduced my hours so much because you don't have that much control over whether you are doing well or badly. (…) And, of course, there was the problem of my sister… (…) So, I decided that… I mean I was still with Marco, the Italian guy. He came to Spain, sometimes I went to see him… and then I thought, 'Okay, I'm going to try it', because here my work wasn't going well, I couldn't pay rent, and my family situation was really bad. It was clear for me that I had to go… because I couldn't live with a person like that or visit a person like that [younger sister]. It's too stressful. So I came here nine months ago… I'm living with him now.*

When taking a closer look at how María's migration project emerged, one can observe a few similarities and differences with Adam's case. Both informants were deeply unhappy in Spain and longed for a change. While Adam felt stuck at his mother's home, María had no 'shelter' she could return to due to the disintegration of her nuclear family. The economic crisis affected María at a different stage in her life, as she had spent several years living and working as an independent adult prior to the financial collapse. Her modest, yet independent existence evaporated within a very short period of time. María was expected to take care of herself and her finances but felt paralysed and unable to do so. Unlike Adam, she was at high risk of losing her accommodation and means of subsistence. Maria experienced her situation as existentially threatening.

What the two informants share is that the idea to go abroad initially emerged out of a family member's intervention. While Adam's mother suggested a temporary stay in the UK as an investment in his English skills, María's aunt wanted to give her niece a break from her difficulties at home. Neither of the participants travelled to Britain with the intention of staying long-term. Instead, they arrived as tourists and then *stumbled* across opportunities that they perceived as a way out of a hopeless situation at home (cf. Salazar, 2020). For Adam, it was the prospect of finally gaining financial independence by getting a job at a hotel in Manchester. For María, who was facing financial and personal ruin in Madrid, Bristol appeared like a safe haven to which she could escape. Her cousin and her new Italian boyfriend, who had both lived in the UK for some time, could provide her with shelter, which was a source of comfort and security.

María's biographical narrative suggests that she was longing for some physical distance from her sister, whose behaviour she described as violent and unpredictable. Her role as a mediator between her mother and father created an additional burden, as their conflict turned increasingly toxic. María's decision to leave Spain can be defined as an action scheme of escape (Schütze, 1981), which is especially visible in her sentence *"It was clear for me that I had to go"*. Her parents did not approve of her decision to migrate and put moral pressure on her to stay and help out. María's migration project apparently was a source of controversy in her extended family.

ARRIVING IN ENGLAND

In contrast to Adam, María was immediately welcomed into existing support structures after moving to Bristol. She could move in with her partner, who shared a flat with several housemates. Although her boyfriend was working in his field of expertise (i.e. marketing) in the UK, his salary was quite modest. He earned enough to cover the bills for one person, but not two. María was therefore under pressure to find a job quickly.

Prior to her departure, María had not made any concrete plans concerning what type of work she would seek in England. In retrospect, she described her English skills at the time as very limited, which for her ruled out the possibility of working in something related to her academic training as a librarian. Eventually, she accepted a job as a kitchen porter at a local university. For María moving to Bristol entailed a drop in living standards. The house, which the couple shared with several other men, was apparently in bad condition ("*there are bugs everywhere*").

THE EXPERIENCE OF WORK

María was not very happy in her new job.

> *It's very hard work. It's hard because it's cleaning… I've never done that before for a living. It's really hard physical work. Furthermore, the Brits… I think they are a bit annoyed by the Spanish people here. We are so many. My boss has seven Spanish workers. He is a typical English guy who talks quite loudly and is a bit narrow-minded. It's hard for us to understand him. Sometimes he yells at us and talks down to us…. He sometimes screams, 'They don't understand me! I don't know what they are doing here!'*

Her biographical narrative revealed a particular vulnerability at this point in time. She had arrived in England completely exhausted from her family and financial problems at home. In Bristol, she was now thrown into a work environment that she experienced as both physically and mentally draining. In interactions with her English superior, María sensed how he reduced her to the status of a migrant worker without a history. She experienced a radical degradation and devaluation of her biography that she had not anticipated.

The majority of María's co-workers (eight out of eleven) were also from Spain. Being able to communicate in her own language, including making some subversive insider jokes when faced with unfair treatment, was a source of relief for her. María emphasised how they had all graduated from university and led quite "normal lives" prior to the economic crisis. She used the term 'normal' to create a contrast with their current ways of making a living. Working as a cleaner in a foreign country *after* graduating from university did not quite fit with the aspirations they had had for their future when they were growing up. María emphasised how this was something that set them apart from their parents' generation.

María described how she believed the conditions of her 'zero-hour' contract (Wood & Burchell, 2014, Wood 2020) to be impeding her integration process. She could never predict how much income she would have by the end of the month, as she was not entitled to a minimum number of hours. María was not able to sign up for language classes because her schedule was constantly changing. English was, however, the shared language of communication at home (with her Italian boyfriend and their housemates), a set-up that put her in an advantageous position compared to other Spanish migrants who mainly socialised with co-nationals.

In order to arrive at a monthly salary of about £800, she and her co-workers would always try to work as many shifts as possible. She often had to work on the weekends, which meant that she did not get to spend much quality time with her boyfriend. The lack of financial security also prevented the couple from getting a separate flat together, which was something that María deemed very important. All of her Spanish co-workers were in their early to mid-twenties, which is why María felt slightly out of place. At age 30, María sensed more societal pressure to reach some form of age-appropriate stability (e.g. a formal job, financial security, a separate flat, family planning, etc.). She felt, however, very insecure about her future and lacked a sense of orientation (*"Some days it gets really hard because I don't want to believe that this is my future."*). María seemed at risk of losing touch with her original qualifications. She had many self-doubts concerning her English skills and therefore chose not to apply for jobs in bookstores or libraries. For these kinds of jobs, she argued, one had to speak English perfectly, a goal that she believed she would only be able to achieve in a few years' time.

In addition to her work as a kitchen porter, María also taught Spanish to young children at a nursery school once a week. This voluntary engagement served as an important source of meaning. By diversifying her activities, she could distance herself from her main occupation as a kitchen porter and feel useful and validated.

MARÍA'S EVALUATION OF HER BIOGRAPHICAL SITUATION IN 2014

María had experienced her family dynamics at home as quite suffocating. Moving to Bristol allowed her to breathe, as her parents did not have as much control over her life anymore. Although she believed that it had been the right decision to migrate, she also expressed disappointment about her life abroad. She was unhappy about living in a run-down flat with many housemates and having to work under such harsh conditions. At our first meeting, María seemed somewhat trapped in 'limbo'. Although she had managed to escape from her intolerable living situation in Madrid, she was lacking orientation in how to move forward with her life.

María was, furthermore, still traumatised by what had happened in Spain. She was taking anti-depressants every day, a secret that she kept hidden from her boyfriend. Although she portrayed her new partner as an understanding person, she was deeply afraid of history repeating itself. Her former boyfriend had ended the relationship after seeing María at her weakest (i.e. falling into a depression). She drew a problematic lesson from this experience (*"guys are guys"*), as she was unwilling to make herself that vulnerable again. María preferred keeping her new partner at arm's length, carefully controlling which parts of her life he would get to see and which ones would remain hidden.

SECOND INTERVIEW: NOVEMBER 2016

After meeting María for the first time in 2014 in the context of my MPhil project, we did not have any contact for over two years. When I sent her a message in November 2016, she wrote back that she enjoyed hearing from me and agreed to a second interview. In the email, she indicated that she was planning to move back to Spain shortly. We arranged a meeting at a coffee shop in Bristol. I asked her to tell me how her life had developed since we last saw each other. She opened up to me very quickly, and I did not interrupt her during the first part of the follow-up interview.

HER LIVING SITUATION

María started her second narrative by informing me that the relationship with her Italian boyfriend had dissolved about eight months prior. The decision was mutual, and she had not experienced this separation as very dramatic. Her cousin, with whom she was very close, had returned to Spain to care for a sick relative. Since María's social life in the UK had previously revolved mainly around these two people, she started to doubt the purpose of her stay in England after the breakup. She reflected and concluded that her current way of life no longer worked. After the separation, María made plans to move back to Spain, but wanted to give herself a bit more time before making another change. The past few months after the break-up had been quite transformative ("*It was quite a drastic change*"), as she believed she could apparently turn her life around for the better.

During the course of their relationship, María had led quite a reclusive life with her former partner. Although she had previously not socialised much with her Spanish co-workers at the university facility, they were there for her at a time of need. One of her colleagues informed her about a free bedroom in their flat share. María was relieved about the offer, as she had found the prospect of finding accommodation for herself quite daunting. At the time of our second interview, she was living with eight Spanish housemates. Despite having to compromise on her living standard, she seemed happy in this new situation. Her biographical narrative revealed that she had never been a very sociable person before, neither in Spain nor whilst she was living with her boyfriend in the UK. María now found herself integrated into a close-knit group of friends with whom she shared her everyday life. This was a new experience that she enjoyed.

THE SITUATION AT HER WORKPLACE

Although María was still working at the same university facility, her conditions had improved. The atmosphere at her workplace had lifted significantly after her former manager was discharged by the university administration. From María's perspective, her former boss had taken advantage of the unfavourable conditions of his workers' zero-hour contracts. They were dependent on his 'good will' to get good shifts and he apparently enjoyed this position of power.

> *And when I would say, 'No, on Sunday I don't want to work...' or 'I'm working all Sundays, please change my schedule and give me shifts on Mondays or Tuesdays.' He would then shorten my hours, or wouldn't give me any. I was so incredibly exhausted, and very sad because I thought that this was so unfair. I never missed work, I never arrived late, I never caused any problems, I have always done a good job. And after two years, it was still the same. Always working on the weekends, at night, almost never in the mornings... and when new people came, English people, at times they had only been working there for a month and they gave them the morning shifts*

> *from Mondays to Fridays. Super unfair, super unfair. We complained. As a group of people we complained.*

According to María, her manager punished her for speaking up by reducing her hours, which he knew would hurt her (cf. 'flexible discipline', Wood, 2020). Throughout the interview, she criticised the university's use of zero-hour contracts *"because you live in fear"*. María was saddened by the perceived lack of reciprocity, as nothing had changed even after two years of doing *"a good job"*. Her sadness turned into anger when she had the impression that *"English people"*, who had joined the team much later than her, were receiving preferential treatment in form of 'scheduling gifts' (Wood, 2020). Similar to Adam's experience at his workplace, the foreign workers' voicing of complaints marked something like a rudimentary beginning of joint resistance. It was, however, just a momentary and unorganised revolt. Although the university administration eventually decided to let go of this manager, María believed it was mainly because of practical reasons. In Bristol, she argued, it was relatively easy to find an informal job somewhere else. Many of her foreign co-workers were therefore unwilling to put up with this manager's behaviour and quit after a short period of time. As the team was often left without staff, her boss was not able to fulfil the tasks that he was required to do. This was a reoccurring pattern that eventually led to his discharge.

After her former manager left, María was offered a position at the university bar, which involved less direct supervision and control. She enjoyed this new autonomy (*"They trust me"*) and the ability to talk to students to practise her English. María also mentioned how she received a labour contract, which gave her more stability. Although her monthly salary was still very modest, it took away the *"fear"* that she associated with her former zero-hour contract. She was visibly relieved about the new working conditions, as she no longer had to worry about whether she would be able to pay her bills at the end of the month.

THE BIOGRAPHICAL RELEVANCE OF VOLUNTARY WORK

María had expanded her voluntary engagement since the breakup. Four times a week, she volunteered as a receptionist at a Citizens Advice Bureau that provided support for vulnerable people in Bristol. Her eyes lit up when speaking about this work, indicating that it had become for her an important source of biographical meaning. María felt very valued at the charity, as the organisers had expressed much respect and gratitude for her engagement. Her descriptions of this work became very dense and detailed, as she vividly recalled encounters at the office that had made a lasting impression on her. For the first time in her life, she was confronted with the topic of illiteracy among the local population. María found herself assisting British people in filling out forms and applications (e.g. for disability benefits). This type of work that made her feel useful and increased her self-confidence. Given how insecure she was about her foreign language skills at the time of our first interview, being able to support native speakers in that way felt like a remarkable achievement. At the Citizens Advice Bureau, María also practised certain skills such as speaking English on the phone, which she hoped might help her find a more formal job after returning to Spain.

María had also tried to reconnect with her academic training by volunteering at a university library. In her free time, she catalogued books in Spanish, Portuguese and Italian. The analysis of María's narrative reveals that she was striving for biographical continuity by trying to reconnect with her professional identity as a librarian. Her motivation to volunteer at the library was two-fold. Firstly, the work gave her a sense of dignity because she told herself that she was still essentially a librarian, not a kitchen porter. María sensed that her ability to distinguish between Romance languages was a unique skill that the British librarians in her environment did not have. They had expressed their gratitude to her, which served as a source of professional recognition, even though she was not paid. Secondly, she hoped that a certificate from the library she volunteered at could help her find a job in her field in Spain.

There are certain parallels with Adam's attempts to reconnect with his professional training by occasionally getting 'audio-visual jobs' at the hotel, where he was mainly engaged in manual labour. Both informants observed their work environments very carefully and developed a keen sense of where their special skills might be needed. This is a theme that also appeared in quite a few other interviews. Even though my participants came across such opportunities only sporadically, they served as a source of biographical continuity. They provided María with a sense of progress.

MARÍA'S DECISION TO RETURN TO SPAIN

Against the backdrop of how much progress María seemed to have made since our last interview, her plan to return to Spain appeared to be somewhat surprising. In Bristol, she had finally reached some financial stability and had a fulfilling social life. She contextualised this decision in the following way.

> *So now... I'm happy. I'm at peace. And okay, I'm going back to Spain at Christmas because I feel that this chapter of my life is coming to an end. I see Bristol as a stage of my life but not a place to settle. I learned all the English I could, I made all the experiences that I could have made and now I feel I should go home.*

Not unlike Adam, María decided to leave when she felt she could not get anything new out of the experience. They shared the frustration of close friends leaving the shared city of residence, making the UK a difficult place to settle and build up a lasting social life. Whilst she was generally content in Bristol, she believed to have outgrown this phase of her life. She reached this conclusion through discussions with friends who were in a similar situation.

María had contacted her former employers at the bookstore in Madrid. They made an informal promise that the next free position would be for her. She was confident that they would hire her back, especially since she had a certificate from her voluntary engagement at the university library. Interestingly, María mentioned how she would eventually like to work in the social sector. She had developed this idea whilst volunteering as a receptionist at the Citizens Advice Bureau in Bristol, which was a new biographical line that she wanted to develop further in the future. After her breakup, it seems that María underwent a creative metamorphosis (Schütze, 2008, 2014, 1981).

María only spoke about her family situation in Madrid after I specifically asked her about it. The textual structure of her second narrative revealed that she had avoided thinking about her problematic family dynamics when making the decision to return. Even though her parents had not explicitly mentioned this possibility to her, she was deeply afraid of becoming her disabled sister's primary caretaker again, which was a role that had previously caused her much unhappiness. Although María appeared to be in a much stronger place than when I first met her, she was keenly aware of the fragility of her personal progress (*"I'm doing much better, much better, and I'm scared that I'll go back to the same... I am really scared"*).

The worst-case scenario (becoming her sister's caretaker) was most likely to occur if María spent a longer period of time unemployed after her return. Although she was generally optimistic about her future, there appeared to be a contradiction in how she spoke about her job situation in Madrid. On the one hand, she seemed to have her mind set on working for the bookstore again (*"I have a job"*). On the other hand, she was aware that the offer was very informal (*"The first free position will be for me. But nobody knows when there will be an open position. Nobody knows"*). As previously mentioned, this company had deeply disappointed María before by reducing her salary by 50% when she was in a situation of despair. Against this background, her newfound trust in her old employers appeared somewhat surprising.

BREXIT? – "IT'S GOING TO BE WORSE FOR THEM!"

Unlike Adam, María was still living in the UK during the EU referendum of 2016. She did not cite Brexit as something that played into her decision to return to Spain. That being said, the collective political developments in Britain had overshadowed her last year in Bristol. María's reaction to the vote was somewhat typical for my sample, as she consistently used the personal pronouns 'we' and 'they'. Her line of argumentation had apparently emerged in conversations with other EU citizens who were in a similar position. She vividly described how she and her friends had experienced the night of the EU referendum, which took place five months prior to our interview.

> *We thought it was going to be negative, that it wasn't going to come out the way it did. We were very sure. And when it came out positive, to me... you had a sensation like, 'They are a little ignorant because they don't realise how much they need us.'*

Even though María claimed to be indifferent about the vote, her argumentative commentaries were quite detailed and conveyed a sense of anger. Her relationship to the receiving society had changed overnight. María and her friends distanced themselves from feelings of rejection by intellectualising the phenomenon. The idea that Brexit would eventually backfire (i.e. hurt Leave supporters) served as a source of solace in this context.

THIRD INTERVIEW: AUGUST 2017

I met María for a third time nine months later in Madrid. When I contacted her, she agreed to another interview right away. We met at a restaurant in a business district, which was close to her current workplace.

A ROUGH START

María started the third interview by recounting how her plans to return to the bookstore had not worked out. She had spent four months hoping to hear from her former employers. When she finally received a phone call from the company, she was disappointed to learn that they only offered her a part-time position that was low-paid. When she tried to negotiate more attractive conditions, her former employers apparently reacted in an unfriendly and uncooperative manner. Given her lack of income, María moved in with her father for several months. She experienced this initial phase of her return migration as quite disheartening.

> *So, I found myself at my father's place, everything was full of boxes, everything, my clothes were in suitcases. I didn't feel, I didn't have a space for myself, I didn't have my things… And that was hard… I didn't feel… I don't know, it was as if this wasn't Spain. Because over there [Bristol]… In the end I wasn't happy, but I was always doing things, and here for three months I didn't do anything, nothing, I was just at home. And that was a bit hard, I had to adapt myself, because I didn't want to do many things either, so I wouldn't spend money, because I didn't have an income, I didn't have a job, I didn't want to spend money. I felt very lost.*

In the first few months, María's expectations and the reality of living in Madrid again diverged significantly. Many of her hopes such as improving her living standard were closely tied to having economic stability. In the second interview (November 2016), María had been under the impression that she could somehow pick up her old life as she had left it, which turned out to be illusionary. Her former employers had moved on, which put her in a more precarious situation than she had been in England. María's impression that "*it was as if this wasn't Spain*" underlines how estranged she felt from her old, yet somehow unfamiliar, environment.

The lack of structure took a toll on María, as she felt that her living situation in Bristol compared favourably to what she had found in Madrid. During that time, she started to doubt whether she had left the UK somewhat prematurely: "*I was really, really sad. I thought I had made a mistake. I thought about going back (…) to Bristol, yes. Because over there I had a job, I had friends, I had a routine.*" In our second interview, María had listed a number of quite general motives for why she wanted to move back to Spain, including warm weather. These pull factors quickly lost their appeal, as she was lacking a strong social circle. María paid a high price for leaving Bristol and developed a keen sense for what she had lost ("*I had friends, I had a routine*").

LOOKING FOR AND FINDING WORK

While María was waiting to hear back from the bookstore, she sent out over 100 applications elsewhere without any success ("*They responded twice to tell me no. The rest didn't respond to me*"). In this harsh economic climate, María's initiatives to carefully prepare her return migration appeared to be in vain (e.g. her voluntary engagement at the university library).

Eventually, María was offered a job at a call centre, which she experienced as intolerable. She was not allowed to speak to her co-workers for reasons she could not understand, a policy that made her job alienating and "*so boring*". This new work environment differed a lot from what she had been used to in Bristol (after the dismissal of her first manager). Even though both jobs could be classified as 'low-skilled', María's work as a kitchen porter in Bristol appeared more humane in comparison. She recalled many playful interactions with co-workers in the kitchen and she missed these daily rituals in retrospect ("*At work, I would always laugh a lot. I always had a good time. I never had a job like this, always laughing*"). Given how unhappy María was at the call centre, she was desperate to find something else. Through personal connections, she eventually managed to find a job as a receptionist at a private company.

> *So then this job opportunity came up. This company is called XYZ, which is private equity. I'm at reception. They have many meetings because they are looking for investors from England, Switzerland, Italy… So that's why they needed a receptionist who*

> *could speak English. Someone who attends the meetings, organises the agenda for the meetings and works at reception… who is there when people call, answers the requests, and receives the mail that arrives. It's been two months and it's very good. I'm happy.*

Although María's ability to speak English was a decisive factor for finding a position she was content with, the process nevertheless had been difficult. She had learned English in an informal way at work and in communication with her former Italian partner. María did not have a foreign language certificate, which made it difficult for her to prove this skill to potential employers. Without personal contacts, she believed her chances of getting invited for an interview would have been close to zero (*"I got invited because the owner is friends with one of my cousins"*). Unlike other informants in this study, María had not migrated to the UK in order to learn English. In retrospect, her language skills nevertheless became important for her reintegration into the Spanish labour market. María described her new work environment as very formal. The hierarchical division of labour in this company appeared to be quite strict, as she was not allowed to approach partners directly if mail arrived. Instead, she had to email them a notification and wait until they approached her. Although these types of formalities took some time to get used to, María felt comfortable and respected at the office. She was also happy about the working conditions (i.e. salary, paid holidays) and appeared to have finally reached a state of stability.

MARÍA'S EVALUATION OF HER PERSONAL SITUATION

After getting the job, María could move back into her old flat. In order to save money, she shared the apartment with her best friend from high school and her teenage daughter. The living arrangement was different from the flat share in Bristol. Her friend had to work a lot in order to provide for her child. Whilst being on good terms, María did not get to see her housemates much and often spent her weekends alone. Although she still experienced feelings of loneliness from time to time, they were not a great burden anymore. For a long time, finding a job had been her number one priority. Now that she had found some financial stability, she expressed an interest in socialising with new people her age. María underlined her belief that new social relationships needed to evolve naturally and required time and patience.

María again only spoke about her family after I explicitly asked her about it. In our second interview, she had expressed her concern about being pulled back into family dynamics that she had experienced as destructive. Her sister was now living in Madrid but remained institutionalised. Her mental impairments had apparently become worse, which ruled out the possibility of caring for her at home. Although María visited her sibling sporadically, their relationship appeared to be extremely distant.

> *Yes, but she doesn't speak. She doesn't look at you. She is… she is a different person. It's like there is nobody inside. (…) She has been ill for seven years, but she had always been a little bit strange. She had things, the beginning of this illness… and we were really distant. And I… I don't feel that I have a sister because we never… I never shared anything with her.*

This sequence suggests that María had cut ties with her sister completely. Considering the biographical context, it appeared to be a coping mechanism to deal with a situation that she would otherwise experience as intolerable. What calls for attention is María's attempt to devalue their shared history prior to the accident ("*I never shared anything with her*"). By dismissing common childhood memories, María constructed her sister as a stranger.

Since returning from England, her relationship to both of her parents had slightly improved. María did not share anything personal with her mother and expressed relief that she no longer pressured her into taking care of her sister. She described her relationship with her father as friendly but also distant. Even though she had lived at his house for a few months, they apparently did not see each other much. María's main support structures were in the extended family, as she spoke very warmly of her grandmother, aunts and cousins.

MATEO LÓPEZ

The following case study is based on an autobiographical narrative interview that I conducted in the summer of 2016 in Berlin. The interviewee, who I have given the pseudonym Mateo, contacted me after reading a post about my research project in a Facebook group for Spaniards living in Germany. His email stood out as he expressed an intellectual interest by asking quite specific questions about my methodology and how I arrived at this topic. After a few email exchanges, we agreed to meet at an underground station in Berlin. It was a very warm night, so we decided to conduct the interview on a park bench close by. The atmosphere of the interview was very relaxed. After I explained the structure of the interview, Mateo started his main narrative that lasted about an hour. I did not interrupt him during that time. After he finished his life story with the coda "*I believe this is everything*", I started asking him questions.

MATEO'S CHILDHOOD AND FAMILY CONSTELLATION

At the time of the interview, Mateo was 32 years old and working as an engineer in Berlin. He was born and raised in Barcelona, but his working-class parents were "*immigrants from Spain*", as he put it, because they had moved from Madrid and Andalusia to Catalonia as children. Later on in the interview, he stated that although he was Spanish he felt "*culturally Catalan*" – a distinction he made when speaking about the uneasy socialising within the Spanish diaspora in Germany. He also has a brother who is four years younger than him. His mother had worked for a German company in Barcelona, an influence that he described as important in his life.

HIS FIRST YEAR AT UNIVERSITY: A PAINFUL DISAPPOINTMENT

Growing up, Mateo was a good student who excelled in mathematics and natural sciences (more so than in subjects like history and languages). From an early age onwards he was interested in planes and air travel, developing the biographical project to work in this field. At age 18, he finished high school and decided to study aeronautical engineering. The only university in Spain that offered this degree was in Madrid, a competitive programme onto which he was accepted after fulfilling the entry requirements. Moving out of his home to a new city brought about many challenges both for him and his parents, who struggled to support him financially. The tuition fees were high and so were the living expenses of his student accommodation. While Mateo had always had excellent grades at school, his results at university were not as high, which was a great disappointment for both him and his parents. After his first year of university, he returned to Barcelona for the summer to study for re-sit exams. During this time, he sensed some discontentment and tensions between his parents, which seemed to be triggered by his low marks at university. In the following narrative extract, Mateo interrupted the main storyline of how the situation at home escalated by inserting a background construction[7] that shed light on the origins of this conflict.

> *So when I finished this year, I went back to Barcelona for the summer to prepare myself better for the exams. But that's when there was already a bit of discontentment at home, in my family and between my parents because of well… my grades.*
>
>> *I always had good grades at school, more than anything because my parents were very strict, very hard on us because they didn't go to university and surely for them it was very important that we would get a university degree and that we would study… because studying was very important for them. It was the most important thing really. So let's say that since I was little, I had a normal social life, but really, it was really… I always got good grades, I was very dedicated to studying and then my parents were happy because I had good grades. So, when I was at university I did the same thing, but what happened is that I was in Madrid and my parents couldn't see me. So that's when they thought that I perhaps didn't dedicate myself enough in my first year at university… and*

> *another thing is that the first year at university is pretty different and every student needs a bit of time to adapt. But of course, this is what my parents didn't see.*
>
> *So after some time, problems emerged at home and it seemed typical that my parents would be arguing… and of course I also felt guilty because I told myself, "Well, maybe I don't know… if it wasn't for my studies and everything maybe they wouldn't be arguing and wanting to split up." I already intuitively felt that this was going to happen (…).*

In this data extract, Mateo reveals a lot about his family dynamics and the painful memories he associated with his first year at university. His parents' expectations were extremely high, which becomes especially visible when he interrupts himself. In the background construction (starting with *"I always had good grades (…)"* and ending with *"But of course, this is what my parents didn't see".*), he illustrated how he had always been under a lot of emotional pressure to perform well academically (*"My parents were happy because I had good grades."*). Although he had a 'normal social life', something seemed a bit different about his upbringing (*"I had a normal social life, but really, it was really (…)"*). When he was unable to achieve the results he had hoped for, it caused a rift not only between him and his parents, but also between his parents, affecting their marriage (which would later dissolve). Although his poor marks might have only been a catalyst for deeper underlying issues in the relationship, Mateo felt guilty and misunderstood. The textual phenomenon of the background construction indicates that Mateo has not fully dealt with some of the experiences he made during that time. Even after more than a decade, remembering how his parents mistrusted him in this situation still appeared painful during the interview. His academic performance and the quality of his parents' marriage seemed intertwined. When he was unable to live up to their expectations, Mateo appeared to develop what could be defined as a *trajectory of suffering*.

TAKING CONTROL BY JOINING THE ARMY

Unable to cope with the mounting pressure at home, Mateo was looking for a way to take control of this situation. After realising how much of a financial burden his studies were for his parents, he decided to quit his degree in aeronautical engineering. Not willing to give up on his biographical project of working with planes, he developed the idea of becoming a pilot. In Spain, he explained, there are two ways of becoming a pilot. As a civilian, one could attend the academy for pilots, a highly competitive programme with an entry age limit of 21. The alternative path is to join the army. As a soldier, it is possible to become a pilot until the age of 27 and receive free training (and later on become a pilot for commercial flights), something that appeared very attractive to Mateo in this situation. In retrospect, he admitted that he was *"very young"* at that stage in his life (he was about to turn 19) and looking for adventure. He therefore voluntarily enlisted in the army, where he was part of the Special Operations section.

When thinking about the structural processes in his life-course that led to this decision, one can observe the following: firstly, joining the army was an attempt to get his trajectory of suffering under control; secondly, it was a way to rebel against his parents (from whom he wished to become independent); and thirdly it seemed to offer an opportunity to pursue his biographical project of working with planes. He did, however, modify his professional ambitions, as he no longer aspired to be an aeronautical engineer but instead a pilot.

Mateo described his experience in the military as *"really intense"*. While there were certain aspects of it that he enjoyed, such as parachuting and courses about ships and tanks, it was a milieu in which he felt alien and out of place.

> *And that time was very hard and that's why I didn't talk to my parents... because in the end, I also blamed them a little bit for what happened. It's because I had spent so much time studying, I had always been a good student, and only because things didn't work out that well at university... I felt I didn't have another solution and that's why I joined the army, where things were really hard. Where all the people, the majority of people that were there, including my bosses, had never studied anything. And I, I had to quit university, a very good university, to join the army. Or let's say, where people weren't very educated and where there were also a lot of drugs and stuff. I am telling you, it wasn't a good environment. And of course, I blamed my parents. I spent so much time studying, getting good grades. I didn't smoke, I never did anything like that, being a good kid… and then I find myself in the army, which is not a nice place to be.*

This data extract illustrates a perceived loss in reciprocity between Mateo and his parents. Always having 'played by the rules', so to speak (i.e. being good at school), Mateo felt deeply cheated by not being able to continue his studies and finding himself in the army instead. His anger and frustration about the situation went very deep, as he broke off any contact with his parents for a few years. As a soldier, Mateo also moved around Spain a lot, leaving Barcelona for other cities such as Madrid, Valencia and Murcia. In a later stage of the interview, he recounted how these years took a lasting toll on his relationship with his younger brother, who never forgot how his older sibling suddenly 'disappeared'.

A FINAL ATTEMPT TO BECOME A PILOT – AND SETTLING FOR AN ALTERNATIVE

After two years in the army, Mateo's contract ended and he decided not to renew it. He did not enjoy the environment and his occupation left him very little time to prepare for the pilot exam. Not willing to give up on his plan of becoming a pilot, he decided to try to enter the aforementioned academy as a civilian. The entrance requirements were high, as hundreds of applicants would compete for very few places. Mateo therefore enrolled in a special one-year programme to prepare for the entrance exam at the academy for pilots. The exam covered many different subjects, including English and mathematics. Mateo did not succeed in the competition, as he only reached position 300 while there were only 19 places available.

While studying to become a pilot, Mateo also prepared for the entrance exams at the police academy. During this time, he also received offers to work for the secret police because he had made a good impression in the army. He was, however, not attracted to this type of occupation.

> *It wouldn't have been like in these James Bond movies, I would always have had to be in places where there is a lot of drug trafficking, spying on people, or sleeping in the car because you're watching them. And I said, "Well, that's not really what I want."*

After passing the entrance exam for the police, he found that without a university degree there were limited options regarding what he could do within this institution. At age 23, he therefore decided to go back to university while keeping the option of becoming a police officer open. By the time he made this decision, Mateo's relationship with his family had slightly improved, thanks to a girlfriend who encouraged him to get in touch with them again.

Since his plan to become a pilot had failed, Mateo opted for a double degree in telecommunication engineering and computer science at the University of Barcelona. Initially, he lived with his parents, an experience he found unbearable after having lived independently for a few years. After one year, he moved out and spent the next three years living in student flat shares or by himself for some time.

REDISCOVERING HIS EARLY TIES TO GERMANY

During his time at university, Mateo's interest in foreign languages re-emerged. Growing up, his parents had always emphasised the importance of studying foreign languages. In his parents' view, speaking English was not enough, and it was crucial to study an additional language. Throughout the interview, Mateo mentioned his mother had worked for a German company for over three decades, something that had an impact on him growing up.

> *And my mother, let's say that now she is already 62 years old, but she spent 35 years working for a German company… and because of that you could say that since I was born, there had always been a German influence in my life because my mother was working for this German company and also we used to see, during our summer holidays… since I was born we would always go camping and that's where I saw many Germans who came to visit… and that's why we would always have contact with Germans and so that was something really exotic for us children, but it was also the first contact with people who weren't Spanish, that is to say, from other countries.*

This data extract illustrates a certain familiarity that Mateo associated with Germany since childhood. When his parents asked him at age thirteen which foreign additional language he would like to study, his intuitive choice was German. He then took private German lessons for two hours a week. In this context, Mateo also mentioned an exchange programme he took part in when he was 17 years old.

> *And so I started when I was 13 years old, since I was 13 years old I studied German for two hours a week in a private school. And so when I was 17 years old, I went for*

> *the first time… I spent a month studying German in Frankfurt, close to Mannheim, and I really had a great time there. I went with more Spanish, talking… and it was the first time that I was away from home and I didn't want to go back because I was doing really well, it was my thing. So this first time that I was abroad was really liberating for me… and that's why when I went back to Barcelona I had the courage to go to Madrid.*

Even though this exchange programme was relatively short, it seemed to have had a lasting impact on his life. Mateo brought up these early experiences when speaking about his time after the army when he was enrolled at the University of Barcelona. The option of going to Germany to work or study seems to have stuck in his mind for many years, as he associated it with positive memories. During his first year at university, he visited Hamburg to see if he could enrol at the local university to study aircrafts. He could not meet the necessary language requirements and therefore returned to Barcelona. This example is quite interesting, as he explored Europe as a space to pursue his biographical project of working with planes. Despite many efforts, it seemed that this path was not open to him in Spain despite extreme sacrifice (being in the army).

The theme of not being able to fulfil one's dream in Spain reoccurs throughout this sample, as many participants moved abroad in the hope of entering the labour market in their field of expertise after graduating from university. Mateo first had the idea of going to Germany when he was still a student. There were several participants in my study who decided to prolong their exchange semesters and finish their studies in Germany, often out of frustration with the Spanish higher education system, which was described as rigid, anonymous and expensive. These participants sensed a certain adversity towards students by the university administration, as the tuition fees were significantly increased in the case of poor performance. This was also the case for Mateo, who returned to Barcelona after his plan to study in Hamburg did not work out.

> *I went back to Spain again and started university there. So, this degree lasts five years and you always have to pay a lot. Well, during my studies I always had to work as a trainer at the gym, giving special classes, or working as a trainer at schools. (…) Apart from that I was studying. It was because I had to pay the university and my parents helped me, but the university was still very expensive. And ultimately, when you don't pass a subject, they raise the tuition fee by 33%. That is to say that they were always charging me more, and then for a third time even more… so it was all a lot of money.*

The programme he was enrolled in was designed for five years. In his fourth year, there was a possibility to earn a double degree from a foreign university in the context of an Erasmus scheme. Among other European countries, there was the option to go to Germany. The scheme appealed to Mateo because it was a way to earn a full degree from a German university (*"as if I was a German student"*) in addition to the one he was already pursuing. Furthermore, he described the programme at the University of Barcelona as *"really tough"* and was therefore attracted to the idea of converting credits he earned somewhere else (where his grades were better).

STUDYING ABROAD IN THE CONTEXT OF THE ECONOMIC CRISIS

The programme entailed three more years at the University of Freiburg. Since many of his courses were in English, he spent one month in England living with the parents of a British friend. In 2011, at age 27, he moved to the south of Germany where he spent three years, finishing with a master's degree. He enjoyed his new academic environment because the workload was more manageable and the professors seemed more cooperative (*"This is something that I discovered at this university and I thought 'How great! What a joy!'"*). In this context, Mateo first brought up the topic of the economic crisis in Spain.

> And I believe that was when, already when I was in Freiburg, maybe even a little bit before that, when the crisis began. So yeah, so because of that the crisis had motivated me to come to Germany, but even before that I always had the idea that in Germany the work is better. It is much better paid and furthermore I also liked German culture because it's more social. That is to say that they are more responsible with their work and things like that. And when I was working in Spain, in the army and in other areas as well… because I worked in many different areas I saw how Spanish culture is more like, 'Yes, I can earn money working but staying at home is better. That is to say 'If I work the least amount possible but earn money, I'm very smart. But Germans don't see it this way. (…) It's cultural. So that's why, since my mother had worked for a German company, I have always seen the difference and she raised me that way too. My mother always told me, 'No, be responsible. You always have to work, you always need to help the company.'

This data extract shows the complexities underlying his migration project and the importance of taking the biographical context into account. Mateo admitted that the economic crisis was one important reason why he was attracted to the idea of working abroad. He described the working conditions for engineers in Spain as very harsh, while the salaries were around half as much as he would earn in Germany. His interest in working in Germany, however, preceded the economic crisis by many years and has its roots in childhood. Mateo's lay theories about the cultural differences between Spain and Germany illustrate a very distant relationship to his home country. Even though he did not mention it explicitly at this stage in the interview, his descriptions of Spanish culture resonate with the narratives of other Catalan participants in my study, who referred to differences in work ethic when drawing the line between Catalonia and Spain. Towards the end of the interview Mateo stressed how he felt 'culturally Catalan' and preferred socialising with other people from his region rather than 'Spaniards'. Given that his parents were originally from Madrid and Andalusia, Mateo's self-distinction and lay theories serve as a good example of how complex identity politics in Spain can be. The economic crisis had quite a dramatic impact on his family, something that he was affected by while living in Germany.

And well, when I was already in Freiburg, well apart from that, what happened later is that my parents divorced and also with everything related to the crisis, they started to have problems with the banks, with the apartment, things like that... The crisis started like that as well – with apartments. And so, when I was already studying in Freiburg, my mother started to have a lot of problems with the banks, because they wanted to kick her out of the flat, because she had to pay a lot of money, because when they bought the flat it was very expensive and later with the housing crisis not even the banks wanted them and the prices were really low. That is to say, you would owe a lot of money and the banks wanted to sell the flats although they were very cheap… just to make money. But of course, if they wanted to sell, they had to kick out my mother. So that's why I, for a long time in Freiburg, I was always looking to write my thesis with a company… like Bosch and other companies, where I could earn some money and help my mother.

In Mateo's family, the macro developments of the economic crisis seemed to exacerbate his parents' marital problems that ultimately led to their separation. In a later stage of the interview, he spoke about how he had not talked to his father for many years. According to Mateo, his father had completely disappeared from their lives since the separation, leaving his mother alone with crippling debt. This example also illustrates the vulnerability of individuals in times of economic crisis. His parents took out a substantial mortgage to buy a flat, trusting in the stability of the housing market. The value of their property evaporated very quickly when the financial turmoil unfolded, a phenomenon that was characteristic of this collective crisis.

The sudden financial destabilisation shifted the family dynamics, as Mateo had to take responsibility for his family and contribute as much as he could. Both he and his brother were studying at the time, which was also very expensive. The problems at home appeared to overshadow his studies because he had to work as a fitness trainer at a gym and did not have much time to invest in his degree. In Freiburg, Mateo found it difficult to socialise, as he was often mistaken for an exchange student who would soon be gone even though he was matriculated full-time.

> *People kept saying, "Oh, you're Spanish! Erasmus!" or like they didn't want to become close friends because they thought that after six months or a year I would leave.*

Within his programme, students could choose to write their thesis for a company, which was paid. Given the financial problems of his family, this option appealed to Mateo, who received an offer by Mercedes-Benz. He then completed a thesis based on research-related topics, which was accepted at the University of Freiburg. The company, however, did not allow him to share his work with the University of Barcelona as it contained confidential information. This example illustrates one of the complications that can occur when universities cooperate with the private sector, especially in an international context. In contrast to dissertations that are written in a purely academic setting, students have to comply with regulations that the company determines. In order to complete his double degree, Mateo therefore had to write a second thesis. Having spent a few years in Freiburg, he was curious to explore different locations at this point. After researching the options that he had, he opted to go to Denmark and write a thesis for a large telecommunications group. This company did allow him to use the thesis for his degree in Barcelona, while paying him for his research. He was happy about this opportunity (*"Ah how great! Amazing!"*) and looked forward to getting to know a new country. The only prerequisite of the Danish company was an English certificate. In order to prepare for the English exam, Mateo spent two months in England living with the parents of a British friend who had a spare bedroom.

After these two months, he quickly returned to Freiburg to collect his belongings and then moved to Denmark. In Copenhagen, he wrote a second master's thesis and finally fulfilled the requirements to graduate with his double degree (Barcelona/Freiburg). During this time, he started dating a Danish woman who was a few years older than him. The relationship got serious quite quickly and they were envisioning a future together. Mateo therefore decided to prolong his stay after finishing his thesis and tried to find a job in Denmark.

I spent four months trying to find work in Denmark, but nothing came of this because my Danish wasn't good enough to find a job. And in the fifth month of not having anything... In this moment I was living with a Danish girlfriend, so yeah I didn't have to pay rent because she helped me. But in the fifth month I was already a bit tired and said, 'well, I will look for work in Germany again', because this is something that has always worked for me.

Mateo's migration project developed gradually, while already living abroad. After graduating from university, he was looking for work both in Denmark and Germany. It is notable that he did not explicitly mention the option of going back to Spain at this stage. Mateo seemed to have some awareness of the working conditions at home. After having acquired cultural capital (Bourdieu, 1986) in the form of a German university degree in engineering, he was certain that he could receive more attractive job offers abroad.

SETTLING DOWN IN GERMANY AFTER GRADUATION

Mateo decided to apply for jobs in Hamburg and Berlin because he preferred bigger cities to smaller towns like Freiburg. After two weeks of sending out applications, a company invited him to Berlin for an interview and paid for his flights and expenses. The interview went very well and they immediately sent him a contract making him an offer to start work the week after. Mateo and his Danish girlfriend decided to separate because they did not want to continue the relationship over long distance.

After receiving the job offer, Mateo moved to Berlin. At the time of the interview he had been working for the company for almost a year. While the transition period involved some challenges, such as finding a flat and building new friendships, he felt comfortable at this stage. This part of the interview was characterised by a longer argumentative sequence, in which he reflected upon the reasons why he decided to leave Spain and how he envisioned his future. Much of his wellbeing, he said, depended on his social relationships. Recently, he had started dating a German woman he had met at the gym three months prior to the interview. Even though this relationship was quite new, Mateo emphasised how he could envision a future with her.

> *So yeah, my idea is to stay here and really spend five or ten or thirty years in Germany, for her… and start a family in Germany. This is something that I regard as very likely because returning to… I know a lot of Spaniards here who tell me that at best they want to spend four or five years here and then go back to Spain. But I wouldn't go back because… maybe because I believe that I struggled a lot with the Spanish system, you know? Being in the army and doing things for the police… So I feel, I have always been doing things, many things for my country, trying to be part of my country and helping. I always felt quite rejected in the sense that they didn't help me at university. They put me through a lot of difficulties with work, with money. So I said, 'How could it be that I get so little help in my country, when I sacrificed so much to support it?' I even wanted to do things like be in the army and this is a service to my country. And in contrast here in Germany and in other countries, it seems to me that they treat me better, with more respect.*

This argumentative sequence illustrates the importance of taking Mateo's biographical background into account. His early experiences of having felt rejected by state institutions shed light on his negative disposition towards Spain. Mateo thereby articulated a feeling that had accompanied him since early adulthood. At the time of the interview, the memory of having to quit his studies in Madrid was still painful. He still seemed to wonder how things would have turned out for him if he had received some financial support from the state in this situation. In this commentary, he also expresses his deep disappointment about a lack of reciprocity, as his service for Spain went largely unrecognised. There is bitterness in how he reflects about his younger self, who had voluntarily joined the army to '*take part*' in society and '*help*'.

While his struggles to get support from the Spanish state started before the recession, the conditions worsened throughout the economic crisis as many social services got cut. Mateo emphasised how he felt ready to start a family. His negative experiences seemed to gain weight when thinking about the future of his children. Mateo's trust in the German state outweighed the benefits his home country had to offer, such as the weather. Spain, so it seems, could not offer him a solid foundation on which he felt comfortable building a future. The labour conditions, he explained, remained very precarious as *"they can fire you from one day to the next"*, while he would earn about half of what he was paid in Germany. Furthermore, Mateo hoped that his children would have an easier time than he did at university, as there seemed to be more funding available. The welfare state was also a factor that attracted Mateo to Denmark because students receive state support independently of their parents' income (*"I knew that if I found something in Denmark, it would really be like paradise"*). Even though he still seemed a bit disappointed about not having found a job in Copenhagen (*"I would have stayed in Denmark. Maybe forever."*), he was also grateful to have been given this opportunity in Berlin. There were, nevertheless, some aspects of his work environment which he criticised.

> *What I noticed being a foreigner, or Spanish for that matter, and not speaking German perfectly... What I noticed is that at work they are sometimes uneasy about it. What I see is that for certain things they don't call me or consult me, or my salary isn't quite what I know it should be. It's because I've been here for a long time and I know Germans that have studied with me and so on... and the salary for a Spaniard or foreigner is lower than that of a German. Yes, and you would think it's because of the language, and you have a point. I don't speak German as a native language, but they pay me as an engineer and the grades that I got... And that's why I got the job, so I don't think they pay me fairly. But okay, they give me work and, compared to Spain, they pay me very well and they treat me very well.*

What Mateo complains about here is an uncomfortable situation many migrants find themselves in. On the one hand, he felt that he ought to be thankful for this job opportunity that is very attractive in comparison to what he would be offered in Spain. On the other hand, knowing he is paid significantly less (about 20%) than his German colleagues appeared to be a source of great frustration. Mateo seemed torn between accepting the situation as it was and expressing his anger.

> *Well okay, I understand that it's not my country... but okay, it's also not, I mean, is this Europe or is it not Europe? From what I have seen it's just my passport and that's it.*

In theory, equality among EU workers is a key value on which the principle of 'free movement' was based. In practice, however, Mateo felt treated like a second-class European. It appears that coming from a poorer member state carried a certain stigma for him and seemingly undermined his negotiating power. In this context, Mateo drew parallels to the situation of women.

> *I don't think Germans are racist, or at least it's not what they want to be, but maybe they are a bit biased without realising it. It's the same thing with… with women. (…) And of course, now they are trying to get more girls to study engineering and all that, but they still don't earn the same. And if that happens to German women – people of the same nationality but a different sex – maybe that's why there is a bit of resistance to the idea that a Spaniard can earn the same salary from the beginning.*

Mateo's migration experience sensitised him to the struggles of women who are also marginalised in certain professional and occupational settings. While trying to reconstruct the reasoning behind his lower salary, he also emphasised how he did not agree with it. "*Underappreciated*" was the term he chose to describe how he felt at work, pointing out that many of his additional skills, such as speaking five languages, (Spanish, Catalan, English, German and basic Danish) go unnoticed. Mateo said that he was about to speak to his manager about it and would start looking for a different job if his conditions did not improve within a year or two. Apart from this problem, Mateo was generally content with his work environment and life in Berlin. His plan was to stay and settle in Berlin and perhaps start a family in three or four years from now.

In this context, he mentioned how the geographical proximity to Spain played a role in choosing Germany as a place to settle. After his parents' separation, he became very close to his mother, with whom he spoke every day. Even though she was no longer dependent on his financial support, he mentioned that they shared a bank account as an example of their closeness. For Mateo, moving to countries such as the United States, as some of his friends from university had done, was not an option. Since his mother had entered retirement age, he wanted to be able to travel to Spain quickly in case something happened to her. The availability of cheap and quick flights to Barcelona appeared to put him at ease when speaking about his plans to settle in Germany.

WHERE TO GO FROM HERE?

The purpose of such single case studies is not only to understand individual life histories, but also to detect phenomena that are of importance to society at large (e.g. social processes in juvenile delinquency (cf. 'The Jackroller' (Shaw, 1930/1966)). By 'zooming in' on the narratives of Adam, María and Mateo, one could gain important insights into the relationship between collective crises and personal biographies. Their lives were deeply disrupted by the financial and economic breakdown of their home country, and they struggled to find their way out of a seemingly hopeless situation. An in-depth analysis of the interviews not only revealed their biographical processes (such as biographical projects and trajectories of suffering), but also how they continuously reflected about what has been happening to them.

The effects of the 2008 crisis on Adam and his friends reveal aspects of their shared generational experiences: the monotony of their everyday life, a distorted perception of time, and a pervasive lack of future opportunities. Sometimes narrators formulate such generalities themselves. After finding only a menial job in Bristol, María commented on the reversal of higher expectations for future generations in Spain. Whilst her parents' generation could aspire to some prosperity in their lifetime (e.g. owning a house, stable income), she believed that people of her age and younger (i.e. her Spanish co-workers) had to settle for much less. Mateo's case illustrated how macro-economic developments and personal relationships are deeply interlinked. The accumulating debt, falling property prices and the threat of eviction exacerbated his parents' marital problems, ultimately leading to their divorce.

Adam, María and Mateo were chosen for the case studies because their biographies differed in important aspects (i.e. age, gender, socio-economic background, education, family constellations, as well as level of success in the receiving society). The in-depth analyses and the (occasional) comparison of the three life histories already revealed important biographical and social processes that are important for this study. Examples of the latter include the different experiences of the economic crisis, how the decision to migrate emerged, work experiences in the receiving society (including the importance of voluntary work), being confronted with Brexit as a new collective crisis, and difficulties relating to one's return migration.

There is, of course, a huge variation in my sample that is not covered by these three cases. When spelling out the commonalities and differences of Adam's, María's, and Mateo's life histories, it was also necessary to take a closer look at other data. Did the foci, generative questions (Strauss, 1987) and first categories, which were developed in a first contrastive comparison of these cases, 'fit' with the diversity of the whole data corpus? Or did they have to be modified? Considering that both Adam and María engaged in low-paid manual labour in England, it made sense to look at the biographies of informants who worked in their field of expertise in the receiving society. This is why I chose Mateo, as he had found a stable job as an engineer in Berlin and was planning to stay in Germany for the rest of his career. By engaging in a contrastive comparison between the case studies and by selectively drawing on other interviews, it gradually became clear to me that it was worthwhile to focus on specific phases and aspects of migration experiences.[8] The following topics will be pursued further in theoretical and empirical chapters by continuously confronting, reassessing and refining initial discoveries and propositions with other data from my sample.[9]

What can be learned about:

1. the biographical problem constellations and processes that lead to the emergence of migration projects?
2. the biographical meaning of work experiences in the receiving societies?
3. the web of social relationships that exists abroad? How do migrants try (and sometimes fail) to maintain long-distance bonds with friends and family at home? What can be learned about newly developing relationships in the receiving society?
4. the biographical significance of unanticipated new collective crises such as Brexit?
5. the experience of return migration?

4. TIME TO GO?

The analysis of the interviews revealed that the migration projects of almost all the participants could be regarded as a response to circumstances that they felt were problematic.[1] The question remains: migration as a response to what? What are the biographical contexts, processes and meanings of the respective migration projects? In the following chapter, I analyse various biographical processes and problem constellations under which 'leaving Spain' emerged as a topic. This is quite different from simply asking for 'motives' for migration. Whilst several interviewees officially presented their migration projects as motivated by the wish to learn a new language, their biographical narratives often revealed that in reality the biographical processes that led to their decision to migrate were much more complex. Sometimes, narrators struggled to explain them in a clear-cut way, which indicates that they were still coming to terms with what had happened in their lives.

Everyone in my sample migrated, but different biographical problem constellations or themes became dominant in each case. By doing a sequential and comparative analysis of the narratives, it was possible to discover and categorise the following biographical processes and problem constellations in which migration appeared as a 'way out': (a) 'going abroad' in the context of one's academic training, (b) withstanding a collective mood of demoralisation, (c) trying to overcome a prolonged period of dependency and stagnation, (d) trying to cope with or escape from a trajectory of suffering, (e) trying to gain professional recognition and adequate pay, and (f) acquiring foreign language skills in order to gain a competitive advantage. These biographical patterns were neither exhaustive nor mutually exclusive as they overlapped in individual cases.

'GOING ABROAD' IN THE CONTEXT OF ONE'S ACADEMIC TRAINING

There were a number of young Spanish migrants in my sample who had first taken part in time-limited exchange programmes at university before deciding to prolong their stay abroad beyond the official time span. The plan to 'really' migrate often gradually emerged abroad, also by continuously comparing one's own (newly discovered) educational and occupational options in the receiving society with the apparently depressing situation of one's peers at home. There were several biographical conditions under which taking part in an Erasmus scheme appeared attractive for various informants.

(a) Gaining a more independent lifestyle

The liberating quality of the Erasmus scheme became especially visible in the case of Sandra, aged 25, who was living in Berlin at the time of the interview. Sandra described her upbringing as very controlling, as her parents did not allow her to socialise much as a child and even as a young adult. Like the majority of my informants, she continued to live with her parents after starting university, which she found increasingly intolerable. She perceived the Erasmus scheme as key to emancipating herself.

> *The problem is that my parents are really close-minded and strict. They never let me travel outside of Spain. They never let me do anything really. You know in my house there were always so many rules. At 9:30pm I always had to be at home. I could only do stuff with my friends once a week. They didn't let me go out more. That's why I felt very controlled and I always wanted to do something different... because it was just too much for me to stay at home almost every day. (...) And then when I was at university they told me about Erasmus and I said, 'Okay, I have to go on an Erasmus exchange! To wherever!' There were a lot of countries but I had always liked Germany (...).*
>
> *So, I came here as an Erasmus student... it was a bit crazy because I had no money, just a tiny scholarship. I could pay the rent and nothing more. Well, I came here with almost nothing, but the truth is that my Erasmus year was also a lot of fun. At last, I travelled. At last, I went out at night and met new people and I could go get a drink with them. Although I didn't always drink something because I didn't have*

> *money, being able to go out was so much fun. I could go out or not go out… whatever I wanted. That's why when I first came to Germany, I loved it!*

Sandra's narrative revealed that her Erasmus semester allowed her to feel 'young' (i.e. going to parties, enjoying life) and 'grown up' (i.e. living on her own) at the same time. This is a striking combination that underlines the biographical significance of her participation in the university exchange programme (Krzaklewska, 2013).

Her relief about finally living independently resonated with the narratives of several other former Erasmus students – even those who had a close relationship with their parents. Although these informants did not describe their parents as quite as strict, they mentioned smaller everyday irritations including well-meaning questions such as 'Where are you going?' or 'When are you coming back?', which they felt did not fit their age anymore (Minguez, 2016).

(b) Feeling frustrated with the Spanish higher education system

Apart from the students' deep desire to live independently, several informants spoke about frustrating experiences relating to the higher education system in Spain that sparked their interest in exploring different academic environments. León, aged 26, first took part in an Erasmus exchange in Bristol as part of his undergraduate degree in history.

> *(…) Then I started university. It was really disappointing, because… humanities in this country [Spain] are very bad. It was the least exciting intellectual environment you can imagine. And I was… I wasn't depressed but I wasn't happy either. In my second year…*
>
> *And then in my third year I moved to England, to Bristol, to take part in an Erasmus course. It was a very nice experience. (…) First of all I really enjoyed the experience academically. (…) In Spain, at university what you do is you go to a class… you listen to a professor talking about something for an hour. You try to copy everything down and then you do that again for the next five hours. (You spend) five hours a day, five days a week at university just taking notes, then you learn them by heart and then in the exam you write [them all down]. And that's it. It's only about memorisation.*
>
> *First, in England I had to… I only had seven hours a week. But, you know, you have to do a lot of reading, you have to prepare your classes, there are a lot*

> *of seminars, discussions. So wow, I was really sad about my studies, I was almost regretting that I had chosen history. And then the Erasmus year made me fall in love with the field again. I really enjoyed it. I had very good grades. That was (also) very good for my self-esteem because in Spain I wasn't getting outstanding marks because of lack of motivation.*

León's descriptions of how he was taught at his home university in Spain were in line with the experiences of other informants. His claim that his home university offered the "*least exciting intellectual environment you can imagine*" sounds harsh and resentful. Whilst Sandra's reasons to take part in the Erasmus scheme were very personal, it seems as if León's motives seemed to be primarily academic. He appreciated being given more autonomy in preparing seminars, which motivated him to make more of an effort. At the time of our interview, León considered pursuing a PhD in history in the hope of eventually becoming a university lecturer. In retrospect, his positive academic experiences as an exchange student made a lasting impact on his life and career choices.

Several informants spoke about being put under a lot of financial pressure at their home universities in Spain. These participants described how their tuition fees were increased if they failed a subject, which sometimes turned into a vicious circle. In order to continue their degrees, some students had to work part-time in order to pay for such penalties, which in turn took away time from adequately preparing for their exams (Rio-Ruiz et al., 2015; Sanchez-Gelabert et al., 2017).

(c) Taking a break from the 15-M movement

In addition to their work and academic commitments, several participants were also very active in organising anti-austerity protests. Tomas, who was 24 years old at the time of the interview, had previously studied mathematics and philosophy in Madrid simultaneously as two full-time degrees. Prior to moving to Hamburg as an Erasmus student in September 2012, he had been very active in the 15-M movement in Madrid. In the interview, he recalled moments in which he felt overwhelmed by the speed of the collective developments at the time, a certain lack of orientation and group pressure.

> *One [person] was in charge of coordinating the camp, another was in charge of the infrastructure, another was in charge of communication and suddenly there were*

hundreds of people working proactively on something that was not well developed yet, that had just emerged… it was a camp. We did not have a very clear idea of what we wanted to do. We worked in an assembly, with assemblies of hundreds of people.

I remember one Tuesday … There was an assembly at 4am in the morning, for example, where 500 people attended. In other words, I was going to hold the assembly, but I saw all the people there and I said, 'I am not going'. In other words, it was 4am in the morning. I had… I was tired. And then they started, like there was an explosion of this way of working, which some groups were already…using then, especially left-wing groups that had had their assemblies, for years now but, suddenly, there was a multitude of assemblies in Sol. And there were like thousands of people and every day there were four to five assemblies where we discussed different topics. Also on the weekends… It was suddenly as if there was an explosion of activism. And people who had no previous experience in activism became involved. I for example was politicised, but no, I had never participated in any political group. And this was a group, which was not a group as such, we were simply people, um… I mean, it wasn't, we didn't support any party, any concrete measure, it was very abstract.

In this sequence, Tomas recalled how he and his fellow 15-M activists struggled to channel the outburst of collective energy and outrage into something productive (Romanos, 2013). Although thousands of young people shared a collective sense of indignity and anger about the current situation, the movement had not yet defined its exact objectives at that point. Somewhat prematurely, Tomas found himself in a leadership position as he was in charge of moderating assemblies with hundreds of attendees. His example of being expected to hold an assembly at 4am illustrates the invasive effect the social movement had on his life at that point. Although he deeply identified as an activist, he started to doubt the purpose of the assemblies, as the content of their discussions was very abstract. By adding the comment "*we didn't support any party*", Tomas contextualised this initial lack of orientation as he was referring to a time before the formation of Podemos in 2014 (Diaz-Parra & Jover-Baez, 2016; Booth & Baert 2018).

For Tomas, taking part in an Erasmus exchange to Hamburg seemed very attractive, as it allowed him to live independently, to reduce his workload at university (i.e. study one instead of two subjects), and take a 'break' from his commitments to the 15-M movement. This was a convenient option, as simply 'quitting' his role would not have been well regarded in activist circles and might have damaged his friendships.[2]

(d) A special professional affinity to the receiving society

Finally, there were some informants for whom studying in the receiving society appeared very attractive due to a special academic and professional affinity to the receiving society. Examples included students in the field of engineering, who had studied with the background awareness of attractive job opportunities in Germany. Apart from the financial incentives (significantly higher salaries), some people also spoke of their life-long passion for the automobile industry and were intrinsically motivated to work on developing cutting-edge technology. For them, being able to study in Germany or the UK, either as an Erasmus or regular student, appeared to be an excellent opportunity to facilitate their labour market entrance in their field of expertise. Firstly, these informants appreciated being given time to learn the language fluently (including technical vocabulary) in an academic environment before entering the 'real world'. Secondly, they hoped that having an affiliation with a German or British university would improve their chances of getting invited for an interview as potential employers were more familiar with these institutions (van Mol, 2013).

WITHSTANDING A COLLECTIVE MOOD OF DEMORALISATION

My informants' experiences with the economic crisis were quite diverse, as they differed in their access to social, economic and cultural capital that could serve as a shield from its worst repercussions (Bourdieu, 1984; Bygnes, 2017). What most narratives shared, however, were detailed descriptions of how the collective atmosphere in Spain shifted. Many interviews included detailed descriptions of urban decay, scenes of mass unemployment and a widespread atmosphere of hopelessness. Several informants also spoke of friends and family members who were unable to find a job and were growing increasingly desperate. They frequently switched to the personal pronoun 'we' when narrating how they experienced the unfolding repercussions of the economic crisis, including the future prospects of young people which were quickly evaporating. This points to important generational differences in experiencing this collective turmoil, as my younger informants' experiences of entering adulthood differed significantly from those of their parents' generation (Holleran, 2019, Mannheim, 1928).

A large number of the interviewees in my sample were still high school or university students when the economic crisis started in 2008. Their experiences differed significantly from the older interviewees in my sample, who had a vivid memory of economic stability in Spain. Contrastingly, the younger participants had grown up with a background awareness of rather depressing job prospects that awaited them after graduation. At the height of the crisis, the wish to achieve even modest financial independence appeared far-fetched. Several informants recalled making a conscious choice to reject the label of the so-called 'lost generation' and stick to their dreams despite adversity. What these participants shared was an intuitive understanding that their road to independence may involve detours, including moving to a different country.

Especially among younger participants in my sample, there was a tendency to draw on the example of others by developing a contrast between 'me' and 'them'. Several participants had a cautionary tale about friends, acquaintances or 'people' in general who appeared to have resigned themselves to the situation of collective unemployment. It seems that the participants' ultimate decision to leave was also enhanced by something like a 'fear of infection', i.e. of not being able to withstand the collective mood of lethargy and demoralisation.

Felipe, aged 23, was working as an au pair in the UK at the time of our meeting. His socio-economic background was very modest, and his family struggled to survive on his father's income as a butcher when he was a child. After graduating from university with a degree in physical education in 2011, Felipe moved back to his parents' home in the village he had grown up in. In the interview, he vividly recalled how the collective atmosphere had shifted as a consequence of the economic crisis.

> *In Spain, everybody is affected by the crisis. Maybe except the richest people, everybody has experienced what the crisis means. Everybody at least has a cousin, a nephew, an uncle, an aunt… who is unemployed. (…) Everybody is scared of the future. So many companies closed down… I lived in a village that depended heavily on construction. This sector completely collapsed. Now, I have tons of friends who have nothing to do because their families are financially ruined. I have friends who sell drugs just to survive. It's just to survive, not because they want to do it. People in Spain are really frustrated. Really, really frustrated. They are also extremely angry at the politicians who are not capable of doing anything. It's hard because in general I think people in Spain are known to have a positive attitude, but now there is so much desperation.*

In contrast to other participants, who had a middle and upper-class upbringing, Felipe and his friends had no shelter that could protect them from the worst effects of the economic crisis. His emphasis on *"everybody is scared of the future"* points to a deep disruption in his village community. Without access to any financial resources, his friends appeared paralysed with regard to moving forward in their lives. He further illustrated the experiences of unemployment by referring to a friend of his.

> *I have friends who sell drugs. I have a friend, it's a very typical case, he… well, his mother works as a cleaning lady, earning maybe €400 a month… and he, his father and two uncles – five people – live off these €400. They all worked in construction before. When the crisis started they all lost their jobs. In Spain, you get unemployment benefits for some time, but after a couple of years you don't get anything anymore. Now, they have nothing but the salary of the mother. So what do you do? You need to eat. So yes, people are really sad as well.*

Whilst this example may appear extreme from an outsider's perspective, Felipe portrayed it as a *"very typical case"* in his social surroundings. His village was especially vulnerable to the financial crisis due to its dependence on the construction sector. When the so-called 'housing bubble' burst, many families suddenly lost their means of existence (Benito et al., 2015). There is something Kafkaesque about this situation, as the entire village community seemed to live in constant fear of the future. Felipe's descriptions of his village resemble Jahoda et al.'s (1933/1972) observations in the Austrian town of Marienthal during the Great Depression. Marienthal was also heavily dependent on a single industry that collapsed during the economic crisis. Jahoda et al. (1933/1972) concluded that prolonged unemployment leads to a state of apathy, as people no longer make use of the few opportunities they are given. What they observed was the emergence of a vicious cycle between reduced opportunities and reduced levels of aspiration.

Jahoda et al.'s (1933/1972) findings also resonated with other interviews in my sample. One example is the case of Matias, a 26-year-old man who had graduated from university with a degree in physical education. After studying in a larger city, he was forced to move back to his hometown in Andalusia, where he only found part-time employment as a children's football coach. Feeling dissatisfied with the situation, he decided to move to London. Matias remembered:

I really didn't want to go by myself, so I asked all my friends. I asked, "Who is unhappy here? Who wants to get out?" At first three people said yes… but what happens is that people are so tired. They have become so, so tired. They are too tired to leave Spain.

Such descriptions about people having become "*so tired*", a common pattern throughout my interviews, resemble the portrayal of the psychological consequences of mass unemployment, which was presented in the study on Marienthal. Matias's quote illustrates this phenomenon as he perceives his friends as not capable of joining him to go abroad despite being initially attracted to the idea. Although there are, of course, other ways of fighting resignation than choosing an 'exit' (Hirschman, 1970), it seems that many people in Spain indeed suffer from the lack of fulfilment of what Jahoda et al. defined as "enduring human needs", such as a structured experience of time and collective purpose.

TRYING TO OVERCOME A PROLONGED PERIOD OF DEPENDENCY AND STAGNATION

None of the recent university graduates I interviewed were able to get a stable job in Spain that would cover the cost of a separate flat or room in a flat share. Due to the lack of financial resources, several informants saw themselves forced to either continue to live or move back in with their parents, which they described as quite depressing. The narratives reveal the widespread experience of multiple and interlinking dependencies and the pervasive feeling of not moving on in one's life (Sironi, 2018).

Some informants had always lived with their parents and were simply not able to change their situation after finishing their degrees. Others had previously studied in a different city and felt forced to move back in with their families after graduation, which entailed a loss of independence with which they struggled to come to terms (Arundel & Lennartz, 2017). The status of being a student had previously provided a shelter from the economic crisis, as it gave my informants a sense of purpose and a valid justification to *not* enter the labour market *yet* in their field of expertise. For these young people, graduation marked something like a rude awakening, as they could no longer ignore the prevalent lack of job opportunities.

Eva, aged 23, tried to find work for over nine months after finishing her degree in tourism. She was working as a cleaner in a small town in Germany at the time of our meeting. In the interview, she voiced her anger about the labour market requirements in Spain, which she perceived as absurdly high.

> *When the crisis began young people weren't hired because you need to have experience. If you have the degree but nobody gives you the opportunity to work, you'll never get the experience. On the other hand, they don't hire people who do have the experience because they tell them that they are too old and that they want young people. It's crazy. If you want people with experience they are not going to be that young. You need to find a middle point. I saw an announcement in Spain for an office job: 'We are looking for an assistant who is younger than 18 with experience.' Well, you can start working when you're 16 because this is the minimum age, but nobody does that. When I saw this announcement, I had to laugh and cry at the same time and I didn't walk in. 'Do you know what you have written there? There are no people like this!!' This is what happens a lot in Spain.*

There is an element of absurdity in requiring applicants to be very young and experienced at the same time. This combination of characteristics excludes almost everybody. Despite her efforts and willingness to compromise, Eva felt unable to reach financial independence due to structural forces outside of her control. To illustrate the gravity of this problem further, Eva gave an example of a newspaper article she once read.

> *I also read an article in the newspaper… It was about a girl I don't remember exactly what she studied but she had a master and a PhD. The title was 'My entire life, my parents told me 'Study, study – so you'll be somebody tomorrow'.' 'Now that I have completed all my education, I don't have work, I'm going to lose my current work as a cashier in the supermarket because I'm overqualified. I studied so much but didn't find anything. I studied my entire life in order to be somebody and now they are punishing me for having studied so much.' That's the story of thousands of people…*

This example reveals an <u>anomic</u> dimension of the crisis for young people (Durkheim, 1897). In the aftermath of the economic collapse, it seems as if previous social norms and values had lost their meaning, causing a widespread feeling of purposelessness and despair. According to Eva, thousands of young people had done everything they were 'supposed' to do. They had followed their parents' advice and invested much time and resources in getting a university degree. The economic crisis, however, shattered the premise of education as a safe pathway to stability. The young woman in Eva's example felt punished for having pursued a PhD degree, as it now created an additional barrier to financial independence (Quintana-Murci et al., 2019), a fate that she apparently shared with many others of her generation.

The phase of having to move back in with one's parents *after* earning a university degree is a stage in life that previous generations had not known since historical circumstances were different. Several interviewees drew contrasting comparisons between themselves and their parents, who they believed had an easier time becoming financially independent. Jorge, aged 25, was working as a warehouse manager in a small town in England at the time of the interview. His migration project was fuelled by the desire to move out of his parents' home.

> *The truth is that I like it here [in England] because I'm not living in my city, with my family, because … in my family I'm the youngest of all and I remember that my parents, for example, when they were my age, I know these were different times… but my parents at my age… they were already married, they were living together, they worked, they began to have children. And then I did not want to be there, in Spain, at that age, just living at home. My family told me, 'Stay, you'll find a job,' but I knew that wasn't going to happen. And then that's why I decided to come.*

Even though Jorge was the first person in his family to move to another country, the excerpt suggests that he migrated in order to follow his parents' footsteps to the extent of becoming an independent adult. His migration could thereby be interpreted as an attempt to restore a 'normal order' in his life-course, as it was common among previous generations (Irwin & Nilson, 2018). Jorge's sense of feeling too old for this sort of living arrangement was in line with the rest of the data. Several participants spoke in detail about how they felt trapped in a frustrating state of 'waiting for adulthood' or 'waithood' (cf. Singerman, 2007).

After graduating from university with a degree in archaeology, Estéban moved back to his parents' home at the age of 30. Despite his willingness to compromise (i.e. being open to working in jobs unrelated to his academic training), he was unemployed for three years before moving to the UK, where he was working as a kitchen porter. In the interview, he described how he found daily life 'at home' deeply frustrating.

> *I lived with my parents again. I didn't pay anything but I was extremely frustrated. 'Mum, can you give me some money so I can go out with my friends?' 'Mum, can you give me some money so I can go out for dinner?' I couldn't afford all that anymore. It was like being sixteen again.*

Estéban's account of feeling like a teenager again after moving back in with his parents is by no means unique as the other interviewees reported similar experiences, which points to a profound disruption in institutionalised patterns of the life course and a collective sense of having to miss out on something one deserves. Many of the younger participants had already experienced living at their family homes as inadequate and frustrating during their university years (cf. previous section). Not being able to change their situation after graduation seems to be an especially bitter experience. All the institutionalised steps, which had formerly led to an independent existence, appear to lead nowhere due to structural forces outside of the individual's control (Arundel & Lennartz, 2017).

As time went by, several informants described how they became increasingly depressed at home. For some people, this came somewhat as a shock as they had previously thought of themselves as optimistic, self-confident and outgoing. The absence of a structured experience of time, combined with lack of purpose (Jahoda et al., 1933/1972) appeared to undermine some of my informants' sense of self-worth, a phenomenon that has been referred to as the 'scarring of unemployment' (Strandh et al., 2014). This disposition of vulnerability was, furthermore, exacerbated by my participants' experiences of rejection by prospective employers, even for jobs that were below their academic qualifications. Against this background, the interviewees' decision to leave Spain as an attempt to end the frustrating state of 'waithood' might be a sign of unusual resilience. Despite having spent many months or even years unemployed, these individuals seized the opportunity to go abroad and thereby actively resisted what Jahoda et al. called a collective 'state of apathy'.

TRYING TO COPE WITH OR ESCAPE FROM A TRAJECTORY OF SUFFERING

Throughout my fieldwork, I encountered several people who had gotten into extremely difficult situations in Spain, and decided to migrate as a form of trying to cope with or escape from different biographical problem constellations. Sometimes, these problems were direct repercussions of the economic crisis as people lost their jobs, homes and, at times, means of existence (Royo, 2014). On other occasions, the source of their deep unhappiness was primarily personal, e.g., painful break-ups, experiences of loss, and family tragedies.

These financial and personal problems overlapped and reinforced each other in single biographies. Examples of the latter include cases in which individuals suffered from personal tragedies, which in turn weakened their productivity and ability to compete on the Spanish labour market (e.g. the case study of María). On other occasions, families lost their means of existence in the context of the economic crisis, which had devastating effects on their relationships (sometimes leading to dissolutions of marriages). In the following section, I will compare and contrast two cases of individuals who got trapped in a deep trajectory of suffering and loss of control (Schütze, 1981, 1995, 2008). Whilst both participants left Spain in an attempt to get some distance from an unbearable situation, their biographical circumstances differed significantly.

When referring to the period of unemployment after graduation, the younger participants underlined how frustrated they were about not being able to progress in life. Being trapped in a prolonged state of dependency ('waithood') can have seriously depressing consequences for individuals who cannot see a way out of the situation. It is nevertheless important to distinguish their <u>frustration</u> about not being able to become financially independent from <u>a trajectory of deep suffering</u> that can develop or is aggravated in a situation of mass unemployment or other collective crises, sometimes marked by a 'destruction of community' (Erikson, 1976). In other words, there seems to be a qualitative difference between being prevented from entering the labour market after graduation and being hit by the crisis midway through one's career. Many of the older participants did not have a 'shelter' that they could return to in case of financial hardships as their parents were already elderly (or deceased), which made the prospect of unemployment particularly threatening.

Juan, aged 42, grew up in the Canary Islands. After graduating from university with a degree in Business Administration, he worked for a bank in Tenerife for a few months. During that time, he developed the idea to create his own company that provided services for elderly people. Launching a firm required a lot of preparation and resources. In our interview, he remembered how in the first three years, he worked seven days a week *"from early in the morning until late at night"*. In 2007, he reached a personal milestone by acquiring two major contracts with a government institution. His life was, however, about to change dramatically due to the financial collapse.

> *And that was in 2005 when I started the company, and the crisis started in 2008. So right when the company started to fly, so to speak, the crisis started. It started with the city council. It all started with the city councils. In Spain, city councils stopped paying their bills to their providers on time, and they were taking a long time, like 20-25 days, sometimes they took three to four months. When the company started to grow, I reached a point where I had 17 employees, 18 actually, that I had to pay each month… and I didn't receive any money from the city council, so that's when I started having problems. I started taking out loans from the banks, I started asking for money from friends and acquaintances. I spent two years like that, until I couldn't take it anymore.*

In contrast to the younger participants for whom the economic crisis often translated into problems entering the labour market in the first place, Juan was affected by it at a different stage of his life. He estimated that during that time he had fixed costs of around €12,000 per month to pay his workers while he was not generating any income.

When comparing the younger participants' experiences with youth unemployment and 'waithood' with Juan's situation at this point, one can see a qualitative difference. Without trivialising the seriously depressing consequences of prolonged youth unemployment, Juan was under much more direct financial pressure. He had no 'shelter' he could return to, but his employees expected him to 'provide shelter' for them. Despite his efforts, Juan struggled to take control of the situation, which took a toll on his mental health.

> *I was feeling really badly at the time, there were moments when I had this anxiety, this anxiety that was related to stress. I went to the doctor a few times and there came this moment when I thought to myself, 'Either you change your life or this will be the end of you because this is not sustainable in the long term.'*

In this extract, Juan expressed how he got caught up in a serious trajectory of suffering and searched for professional help for his stress-related anxiety attacks. After two years working under these extreme circumstances, Juan took action and dissolved the company. Despite being left with a debt of around €50,000, he felt relieved about his decision. Shortly before selling his company, Juan met a woman and started a new relationship. Together with his new girlfriend, Juan developed a plan to temporarily move to Scotland.

> *(...) And the truth is that I went from having many hopes with the company, from having many ideas, from wanting to do a lot of things…to being disappointed. I reached a point where I said to myself, 'I don't want this anymore, I'm not happy with this… with what I'm doing'. (...). And then I met a person, a girl, I started going out with her and I always had in mind to learn English, I wanted to learn a little English, for a long time, but with the company I could not go abroad and all that. And she also wanted to go abroad, to learn English, so we started to speak, we started to see the possibility of going away and we started going out in February and in August we decided to leave, that is, six months later or less. We chose Scotland because we both liked outdoor activities, hiking, running, cycling and all that, and in Scotland there is the possibility to do those activities, and we decided to choose Scotland, we researched how to start. I didn't mind working [in any type of job], because I don't care, I don't care.*

This quote reveals how several biographical patterns merged in this particular case, making a temporary migration to the UK very attractive. Juan's company had gone bankrupt due to structural forces outside of his control. The relationship with his new girlfriend was a ray of hope in his life, as it appeared to give his life a new direction. Like many people in Spain, she had the idea of improving her English via a temporary stay in the UK.

Although it had not been a priority in his life, he indicated that learning "a little English" had also been something that he had been interested in for a while. In this context, studying a new language was a pretext to justify a temporary 'time out' together with his new girlfriend. His biographical narrative contained, however, several indicators that he had the urge to get out of Spain in order to recover from his personal crisis and to come to terms with the loss of his life's work.

Several interviewees went into detail about the difficult times in their lives prior to their migration in which they felt confused and paralysed. These included painful experiences of personal loss, breaches of trust and dissolutions of relationships. Their decision to leave the country seemed fuelled by a desire to also gain some physical distance from places that reminded them of bad experiences (Bagnoli, 2003).

One example is Ander, a 29-year-old tax advisor who had spent six months in England before returning to his native Basque Country. His parents, who had one severely disabled biological daughter, had adopted him and his younger sister as infants. They opted for what has been referred to as a 'closed awareness context'[3] which means they did not inform their children about their adoption. Ander, however, grew up within a 'suspicion awareness context' (Glaser & Strauss, 1965), as he intuitively sensed that some information about his heritage did not add up (lack of photographs, diffuse memory of picking up his younger sister at an orphanage). Early attempts to confront his parents about the subject were ignored or playfully treated as a joke.

His mixed emotions and confusion about his adoption became visible in the particular textual structure of his narrative, as he revealed this part of his life only halfway through our interview – at the point when he and his sister were informed by their parents that they had been adopted. Until then he had presented his life-history as if he were the biological child of his parents. Ander's biographical narrative indicated that his downplaying of the importance of the topic in front of his parents, after his doubts were confirmed at age 22, hid the complexity of his true feelings ("*I told them… for me that's brilliant, that they were my parents and that I wasn't interested in anything to do with my past*").

The second important theme of Ander's narrative was the early death of his sister, who was his parents' only biological child, when she was a teenager. The data suggests that his parents had put their own feelings of grief aside to some extent in order to do 'what is best' for their remaining children. These repressed feelings, however, resurfaced years later, which Ander found overwhelming.

> *From there, last year… it will be almost a year, I decided I'd had enough. Because of many circumstances, ehm… I had a difficult personal situation (…) In my family… what happened is that my mother, about 10 years after the death of my sister, my mother was diagnosed with depression. I wanted to get out and I left!*

> *There was a moment, you know, I was working a lot, and my head was like this… I spent more time taking care of my parents than living my life because, for me, my parents are my life. If it wasn't for them, I don't know where I'd be today. Also in matters of relationships with girls or women… I always felt like a fool. It's like this phrase if you're a good guy you're foolish… I felt a bit dissatisfied with my life in general. I had three long relationships and did not*

manage to maintain any of them. Three years with one girl, five years with another and then two years with another one. They all left me. And then my mother got sick, and I never managed to get along with my little sister… and at work I started to feel uncomfortable, and therefore I exploded! I felt that I was living a life that was not mine. And I decided to give it all up, and that's what I did. I talked to him, my business partner. I told him I was fed up with everything, including him, and that I needed to leave. My business partner, who is still one of my best friends… In May last year, I told him, 'I need to go.' 'When?', 'Next month.' 'But what about all the clients you have?', 'I'll help you with anything… I need to go. I need to leave because if I continue like this… I'm going to have a problem and it's going to affect everyone.' (…)

Then I said, 'I'm going to England!' (…) Then they asked me, 'Where are you going?' and 'I'm going to look at apartments in Brighton' because I also took a little trip there before. 'What's in Brighton?', 'I don't know…' and 'Why there?', 'Well, it's close to London', and 'What are you going to do there?', 'Study English and live…which is what I need'.

The depth of Ander's pain in this situation is visible in the textual structure of this sequence, as he interrupts his main storyline after the first paragraph (*"I left…"*). At this point in the interview, he realised that he needed to insert further information in the form of a background construction (Schütze, 2008) about how he reached the decision to leave Spain in order for his story to 'make sense' from an outsider's perspective. In Ander's life, his mother's collapse could metaphorically be compared to the opening of the 'Pandora's box', as it unlocked identity issues he had ignored for a long time. His expression, *"I wanted to get out and I left!"*, entails a notion of panic, as he felt threatened by the developments in his family. Ander felt overwhelmed by his newly assigned responsibilities of taking care of his parents, to whom he felt deeply indebted. His comment *"If it wasn't for them, I don't know where I'd be today,"* reveals a sense of vulnerability in the context of his adoption. Despite having previously claimed that he had no interest in his past, Ander seemed to have considered alternative scenarios in his mind about what his life would look like if his parents had not adopted him.

When Ander said, *"I felt that I was living a life that wasn't mine,"* he points to the development of a deep identity crisis and trajectory of suffering. On top of his sister's death and his adoption, Ander brought up the topic of his failed relationships with women, which he had also struggled to come to terms with. Ander sensed how he was about to "*explode*" if he continued to pretend that everything was going well. The way he recalled his conversation with his business partner underlines a sense of urgency he felt in the situation. Ander sensed that he would become an additional burden for his parents if he broke down before their eyes, possibly exacerbating his mother's depression.

After having shed light on the arguably messy and emotionally confusing process leading to his decision to leave Spain, Ander returned to his main story line. It is very interesting that he chose England as the destination for his time-out, as it provided a perfect 'ancillary motive' (Mills, 1940) for his temporary migration. In the context of the economic crisis, thousands of (young) people opted for a temporary stay in the UK to learn the language, often in the hope of gaining a competitive advantage once they returned to Spain. For Ander, however, 'learning English' appeared to some extent like a cover-up to conceal his deeper desire to get away in order to deal with a personal crisis. At extended family gatherings and/or work-related situations, Ander could easily portray his temporary stay in the UK as a conscious investment in his professional career, a socially acceptable justification unlikely to provoke further questions.

One may ask why I decided to discuss these two cases of Juan and Ander in one section, given the striking individual differences (i.e. economic crisis vs. family related causes of despair). Against the backdrop of my diverse sample, I realised the importance of exploring different biographical problem constellations that can contribute to trajectories of suffering. When comparing these two biographical narratives, one can detect how both informants experienced their living situation in Spain as suffocating. What they shared was reaching a moment where they could not continue their lives as they were and needed to 'get out', a decision that can be conceived as an action scheme of escape.

IN SEARCH OF PROFESSIONAL RECOGNITION AND ADEQUATE PAY

A few interviewees in my sample migrated due to their expectation of better working conditions abroad. These informants already had considerable work experience in their occupations or professions, high self-esteem with regard to their qualifications, and they developed expectations about what they deserved (symbolically and materially) due to their skills – expectations that were not met in the current situation in Spain (Bygnes, 2017). These migrants were not directly affected by unemployment but reported how their working conditions gradually worsened throughout the crisis. They felt deeply cheated, as their work environment did not reflect their self-perception as competent experts or professionals (Markovitz et al., 2014). Ignacio is a 36-year-old computer scientist who was living in Exeter at the time of our interview. He started his career many years before the economic crisis, had a stable job in Madrid, but was unhappy about the working conditions: *"So many overtime hours, which were not paid. Furthermore, they don't care about the team and don't treat their employees well."*

Against the background of the economic crisis, several informants described how their last employers in Spain made them feel as if they 'ought to be grateful to have a job'. Given the widespread unemployment, these participants felt that they could not speak up about perceived injustices including unpaid overtime hours and salary cuts. Furthermore, they perceived the opportunities of advancing their careers to be very limited in Spain. Although these informants usually earned enough to pay their bills (see the phenomenon of 'mileuristas')[4], they were curious about exploring seemingly more attractive job opportunities abroad.

One example is 30-year-old Diego, who was working as a nurse at a public hospital in England at the time of our interview. He had graduated with a university degree in nursing in 2008, just before the onset of the economic crisis in Spain.[5] At first, he had no trouble finding work as he received a job offer only six days after finishing his degree. In Spain, as he explained to me, nursing graduates start their careers by substituting state employees who are on maternity leave or vacation. Therefore, he only received short-term contracts for periods lasting two and a half months. However, in the first two years after his graduation, he was almost constantly working as *"these were different times – people in my profession didn't need to go look for work because employers were actively looking for us"*. Diego even declined some job offers in order to have more time to play football. His working conditions however got gradually worse as the economic crisis unfolded (Galbany-Estragues & Nelson, 2016). When discussing how the idea to migrate came about, Diego recounted:

> *The most important reason, I think, was the precariousness of the work I had in Spain. It became harder and harder to find work there. They started reducing the*

> *contracts a lot. (…) What happened is that the government started cutting the budgets. They reduced it so much. Now, when the state employees are not working, if they are on vacation or maternity leave, they don't substitute them anymore. They just work with less staff. (…) They started giving me worse contracts compared to the ones I had when I first graduated from university. (…) During the first two years I didn't spend much time without work. I had a contract… when the contract ended, I would spend some days at home, but then I would get another one. It was always a matter of one or two weeks. But when time passed… my contracts evolved inversely with regard to my work experience. I had more experience but my contracts became shorter.*

Diego's impression that his career evolved "*inversely*" with regard to his experience resonated with the experiences of other interviewees (cf. Riemann, 2019). The combination of becoming more experienced at one's job while receiving less attractive conditions served as a source of frustration and anger. It seems as if the economic crisis blocked their professional development, confining them to the status of 'perpetual beginners'. Diego was frustrated with his work situation in Spain, which is why he started to look for opportunities abroad. When evaluating his options, he learnt about an EU programme for medical professionals encouraging them to work in public hospitals within Europe. Within this system, doctors and nurses can earn points while working abroad. These transferable points are then used to determine the salary bracket of the employee because in many European countries nurses earn more as they gain more experience (Bach, 2010). Diego learned that his prospects of finding work abroad were very good as there was a great demand for nurses in many countries such as Germany, the Netherlands and the United Kingdom. He illustrated the urgency with which foreign hospitals were looking for nursing staff from southern Europe by giving the example of how he got recruited.

> *The directors from my hospital here in Bristol went to Porto and Madrid looking for staff. They spent three or four days interviewing a lot of people… and then they went to Madrid and did the same. They offered me the job and I accepted.*

Diego could choose between various attractive offers prior to his departure, which put him in an advantageous position over most other informants in my study. Migrants such as Ignacio or Diego could realistically expect to immediately continue their professional lines on a higher level as compared to what they were offered in Spain (with regard to working conditions, pay and symbolic gratification). What sets these migrants apart from the rest is that they are generally trained in occupations that are highly sought after (e.g., nurses, computer specialists), which do not require flawless English skills, in contrast to the work of lawyers, for example (Meinardus, 2017).

ACQUIRING FOREIGN LANGUAGE SKILLS IN ORDER TO GAIN A COMPETITIVE ADVANTAGE

Some interviewees went to the UK – and to a lesser extent Germany (Glorius, 2017) – with the sole objective of learning the language, hoping it would give them a competitive advantage when returning to Spain. The data suggests that throughout the crisis foreign language skills have gained symbolic value in Spanish society. Employers often require applicants to be fluent in English for positions that are traditionally not linked to foreign languages. Pumares (2017, p. 141) observed that in the context of the crisis, the requirements of employers have become "limitless" and have come to include English, "whether necessary or not, if only as a way of clearing out CVs piling up on their desks". In response to these new requirements, there has been a collective revaluation of foreign language skills that seems to shape how people think about their future and make plans. In many narratives in this sample, speaking English fluently was referred to as a 'universal' door opener both in Spain and abroad. Some participants believed it to be the only obstacle to finding a job in their field of expertise, thereby seemingly fading out other important factors such as lack of work experience.

Almost all interviewees expressed anger about their English training, which they had received at high school, arguing that they learned close to nothing due to the lack of practical exercises. It seems that there is a general sense of having been let down by the Spanish state, which failed to sufficiently prepare recent graduates for the current situation (Bygnes, 2017). A temporary migration with the sole purpose of learning the language can therefore be understood as an attempt to catch up on the rapidly changing labour market requirements.

Óscar, a 29-year-old engineer by training, claimed that "*in engineering, it is now mandatory to speak English*". Due to a case of illness in his family, Óscar had to work in his parents' shop during his studies, which is part of the reason why it took him six years to complete his undergraduate degree. In Spain, he argued, it is not that uncommon to take a few years longer to finish a university degree. In the context of the economic crisis, however, the entrance requirements for the labour market seemed to have increased significantly. Óscar was now in the position of having to compete with younger applicants who possessed the same academic qualifications as well as people his age and people who were older who had more work experience. In the interview, it became clear that he grew increasingly worried about losing touch with his professional identification, as he had not been able to gain any practical experience in the two years after his graduation. In this situation, learning English seemed like the only way to gain a competitive advantage on the job market in Spain.

Óscar therefore decided to move to England with his girlfriend, a nursery schoolteacher, with the initial plan to stay eight months working as au pairs before returning to Spain to look for jobs in their fields. This plan did not materialise in the end, as the couple decided to stay longer after having completed their work as au pairs. While Óscar's partner eventually succeeded in finding work as a nursery schoolteacher in the UK, he started working as a cashier in a fast-food restaurant, hoping to further improve his language skills. Óscar contextualised his current ways of making a living with reference to his Spanish co-workers, who apparently had similar objectives.

> *Most of the Spanish people I worked with at McDonald's come for a little while to learn English and then they leave again. I mean, in Spain, we are quite family-oriented. It's important to live close to our families. Most people come here to learn English and then look for a job in Spain – more prepared!*

Óscar and his colleagues seemed to hope that a temporarily limited stay abroad could somehow translate into cultural capital when returning to Spain (Bourdieu, 1984) and could help them to acquire qualifications that could make them stand out in the labour market at home. While British university degrees are widely accredited and appear useful in this regard, it is unclear if temporary migration to learn English really translates into a significant advantage in the Spanish labour market. There is a risk that future employers might perceive these periods spent working in odd jobs as gaps in an applicant's CV, rather than a real enhancement of skills.

5. ON STUDYING AND WORKING ABROAD

EXCHANGE PROGRAMMES AS PATHWAYS INTO A LONG-TERM STAY

The majority of the participants started working immediately after moving to the UK and Germany. There were, however, a number of informants who first arrived in the new country as exchange students and later decided to stay – sometimes for an indefinite period (King & Ruiz-Galices, 2003). Others started their migration project working in menial jobs but later enrolled in master's programmes at British or German universities. Especially in the case of (former) Erasmus students, it was sometimes surprising how the participation in a time-limited exchange programme evolved into a permanent migration. After having discussed various problem constellations that led to my informants' decision to leave Spain, I now turn to their experiences in the new country. What were the <u>binding forces</u> that made them want to settle in the receiving society?

(a) Fear of losing one's newfound independence

As discussed in the previous chapter, many of the younger participants longed for a more independent lifestyle, which they associated with adulthood (e.g. trying to overcome 'waithood' in the sense of Singerman, 2007). The (former) exchange students were no exception in this context, as all of them had been living with their parents prior to taking part in the Erasmus scheme (Krzaklewska, 2013). Various informants only realised how much they enjoyed living on their own during their semester(s) abroad. They had gotten a 'first taste' of freedom and found the prospect of losing this new independence after returning to Spain quite depressing.

Tomas, aged 24, first moved to Hamburg as an Erasmus student. After finishing his 'year abroad', he decided to remain in Germany to pursue a master's and, later, a PhD degree in mathematics. In our interview, he reflected openly about how this decision emerged in his biographical context.

> *And then, I realised how comfortable I was here, living independently… and then I decided that I was going to try to stay. (…) If I returned to Madrid, I wouldn't be able to live outside my home. Or it would be very complicated… and being here like,/ obviously, I live away from home because I'm in another country.*

This short narrative sequence reveals Tomas's fear of being drawn back into structures of familial dependency in Spain. He knew that his mother, who was a single parent, would take it very personally if he had decided to move to a different flat in Madrid. His expression, "*being here like,/ obviously, I live away from home because I'm in another country*", reveals how he needed to legitimise his decision to live independently. His participation in the Erasmus scheme and subsequent decision to stay in Germany for a master's and PhD degree offered a way to avoid damaging his relationship with his mother under the pretence of purely academic and cultural motives. If a family member asked him why he was living in Hamburg, Tomas could easily refer to ancillary motives (Mills, 1940) such as wanting to work with a specific professor and/or improving his German skills. Whilst his appreciation for the new academic environment seemed authentic, the driving force behind his migration was his wish not to live with his mother anymore, which he could not openly admit to her without causing offense. Although the Erasmus programme was primarily designed to foster an academic and cultural exchange between young people across Europe, several of my informants perceived it as key to emancipating themselves from their families. While it is impossible to make any quantitative claims, their experiences as exchange students seemed to differ significantly from those of other exchange students who had already lived independently prior to going abroad.

(b) Attractive academic opportunities

Apart from living more independently, my informants also expressed a deep appreciation for the academic support they received during their Erasmus stay. In this context, they frequently engaged in contrasting comparisons between their home and host institutions. The Spanish higher education system was thereby often described as impersonal, 'school-like', conservative and expensive (Arce et al., 2015). Some students experienced their Erasmus year as liberating, as they were generally given more time and autonomy to prepare seminars. Furthermore, they felt encouraged to engage in critical discussions and develop their own research projects.

When speaking about how their Erasmus semester evolved into something long-term, several participants spoke of sympathetic academic mentors at their host university, who indicated that they recognised my informants' special talent and potential. These professors not only encouraged them to stay, but also facilitated their transfer by offering support in their application for stipends and/or assistant jobs. My informants sensed that their mentors thought highly of them, i.e., that held positive and encouraging me-images towards them (in the sense of George Herbert Mead's (1934) 'me'), which was decisive for their confidence in their own abilities and their self-identifications as a (future) designer, mathematician, etc. For many students, having such close contact with a professor was a new experience, as they frequently described their study programmes in Spain as much more anonymous.

(c) Extracurricular activities and new social relationships

During their Erasmus year, some people engaged in certain extracurricular activities such as playing in a band, volunteering with migrants and refugees, or creating a cafe at university. Although the projects differed widely, these participants shared a sense of pride in what they had achieved in a short amount of time and how they had set down roots in their new environments. In this context, they frequently drew symbolic boundaries between themselves and 'ordinary' Erasmus students, who they claimed were mainly interested in drinking, partying and socialising exclusively among each other (cf. van Mol & Michelsen, 2014). By working together with others for a common cause, some informants developed quite close friendships (Mitchell, 2012). Being part of a team that had long-term objectives often evolved into a 'binding force', which made it difficult to leave the host institution after one or two semesters. In a few narratives, my informants also spoke of intimate relationships that had formed during their exchange year. Although it was rarely the only reason, envisioning a common future with a new partner also had an impact on my informants' ultimate decision to stay in the receiving society (Gallucci, 2013).

(d) Career prospects in the receiving society

The aforementioned 'binding forces' illustrate how some participants somewhat 'stumbled' into a more permanent migration project. In contrast to that, there were a few participants who thought of their higher education more *strategically* as a tool for finding a job in the host society. One example is Nora, aged 29, who had migrated to London after finishing her undergraduate degree in business administration in Madrid. After one year working in various menial jobs, she decided to go back to university. With the financial help of her parents, she enrolled in a master's programme in human resource management at a public university in Brighton. After graduation, she quickly found her *"first serious job in England"*, working for a big tourist company in Brighton. Based on her previous experiences in London, she expressed her suspicion that foreign credentials such as a university degree from a Spanish university, often get overlooked by British employers: *"you study in your country, but for them it's nothing, your degree is not worth anything"*. She shared this belief with several other informants in my sample who were currently engaged in menial labour.[1] By earning a degree from a British or German university, a few participants could make themselves appear 'less foreign' on paper and gain their employers' trust (Salt, 2011).

The narratives revealed that it was often a combination of these four different yet related 'binding forces' that made it unattractive for the (former) Erasmus students to leave the host-institution after one or two semesters. This is why several informants transferred their credits from Spain and enrolled at their exchange university full-time. Others temporarily returned to their home universities to finish their undergraduate degree but had the clear intention of moving back to Germany or the UK to pursue postgraduate studies (mostly in the form of master's or PhD programmes).

ALTERNATIVES TO WAGE LABOUR

Au pair work

While earning a university degree at a foreign university could be considered the 'classic' path to prepare oneself for entering the new labour market, it also required a significant amount of both economic and cultural capital. Quite a few informants took part in au-pair schemes after graduating from university, which seemed to be a more affordable way to learn a new language in a sheltered environment. Whilst some participants planned to stay only for one year to improve their chances at getting a job in Spain, others perceived their au pair work as a way to ease themselves into the labour market of the receiving society. In other words, they wanted to give themselves a year to learn English or German properly before applying for a job in their field of expertise.

The term 'au pair' is French and translates into 'as equal', referring to the idea that the person should be treated like a family member rather than a domestic servant. The scheme is designed to allow for a cultural exchange for young people and provide help to families with young children (Cox & Narula, 2003). While this set-up appears like a win-win situation in theory, such 'quasi-familial' or 'false kin' relations can be problematic (Anderson, 2000). Although my informants' experiences with their host-families differed widely, their narratives revealed a number of common problem constellations: (a) ill-defined roles in the host family; (b) isolation and difficulties meeting people one's own age; (c) 'empty' time and boredom when the children are preoccupied; and (d), feeling 'overqualified' for one's tasks.

These themes became visible in several interviews, including that of Pedro, who was 23 years old when we met. Pedro was born in Colombia but his parents decided to move the family to Spain in the early 2000s, due to safety concerns in Bogotá at the time. This first migration project entailed a loss of socio-economic status, as the family had to share a small one-bedroom flat in a suburb of the Spanish capital. After finishing high school, Pedro started a degree in fine arts in Madrid but he was forced to drop out because of financial problems. Not knowing how to proceed, he asked his older sister for advice and she suggested a temporary stay as an au pair abroad, as he would "*be taken care of*" (e.g. accommodation, food) and would also learn a new language. Pedro agreed to the idea and quickly found a host-family online. He then moved to a city in the south of Germany where he was in charge of taking care of two young children. Pedro was relieved about having gained some economic autonomy even though he only received some pocket money.

> *Also economically speaking, it was really good because I didn't have any expenses because I had a place to sleep, I had food and they gave me money to spend on whatever I wanted. I sent some of the money to my family, the rest was for me. For me this was a strong contrast, the power to… for example, walk down the street, pass by a bakery, see a piece of cake and just have the power to buy it.*

In contrast to the vast majority of other participants, Pedro sent some of his pocket money to his family in Spain, indicating that they too were struggling financially. The work arrangement had some disadvantages, as he felt quite isolated in the first month of his stay in Germany. Furthermore, taking care of two young children without speaking the language proved to be very challenging.

> *They had two children, the boy was three years old and the girl was five. In the beginning it was hard because, when I came, the mother was at the hospital three or four days a week and the father worked all day. I didn't speak German and the children, one of them, the boy, was super naughty. And I had to take them to school and to the nursery and I always tried to take them… and in general I get along with children because I know how the mind of a child works, but without being able to communicate it was hard. (…) The boy didn't want to walk, he didn't want to help or behave, for example, on public transportation. That really frustrated me at first because I didn't see myself as capable of managing the situation.*

There is an element of resignation and perhaps even shame in admitting that he did not see himself *"capable of managing the situation"*. Pedro was furthermore asked to do certain tasks, which he believed were not part of his role.

> *They also abused the role of an au-pair a bit, they made me their cleaner too. (…) And later on the mother would tell me, 'No, I told you to do this, I told you!' and we would have conflicts because she would ask me to clean much more than would be expected. Including delicate things… If you have a couch that is full of dog hair*

and food and dog piss, why would you get a person coming from abroad to clean it? It didn't make sense to me.

Pedro expressed how uncomfortable he felt about the work setting as his role seemed to be ill defined (Cox & Narula 2003). His example of the dirty couch also illustrates the discomfort of being drawn into somebody else's private sphere. The isolated nature of his work seemed to undermine Pedro's negotiating power because he did not have any co-workers who could support him in situations of conflict.

Since being an 'au pair' is not designed to be a full-time occupation, many informants spoke of longer periods when they had little, or nothing, to do. This was especially true in families with school-age children who were also involved in a number of extracurricular activities in the afternoon. Ana, aged 24, had a degree in physical therapy and was working for a family in Cologne at the time of our interview. Although she was generally content with the working conditions, she grew increasingly frustrated about her situation.

The contract is for one year but I hope to get out of it earlier. It's kind of empty work. They always include you in family things but in the end you are kind of a servant who is there when the mother is working and the father goes to soccer. (…) Despite the positive aspects, for me it's not great work. It's okay for some time, but as the months go by it gets weird. When the mother is at home, I have nothing to do because the kids are with her. It's weird.

Ana felt uneasy about the 'false kin relations' (Anderson, 2000), i.e., being regarded as somebody in between a family member and a domestic servant. Later on, she also voiced her frustration about having to be available for the parents in case they spontaneously decided to go out at night. On many occasions they ended up not needing her services. This pattern was frustrating for her because she could have used the time to socialise with her friends.

Ana's observation that au pair work gets *"weird"* as *"the months go by"* captures a sentiment that almost all informants shared. My interviewees differed in the ways they made use of their free time. Some people had developed a routine of studying English or German while the children were away. Others engaged in voluntary work in the hope that it would facilitate their labour market entrance after the au pair assignment was over. There were also a few interviewees who took on part-time jobs (or internships) outside the family setting, such as working in a bar once or twice a week. By diversifying their activities, my informants could counteract feelings of isolation and boredom (Stubberud, 2015). Most people were looking forward to 'moving on' to the next chapter in their lives. Much like Ana, who strongly identified as a physiotherapist, these informants were keen to gain some work experience in their field of expertise. Working as an au pair was thereby regarded as a means to an end, i.e., as a way to learn a language before entering the 'real world'.

Alternative economic practices

Au pair work is based on exchanging labour (childcare) for accommodation and food, as the financial rewards remain symbolic in the form of 'pocket money'. Apart from working with children, various participants engaged in other alternative economic practices as a way of sustaining themselves abroad (Castells & Hlebik, 2017).[2] After losing his company in the context of the economic crisis, Juan decided to move to Scotland together with his girlfriend. Bankrupt, the couple tried to find a way to sustain themselves with as few expenses as possible. They found a website where people who had local businesses were looking for workers. In exchange for their labour, they would receive free accommodation and food but no (or very little) money. Juan and his partner were attracted to this concept and decided to give it a try. At first, they were working for a bed and breakfast and, later on, a bakery.

> *An artisanal bakery, we started there, we talked to the owner, and we discussed that in exchange for working Thursdays, Fridays, Saturdays and Sundays, we would stay in the flat that he owned. They would pay for all the food. So we decided to try it for a month and see how it goes. The job at the bakery was fantastic. It was such a wonderful way of working, one of the best jobs that I've ever had. It's hard, but it's very rewarding. It's hard because you get up at 4am, start making the bread at 5am. Furthermore, we made it in a very artisanal way, without using chemicals. It was a very slow process, making the dough, letting it sit and all that, right? To be honest, the owners of the bakery helped us a lot. It was incredible. We worked with them and in exchange we could live and eat there. There was no money involved.*

This exchange illustrates the existence of alternative solidarity networks across Europe. The emerging friendship between a formerly successful entrepreneur from the Canary Islands and a Scottish family who owned a traditional bakery seemed initially unlikely. The set-up was, however, beneficial for both parties as Juan and his partner did not have any expenses and could enjoy their stay in Scotland. While the work in the bakery was manual, Juan perceived it as a culturally valuable experience. Even though the assignment was originally meant to last only four weeks, the couple stayed at the bakery for over seven months.[3]

Juan was one of the participants hit hardest by the economic crisis in Spain. Despite years of hard work, he could not save his company due to structural forces outside of his control. When evaluating his first experiences in Scotland in the context of his whole biography, he "took time out" from capitalist work structures by temporarily engaging in alternative forms of production and exchange (Castells, 2017). Before moving to Scotland, Juan had struggled with anxiety attacks and insomnia related to his bankruptcy and accumulating debt. Working in the artisan bakery seemed to have had a positive effect on his mental health, perhaps because there "*was no money involved*".

'UNSKILLED' LABOUR?

The majority of my participants were engaged in what could officially be classified as 'unskilled' labour at the time of the interview. I put the term 'unskilled' in quotation marks as their narratives revealed how this type of informal work was commonly experienced as economically, physically and emotionally challenging. Dealing with such hardships required my informants to develop a certain skillset as part of their survival strategy, which included resilience and an ability to stand up for oneself in difficult situations. In the next section, I will firstly discuss some obstacles my participants associated with specific labour contracts both in the UK and Germany. Secondly, I will raise questions about how Spanish migrants experience their everyday work routines and environments. This includes a discussion on certain vulnerabilities and attempts to resist. Finally, I will conclude with a note on how my participants reflected upon menial labour in the context of their biographies.

Precarious labour contracts: two examples

In the UK, 'zero-hour contracts' are defined as an "employment contract in which the employer does not guarantee the individual any work, and the individual is not obliged to accept any work offered" (Wood & Burchell, 2014, p. 3.). Even though these contracts were originally designed to benefit both employers and employees to facilitate a better balance between home and work life, the lived reality of 'flexible scheduling' paints a different picture. Wood (2020) observed that workers often suffer from feelings of powerlessness and are unable to plan their lives. This was a theme that also appeared in my sample, as various informants expressed how this type of contract took a toll on their wellbeing. The constantly changing work schedules prevented some participants from signing up for English lessons, which seemed to impede their integration process. Being dependent on their managers' good will to receive shifts seemed to seriously undermine my informants' negotiating power in situations of conflict (Wood, 2020). Not knowing how much they would earn each month furthermore prevented some migrants from seeking better housing, which they experienced as depressing (see the case study of María).

In my German sample, some informants expressed their disappointment in only finding so-called 'mini jobs', which entitle workers to a tax-free maximum monthly income of €450 (Jaehrling & Mehaut, 2012). A number of people felt somewhat deceived by Germany's comparatively low unemployment rates (cf. introduction). Prior to their departure, these informants believed that it would be easier to find full-time employment based on these statistics. A few interviewees admitted working illegally (e.g. by cleaning bars at night) to supplement their 'mini job' income.

Biographical rupture and devaluation

The vast majority of informants who were engaged in menial labour were (recent) university graduates who had never worked in a similar position before. After arriving in the new country, many informants experienced a shock. Manual labour was not only physically exhausting but often also took some emotional adjustments. The category of 'unskilled' labour is an umbrella term that encompasses a wide variety of different types of work ranging from being shop assistants in clothing chains and working as kitchen porters in restaurants to cleaning hotel rooms. There were a number of challenges that were quite specific to certain types of labour, such as feeling disgusted by having to clean other people's bodily fluids. Some jobs were much more isolated than others (cleaners vs. waiters), which made a difference in how my informants evaluated their stay abroad.

Many narratives from these participants contained detailed descriptions of experiencing hard physical labour under difficult circumstances. In trying to understand my participants' work experiences, the following themes could be discovered: (a) feeling detached from one's own labour; (b) experiencing physical exhaustion; (c) a lack of workplace solidarity; (d) feelings of repulsion about certain tasks; (e) isolation; and (f) a perceived devaluation of previous biographical achievements. These themes became visible in the narrative of Laura, aged 25, who moved to Glasgow immediately after graduating from her Spanish university with a degree in social work. Her English skills were limited in the beginning, which is why she took on a position as a cleaner in a hotel.

It was horrible, or like there were moments, there was a day when I couldn't even open a bottle of milk. I had no strength in my hand. That was the worst experience of my life. The only thing I would do is to go to work, sleep and go to English classes. Work, sleep and go to classes. (…). Sometimes we had to clean 15 or 16 rooms, and between them there were like 10 exits. So what I did is, when I arrived, the day before I would have prepared the trolley with the towels, the soap, milk, coffee, sugar, bin bags… everything a hotel room can have. And then you would go to the office, they would give you a paper with the hotel room numbers. I would never understand why they wouldn't give you rooms in the same place because sometimes they would give you one here and the other one on the third floor and another one on the ground floor. You lose time, move around the trolley that weighed at least five kilograms and then, you enter the room, you make the bed, you clean the bathroom, you change the towels, you clean the floor… Often I couldn't even catch a breath. It was like a factory, you know what you have to do, and you are being controlled. Sometimes I felt really alienated. (…) One time, they made me work eleven days in a row. Eleven days, it was killing me.

Prior to her migration, Laura had spent several years at university, which she had experienced as a sheltered and enjoyable environment. After arriving in Glasgow, she was suddenly drawn into structures of what she compared to a "*factory*", where she had very little agency over her own time. Laura's work at the hotel was physically exhausting, as she had to carry heavy cleaning equipment and work under extreme time pressure (McDowell et al., 2007; Janta et al., 2011). She sensed that her previous academic achievements were met with indifference as she was reduced to her physical labour. She felt deeply out of place at the hotel, which she underlined by using the Marxist expression of feeling "*alienated*".

Laura's experiences resonated with what was expressed in quite a few other interviews as many participants, both in Germany and the UK, worked in very similar work settings. Most interviewees regarded this type of work as a temporary activity to learn the language before moving on to find a job in their field of expertise. A perceived lack of English or German skills seemed to take a toll on my participants' self-esteem, as they shied away from applying for more attractive positions at the time of our interview. Despite having attained high academic qualifications from Spanish universities, they doubted that they would stand a chance in getting a job in a more formal environment. Furthermore, some participants seemed to suffer from what has been referred to as the 'scarring effect of youth unemployment' (McQuaid et al., 2014) as their attempts to become financially independent in Spain had failed. After having received many rejections from employers back home, these informants tended to hold on to their menial jobs for prolonged periods of time.

However, cleaning jobs in particular were less than ideal for practising one's language skills because people worked in very isolated settings. This became visible in the narrative of Fabian, aged 25, who moved to Glasgow after graduating from university with an honours degree in chemistry.

> *In the morning, I had to go clean the cinema, so my timetable was from 5.30am to 8.30am, six days a week. It wasn't many hours, because it was three hours a day, but the fact that I had to start at 5.30 in the morning, that was… that was killing me. (…) It was quite frustrating because you work too early, so your social life, even if you don't know many people, you don't feel like going out, because by 7pm or 8pm you're already sleepy and want to go to bed. So you don't go to the bar to meet people if you feel like going to sleep. (…) So, I've lost a lot of my social life. I made a few friends while I was at work, but most conversations were like, "Hello, how are you?", I go to my room…I come out… "How did it go? Was there a lot of popcorn on the floor?" There wasn't much to talk about, so it was a bit frustrating. And then, it was always dark. Because being there in the dark room, with the torch there trying to get the popcorn out from under the chair. Ehm… I don't know, then you go in there, once I went in there… and there was vomit, this big, in the corridor. (…) You open the door, first thing in the morning, 5.30am in the morning that smell hits you. (…) Then of course, you feel a bit shitty because of the work. And then you say, "I've got a chemistry degree, what am I doing here cleaning up shit?"*

Fabian's descriptions of his everyday work at the cinema paint a depressing picture of a job that he experienced as unattractive and even disgusting.

Despite only working three hours a day (earning minimum wage), the demanding schedule impeded his integration efforts. Although Fabian had accepted the job in the hope of becoming fluent in English, this cleaning job afforded him hardly any opportunities to practise his language skills. There was, furthermore, a degrading quality to this type of labour. Not only does it involve working in total darkness and isolation, but it also involves tasks that most people find physically repulsive. Fabian's self-directed question underlines the frustration of feeling overqualified for a job. He experienced a sense of alienation and biographical rupture that he shared with many others in my sample (cf. Serra, 2014).

The experience of manual labour does, however, vary depending on the types of work arrangements and occupations. There were important differences between the experiences of informants working as cleaners and those who worked as, e.g., kitchen porters in the hospitality sector. The latter commonly work in teams, which can ease feelings of isolation and give them some leverage in conflict situations with superiors. That being said, my participants' experiences with co-workers differed widely. Some people described the atmosphere at their workplace as generally positive, whilst others reported incidences of micro-aggressions by co-workers and superiors, a phenomenon discussed in the next section.

On the experience of being *othered*

Several informants in my sample described situations at work where they felt discriminated against and excluded because they were Spanish or because of specific features of their English and German. These sequences were often highly detailed, which points to the depth of pain such interaction patterns were causing them. Oftentimes, they felt *othered* by their colleagues and superiors, who apparently used my informants' weak spots (i.e. not being native speakers, self-consciousness because of alleged cultural differences) against them. The intensity of such perceived micro-aggressions varied across the sample, as some informants felt bullied on a daily basis whilst others were simply suspicious of potentially becoming an object of gossip in their workplace. There was, furthermore, a notable difference between informants who worked with other Spanish migrants and those in more isolated settings. The latter seemed much more vulnerable to othering practices, as they became quite isolated laughing stocks. They did not have a team of co-nationals who shared or mitigated this burden. What these informants shared was a sense of mistrust in their interaction partners who, they suspected, were vindictive and manipulative. They felt that anything they said or did could potentially be taken out of context and used against them in situations of conflict – something that could be compared to an 'awareness context of suspicion' (Glaser & Strauss, 1965). Many of them felt trapped in these difficult situations due to a perceived lack of alternative job opportunities.

Beatriz, aged 28, was studying engineering at a public university in Berlin at the time of the interview. She was one of the participants who spoke German quite well, as she had attended a German-speaking school in Spain as a child. Her status as a Spanish citizen did not entitle her to student financing (i.e. BAföG) from the German state. In order to sustain herself, she took on a part-time job as an assistant to an administrative manager at her university. She described her everyday work as follows.

> *And I'm also working for this person… because I always have such bad luck working for people that are so weird. Well, in the beginning it was very good… but then later she started saying things like, "Ahhh! You're late because you're Spanish, right?" and I was like, "No, I don't know." And things like, "You forgot what I told you before!" and oftentimes I hadn't forgotten about anything, she just hadn't told me anything about it. So what I started to do is write down everything she said on a piece of paper. If it's not written down, she hasn't said it. I'm not an idiot. I know what she told me and what she did not. But yeah… these types of things started happening. (…) And so… this type of work is like… I know that I have to leave because it's harming me. Staying there is masochistic, but I haven't left yet because I'm in this situation… I'm an immigrant and it's hard for me to find another job. Now that I have a job, I want to hold on to it, but I'm anxious all the time. (…) It's destroying me emotionally; she makes me feel like an idiot. When I come home, I don't feel like studying… I feel like I want to die. (…) It had been really hard for me. I reached a moment where I just want to quit, even if it means dealing with hunger. I'd rather be hungry than there.*

Beatriz felt 'gaslighted' by her superior, a reoccurring interaction pattern that took a serious toll on her mental wellbeing. Her boss apparently drew on national stereotypes to express her discontent, which is something that she had not anticipated prior to her migration. After working there for some time, Beatriz developed the strong suspicion that her superior played with her memory and perception of reality on purpose. Even though she tried to defend herself by documenting each conversation, these types of interactions seemed to undermine Beatriz's trust in her own cognitive abilities and self-worth.

The psychological consequences of what she experienced as endless mind games should not be underestimated. This is especially visible in Beatriz's comment that she would rather deal with hunger than continue working for this woman.

There were several other informants who felt victimised by their co-workers and superiors, which made their everyday life intolerable. Pablo, aged 52, was working as a kitchen porter in Glasgow at the time of our interview. Prior to moving to Scotland six months before our meeting, Pablo had spent "*two hard years*" in London, where he had worked as a kitchen porter in a cafe. He used the interview situation to reflect on quite traumatic experiences at his former workplace, which he was still trying to come to terms with ("*It still hurts a lot.*").

> In this place where they fired me… I started to notice that this Polish guy, for example, he always manipulated situations so that he could claim, 'You're shouting!' And I would say, 'I'm not shouting, I am complaining' and he would say, 'No! You ARE shouting!' And then I talked like this (whispering), 'No, I am not shouting' but I noticed that he would always try to manipulate the situation so that he could later claim, 'Pablo was shouting'. Well of course… it's a delicate issue because in the hospitality sector you can't shout in front of clients. In Spain you can… because over there we shout a lot… so he [Polish co-worker] used this against me. This is why I started to be super careful because I realised how easily things I say could be manipulated and translated in a way that is out of context. And he was, well, he was the one who would communicate with the superiors because he spoke English well… so he was in charge many times when the manager wasn't around. She put too much trust in him.

Pablo sensed how his communicative resources and prosodic features as a Spaniard, i.e. the sound of his voice in English, were used as 'ammunition' against him in situations of conflict. This daily interaction pattern hurt him quite deeply, as his forms of expression (i.e. accent, intonation, pitch, volume) were not something he could control easily. In Spain, Pablo explained to me, "*we shout a lot*", which he used to contextualise why his mannerisms were apparently perceived as disruptive in England. The data extract suggests that there was something like a linguistic hierarchy in the cafe, as his Polish colleague was fluent in English whilst Pablo's vocabulary was very limited. The Polish employee seemed to be in charge of reporting to the manager what was happening 'on the ground'. In Pablo's eyes, this was a privileged position and the Polish employee was taking advantage of it. Pablo sensed he could be accused of being 'too loud' as soon as he opened his mouth, a shaming mechanism that prevented him from speaking up.

Pablo's biographical narrative revealed how he experienced his former work environment as very hostile.[4] The intercultural communication between co-workers of different nationalities, which he vividly described in the interview, entailed a potential for conflicts, including systematic miscommunication, intergroup tensions, and intensified national stereotyping. This is an area of research that has received much attention in the field of ethnography of communication (Keating, 2001).

In his socio-linguistic study on different forms of politeness in Europe, Hickey (2005, p. 321) writes:

> the imperative in Spanish is not inherently impolite. (…) In commanding or requesting, Spaniards (…) use indirect forms sparingly ('Could you close the door? It's cold in here.'), preferring direct alternatives ('Close the door'), sometimes with a compensator, as in 'Close the door, woman' (*Cierra la puerta, mujer*) or 'Shut up, man' (*Cállate, hombre*), where the 'man/woman' tag compensates for the directness by showing sympathy for the addressee.

Hickey's observations illustrate the potential for miscommunication between Spaniards and English native speakers. In British English, the well-meaning 'man/woman' tag (Hickey 2005) sounds quite inappropriate because it comes across as too direct and violates gender sensitivities.[5] Without knowing details about Pablo's communication patterns with his co-workers, it is possible that clumsy direct translations from Spanish to English (such as using the imperative) may have unintentionally caused offense.

Pablo stressed that *"nothing like this would have happened in Spain"*, as he would have had the tools to defend himself in his mother tongue. Being in a foreign environment seemed to significantly undermine his self-esteem. He was unsure how he fitted in at his workplace because his English was extremely limited and his co-workers (including superiors) were about half his age with different cultural backgrounds. His biographical narrative revealed how he felt like the 'odd one out'.

The form of othering Pablo experienced in everyday encounters is quite different from being confronted with general xenophobic attitudes in the tabloid press. In his daily interactions at the cafe, he sensed that his image as an allegedly 'loud Spaniard' was constructed as a problem and source of embarrassment. This was a very painful process, especially since he had never thought of his personal communicative style as something to be ashamed of prior to his migration. Instead of offering constructive criticism on Pablo's work, his colleague seemed to target the 'essence of his being'. Furthermore, Pablo felt victimised by a *Polish* co-worker. Their common denominator as 'EU migrants in Britain' did not guarantee any form of solidarity or trust.[6] Instead, he had the impression that his colleague defended his privileged position at the workplace (due to his superior English skills) by portraying Pablo in a negative light in front of their manager.

Beatriz and Pablo shared the experience of constantly being *on guard* at work with quite a few other informants in my sample. Having to deal with stereotypes and bias was not confined to those engaged in informal labour; people working in all kinds of positions experienced this. Several informants expressed their shock about encountering bias specifically against *Spaniards*, which undermined their self-perception as EU citizens of equal rights and status. A few interviewees argued that this experience had sensitised them to the plight of migrant workers in Spain (e.g. from Latin America, Africa and eastern Europe), a group to which they had not previously paid much attention.

Health-related problems

There were a few participants whose narratives revealed certain vulnerabilities, which exacerbated their experience of physical labour. They experienced different kinds of trajectories of suffering (Schütze, 1995, 2008, 2014), which sometimes had to do with failing bodies and/or problems that they referred to in psychiatric terms.

One example is Carmen, aged 25, who had developed lupus in her early twenties, a serious autoimmune disease that caused her to be in constant pain. In Spain, her disease had become so severe that she could not leave her bed for over a year. In the interview, she remembered how she fell into a deep depression during that time. After receiving specialised treatment, Carmen's health improved. She was keen to explore a new culture and improve her English. Furthermore, neither she nor her boyfriend could find full-time employment in their hometown in Andalusia. Despite still being physically frail, she decided to move to the UK together with her partner.

In Brighton, Carmen took on a physically exhausting job as a cleaner in a hotel ("*me and a Polish girl were supposed to clean 37 rooms in seven hours.*

It was horrible"). Due to her physical condition, she described this work as "*seven times as hard as it would have been for any other person*". Despite being in constant pain, she decided not to inform her superiors about her illness. This decision had partly to do with her fear of losing the job but also because it would have diminished her self-confidence ("*If you don't believe it, it's over*"). From living with her disease, Carmen had developed a sense of resilience. In this context, she described several survival strategies she used to detach herself from what was happening to her body. Apart from mental exercises, she also relied on medication, including a number of antidepressants. Her narrative also revealed that despite having a university degree in statistics, she took pride in what she had achieved in the UK: "*You know, before I was always depressed about not being able to travel and in this situation, although I was only working as a cleaner, I felt really proud of myself.*"

Carmen's emphasis on taking pride in her work illustrates the complexity of doing hard manual labour. Despite all the hardships associated with this type of labour, she was happy about having made progress in her life, including being able to travel and live independently. That said, her confession that this type of work was "*seven times as hard*" for her as for a healthy person revealed what she had endured.

Apart from Carmen, there were several other participants who spoke of serious health problems (e.g. a history of anorexia) that impeded their own (or their loved ones') migration experience. As discussed in the previous chapter, the migration of some informants can be categorised as an 'action scheme of escape from a trajectory of suffering' (Schütze, 1981). Due to personal losses (including difficult break-ups and family tragedies), their living situation in Spain had become unbearable. These interviewees often still suffered from the repercussions of what had happened back home and were therefore especially sensitive to workplace discrimination.

Attempts of resistance

Many informants, who were mostly engaged in manual labour, spoke of incidences and situations in which they felt they were treated unfairly. In this context, they often mentioned managers who apparently gave preferential treatment to their British or German employees. In other cases, my participants were not paid for their labour or received a salary that was much lower than promised. How did they deal with such situations? As a first step my informants engaged in what could be called 'pre-forms' of resistance, such as everyday practices of keeping a distance. The narratives revealed how such tensions sometimes escalated, requiring migrants to take more decisive measures.

Firstly, various participants reported to have taken action against unjust treatment together with other co-workers. As shown in the case studies of María and Adam, migrant workers seem to have some leverage in resisting unfair treatment once they unite with others in the same situation. Secondly, there were several informants who worked in more isolated settings. These migrants seemed especially vulnerable to exploitation, as they were not part of a team that could support them in their pursuit of justice. In these situations, they sometimes turned to self-help solidarity networks that were specifically designed for Spanish-speaking migrants abroad (Roca & Martín-Díaz, 2016). One example of the second form of resistance became visible in the case of Sandra. After completing her Erasmus year, she moved to Berlin where she started working as a waitress in a small cafe.

> *With my female supervisor it was difficult because she only spoke German and she called me stupid and things like that. And I (pause) I didn't know how to respond or defend myself because I didn't understand German perfectly. (…) I was working there for some time as a 'mini job', but I was treated really badly and one day they told me, 'Don't come back!' And I said, 'Okay, but first pay me!' and then they told me that they weren't going to pay me.*

After learning about her employers' unwillingness to pay her for a month's work, Sandra decided to take legal action. She contacted one of the aforementioned Spanish-speaking self-help organisations in Berlin[7] and was positively surprised about their quick and efficient way of intervening.

> *In this office there was a lawyer who told me that I don't have to pay for anything because he is paid by the state. And he said he would do everything possible, without money. So he wrote up this letter and sent it to the people I worked for. When they got the letter, they got really scared. I don't know exactly why. What I do know is that they paid me in the end and this man helped me so much. They work, they help you and everything is voluntary I think.*

Witnessing or imagining her employers' response to the letter *("they got really scared")* was rewarding, especially since Sandra had felt quite helpless before. By providing migrants with legal advice in their own language, volunteers such as the lawyer in question appeared to have found an effective way to counteract incidences of exploitation.

The biographical significance of menial labour

The vast majority of interviewees who were engaged in menial labour had higher qualifications, mostly in the form of university degrees (Wassermann et al., 2017). On top of that, several people had gained relevant work experience in Spain. After moving to Germany or the UK, many participants had to start 'from scratch' again as their cultural capital did not easily translate to a foreign context. This transition was not easy, as some informants struggled to reconcile their previous biographical achievements with their current work as cleaners or kitchen porters. A case in point is the aforementioned Juan, who worked in the artisanal bakery at first. In order to pay off some debt, he eventually accepted a job as a kitchen porter in a Spanish restaurant close to Glasgow. In the Canary Islands, he had formerly owned a company with eighteen employees, which he lost as a consequence of the economic crisis. When he was offered work washing dishes, he took a moment to reflect about how his career had developed.

> *So he called us and offered my partner a job as a waitress and me a job as a kitchen porter. No problem, I thought, because I wanted to start working and in Spain they don't teach you a high level of English. When you arrive, you notice that it's even lower than you thought it was. So that is why I didn't aspire to much, despite all the work that I had done in Spain.*

> *I didn't tell you that I created another company in Spain, in addition to the one that I already had. With a business partner I created a further education company, to be able to… when things go wrong, to have some income from that side. I got together with a business partner and created this training company, and we offered various courses and so on. So yeah, I also worked as a lecturer, giving courses for employees in companies. For example, giving classes on marketing, selling techniques, e-commerce and things like that. I also worked as a work assessor for a project that helps people who are socially excluded to look for work, so I was also involved in this project. What I'm saying is that I liked trying a bit of everything. If they offered me something I tended to say yes and try it.*

> *So, with all that… with all these skills I had, all the professional experience, I could have told myself, 'And now you're washing dishes?', but yes, to be honest I didn't care in that moment because, with my level of English, I couldn't aspire to much more in that moment.*

At this point in the interview, Juan took a moment to reflect about his career and the prospect of having to 'start from zero' again. While the work in the bakery was also 'manual labour', its artisanal quality and the fact that it was only symbolically paid made it a culturally valuable experience. In contrast, working as a kitchen porter in a Spanish restaurant in Scotland required Juan to re-evaluate his biographical context.

When trying to reconstruct what Juan went through during this time, it is worth taking a look at the formal features of this data sequence. His self-interruption and background construction, which started with "*I didn't tell you*", points to painful memories of trying to reconcile his previous professional achievements with his current position as a dishwasher. Juan's biographical narrative revealed that he had always been a very ambitious and hardworking man. In this data sequence, he listed his additional professional experiences and achievements that also served as a source of self-respect. His self-directed question, "*And now you're washing dishes?*" contains elements of biographical resignation: 'Where am I now in comparison to where I once was?' Even though he gives the impression of having reconciled himself with his situation ("*I didn't care in that moment*"), the fact that he introduced this detailed background construction still signifies his awareness of what he had lost.

Juan, like other participants, took solace in the fact that it was due to his lack of English skills. It seems that being in a foreign country somewhat mitigated feelings of social degradation, as he decided to regard it as a temporary activity to learn the language first. There were, however, several participants who had been engaged in manual labour for much longer periods than they had originally anticipated. This took a toll on their self-esteem, as they worried about losing touch with their academic qualifications. Most informants had initially regarded menial work as a temporary break from, or a preparation for, their career development. As time went by, some of the older participants slowly realised that this was a self-deception. Their chances of eventually finding a job in their field of expertise appeared to become slimmer and slimmer each year. Instead of temporarily working as a cleaner to learn English or German first, they sensed that they were indeed 'becoming a cleaner'. This was a slow realisation, which some participants struggled to come to terms with.

Taking pride in 'unskilled' skillsets

I already alluded to the fact that although some jobs are officially classified as 'unskilled' labour, they should not be regarded as 'simple'. Several interviewees took pride in the manual work they were engaged in, as it required a special skillset that they believed not everybody possessed. Sara, aged 25, graduated with a degree in journalism in Spain but could not find a job in her field. She worked in a cafe in Bristol before moving to Edinburgh, where I interviewed her.

> *I was looking for work as a waitress, and I found a job in a restaurant close to Edinburgh castle (…) but I don't like it. (…) They pay me well… they pay very well. When I first arrived in Bristol, since I was younger than 25, I earned £6.20 an hour. Later it was increased to £6.60 and later £6.95 and now it's at £7.05 an hour. But at this restaurant in Edinburgh I earn £8.80 an hour, or like £1.60 more. They pay me very well, but I'm doing a job that is below my qualification. (…) In the restaurant in Bristol, (…) I took reservations, I was at the bar, I made coffee, I prepared cocktails, I served wine, I knew how to pour beer and I also served tables. And here in contrast, all I do is collect the plates from the tables…I don't even serve food. (…) Apart from being boring, it's also less than what I know how to do. So tomorrow I have a job interview at another place. They will pay me less, but at least I will feel more accomplished.*

Her evaluative comment illustrates that workers do not always perceive so-called 'unqualified' labour as such. Sara took pride in the different tasks she was managing at the restaurant in Bristol, which she regarded as *qualifications*, even though they had nothing to do with her academic training as a journalist. It is significant that she decided to work for a restaurant that paid less but offered her a more diverse range of tasks that made her feel *"accomplished"*. Sara's case illustrates that the classic distinction between 'skilled' and 'unskilled' labour does not always capture the complexity of how people evaluate their ways of making a living (Perry, 1978/2017; Lulle et al., 2021).

Sara's attitude illustrates a sense of dignity in seemingly 'simple' occupations. Despite many hardships, several participants also expressed pride in what they had achieved in a new and foreign environment (cf. Morosanu et al., 2021). Even though working as a cleaner or a waiter may officially be classified as 'unqualified' work, my data suggests that these jobs frequently required special skills including physical endurance and the ability to work under much time pressure.

SKILLED LABOUR

A few interviewees succeeded in finding work that was in line with their academic qualifications.[8] Some people had received job offers from abroad while still living in Spain (or in a third country). Others had previously worked in menial jobs in the receiving society but eventually managed to find a job that suited their occupational profile. 'Skilled' labour is an umbrella term for a vast number of occupations. This variety was also reflected in my sample. Whilst there were many differences between the work environments of nurses and engineers, their narratives revealed a number of common themes.

Firstly, they were usually trained in technical occupations, which were highly sought-after in the receiving society. Secondly, they often had work in Spain, but were offered more attractive positions in the receiving society. Thirdly, some people reported to have been paid less than German or British colleagues in similar positions. Fourthly, several informants felt under pressure to 'perfect' their language skills in order to exercise their responsibilities and to 'fit in' in their work environment. And finally, a few interviewees drew symbolic boundaries between themselves and 'ordinary' (i.e. less successful) Spanish migrants (Bygnes, 2017). The heterogeneity of my sample gives rise to several questions such as how the narratives of professionally successful migrants differ from those engaged in menial labour, what common obstacles these migrants encounter and how they position themselves within (or perhaps outside) the Spanish community?

The case of nurses

Healthcare workers, and especially nurses, are a sought-after group in various countries across Europe. According to officials of the National Health Service (NHS), there are over 40,000 vacancies for nurses in England alone (Oliver, 2019). The situation in Germany has been similarly severe, something that has been referred to as 'Pflegenotstand' or 'nursing crisis' (Kraft, 2019). With ageing populations in both countries, politicians and health care experts have raised concerns about how to tackle this labour shortage, which is especially urgent against the backdrop of the current coronavirus pandemic. Many healthcare employers have started to recruit staff from other countries actively in Europe and overseas.

Despite the comparatively smooth transition into the German and British labour market, working in the healthcare sector in a foreign language presented unique challenges. Daniela, aged 27, migrated to Frankfurt together with a friend.[9] The two women, whom I interviewed at the same time, had chosen this destination after considering various options across Europe, including the UK but *"England didn't make it as easy as Germany"*. The hospital where they were currently employed had offered them an attractive package, including a language course, a decent salary and subsidised housing. Despite having completed a crash course in German, Daniela and her friend described their language skills as limited in the beginning. Working at a hospital seemed daunting at first, as she described being scared about putting patients at risk.

> *Man, the bad thing is when you call 112, which is where we answer… You want to say something about something serious that's going on, I don't know, about someone who's very ill and they don't understand you, then you say, 'Fuck, what do I do?' Then, well, you have to call another co-worker and… we had a lot, well I think I also had a lot of luck, we've been very lucky with the co-workers we've had, because they've always helped us.*

By the time of our interview, Daniela had already greatly improved her German and was not as nervous about phone calls anymore. This data sequence illustrates, however, how the hypothetical scenario of an emergency overshadowed her work experience at first, which is a theme that also appeared in my UK sample. In contrast to other participants who worked as cleaners, Daniela had significant responsibilities because mistakes based on linguistic misunderstandings could lead to very serious consequences for patients.[10]

The occupational profile of nurses in Spain differs from that in the UK and especially Germany, where nursing is an apprenticeship and not a university degree (Kuhlmann & Jensen, 2015). In my German sample, various participants voiced their frustration about not being allowed to do tasks that they were trained to do. Furthermore, they felt that nurses did not receive the same recognition as in Spain, which was something they struggled to accept. Irene, aged 28, worked in an elderly home in a small town close to Frankfurt. In our interview, she said:

It's just, really, this is a message to the world. Nursing in Germany is a catastrophe! (…) It must be the only country in the world, record me, this is very important/ it must be the only country in Europe where nursing is not a university degree. It is…in Ukraine, in Greece, in Bulgaria, everywhere it is a university degree. Not in Germany. So what happens, they cannot have the same skills as a university graduate. So for a Greek, a Spaniard, a Portuguese, or a Romanian, who do everything in their country, they arrive here and you can't even do half of it. They take away your responsibilities. (…)

I think that nursing in Germany is, it is seen as a work of…like (…) Yeah… no, it's not valued. And in the rest of the countries, we are very valued. I don't understand why, in other words, here you see it, in fact we saw an advertisement for an academy, which said something like, 'Are you going to let your children be nurses? No, support this academy, let them study more', like…as if to say, the worst thing there is to be is a nurse. And then, study to be anything else, a banker, an economist, whatever you want, but not a nurse. And that made me very indignant. Because, of course, it's my profession because I have a vocation. So, to see someone throw it on the floor like that, I don't like it. It's super degrading. It's not valued.

What Irene expressed in this argumentative sequence was resentment about the lack of symbolic recognition she felt her profession received in Germany. She felt quite strongly about the topic, which is visible in her request, *"record me, this is important"*. Her choice of other countries (Ukraine, Greece and Bulgaria) is quite specific, which indicates that she had discussed this topic with her co-workers from other European countries. When trying to reconstruct her anger about the lack of recognition, it is important to take her biographical context into account. Irene took great pride in her profession, also because she had cared for her dying father. In the interview, she narrated how this painful yet rewarding experience led her to the decision to specialise in palliative care. The metaphor of her *'vocation'* being *'thrown on the floor'* illustrates the depth of her disappointment.

The nurses in my sample spoke highly of the training they had received at university in Spain. In Germany, many medical tasks are reserved for physicians. Some informants voiced their frustration about not being allowed to apply their knowledge about prescribing medication for small wounds and infections (van Eckert et al., 2011). Furthermore, they were surprised about being put in charge of washing patients, which is something that family members are commonly expected to do in Spain (Kuhlmann & Jensen, 2015).

Most healthcare workers in my sample described their current position as significantly less stressful than their last job back home. Due to the economic crisis, many public hospitals in Spain underwent significant funding cuts that forced them to work with fewer members of staff (Galbany-Estragues & Nelson, 2016; Acea-López et al., 2021). One participant in the UK remembered that in the night shift before the interview, he had to take care of four patients. In contrast to that, the number had often exceeded seventeen at his last job in Galicia. Working in Spain was portrayed as not only precarious due to short-term contracts, but also as carrying the risk of exhaustion due to the high number of patients per nurse (Manzano-Garcia et al., 2017).

Adjusting to formal work environments

Apart from the nurses in my sample, there were several other participants who succeeded in finding work in their field of expertise (e.g. engineering, finance, computer science etc.). Some could immediately continue their career path after migrating to the new country. Others started their journey working in informal jobs, and later reconnected with their academic qualifications and long-term biographical projects. These participants often drew contrasting comparisons between their current position and the working conditions back in Spain. For example, engineers in Germany were frequently offered a salary that was twice or even three times as high as what they would earn in a similar position in their country of origin. Against the backdrop of these income disparities, some participants felt uneasy about voicing their discontent about certain aspects of their jobs, such as earning less than their German or British colleagues in similar positions. The narratives suggest that coming from a 'weaker economy' somehow undermines one's negotiating power, as they felt they ought to be grateful for earning much more than their friends from university who had stayed in Spain (Yu, 2019).

The issue of not being treated equal to their British or German colleagues often revolved around language skills (Vijande Rodríguez & Ruiz Yepes, 2018). Various interviewees felt that their managers underestimated their abilities due to their accent or imperfect grammar. These participants felt frustrated about not being approached for expert advice on certain projects, even though they felt qualified to provide it. The engineers in my sample frequently described their position as purely technical (cf. technical drawings, working with specific machines in isolated settings), while they felt somewhat excluded from the more social tasks such as networking with clients. In contrast to others working as cleaners, these migrants felt a unique pressure to 'soften their accent' and present themselves as 'professionals'.

Magda, aged 31, was working as a civil engineer in Glasgow at the time of our interview. Prior to this job, she had worked for three years as a waitress in London before enrolling in a one-year master's programme at a British university. Magda was therefore in a unique position to compare informal and more formal work settings. In the interview, she described her office environment as follows.

In my office, they are all Scottish. It is the first time that I am surrounded by so many Scottish people and it is a strange sensation because it attracts attention, that is to say, when I speak, people stare for the first time... you don't expect my accent and it stays that way... and then they talk to me. But...I mean, they look at me like I'm weird. And it's a problem, I mean, I feel very self-conscious about my accent and my way of speaking (...). I'm also the only woman in my office. Before, there were more women in my office but they left the company. I mean, I'm not the first woman (...) But now I am alone... and there are only the secretaries, who are sometimes called 'the girls'...

While Magda stressed that she was satisfied with the working conditions and felt generally respected, her status as the only foreign and female engineer made her feel somewhat uneasy. This was a problem that she had not encountered while working as a waitress in London. In her previous job, she had blended in with her co-workers, who mostly also had a migration background. Having a foreign accent was the norm rather than the exception. In this context, she drew contrasting comparisons.

In London I had this street experience... the way people talk on the street... the things they laugh at. It was something else, but here, as I have to take good care of my language and explain myself well and so on, it makes me work harder and it makes me improve my English massively. Still, I have problems with my accent.

Although Magda had become fluent in English whilst working as a waitress in London, she had picked up a mostly colloquial vocabulary, which she sensed was inappropriate – or insufficient – for an office environment. It is quite telling that she believed she had learned more English in one year working as a civil engineer than in her three years in London, where she was mostly engaged in manual labour. This is an important observation, especially since many of the other participants planned for a transition period working either as au pairs or in restaurants before looking for something related to their academic training.

Magda repeated several times how self-conscious she felt about her Spanish accent, which she struggled to improve: *"The other day after work, they were making jokes with an Indian accent. And I thought, 'if you're laughing and imitating an Indian accent, then you'd also be capable of imitating me if you wanted to.'"* Although Magda had never experienced any xenophobic or sexist remarks that were explicitly directed against her, she felt uneasy about how she fitted in after overhearing comments about *other* people. She did not like her colleagues' habit of referring to the administrative staff *as "the girls"* as it had patronising and sexist undertones. Magda took her colleagues' jokes about the Indian accent as a sign that her way of speaking could potentially be a source of gossip. Despite feeling confident about her technical skills, she was under the impression of not having the *"same tools"* as her colleagues when it came to networking with business partners, architects and clients. Although Magda had succeeded in finding a well-paid job as an engineer, she sensed that there were linguistic, cultural and gender barriers that she believed were difficult to overcome (Gropas & Bartolini, 2016).

Transnational mobiles

During my fieldwork, Daniel, a 40-year-old man who worked for a multinational company, contacted me and we met at his office on the outskirts of London. Prior to the official interview, he stressed that he wanted to participate in my project to show me that not all Spaniards in the UK were there to *"learn English"* but that there were a few, *"admittedly not many"*, who were very successful business people. When seeing the consent form of my project, he was slightly irritated at the title of my dissertation, which included a reference to the economic crisis. He felt that this was a stereotype of Spanish migrants he wanted to counteract (thereby resembling Bygnes' (2017) Spanish interviewees in Norway). In this context he referred to his wife's grandparents, who had migrated to Mexico due to the Spanish Civil War. He drew a contrasting comparison between the grandparents, who indeed migrated in *"difficult times"*, and himself, who simply wanted to explore company cultures.

I have had many foreign bosses and always in the work environment I have been connected to many foreign people. And I believe that the Spanish management style, I don't mean multinationals, I don't mean Spaniards who work in multinational companies. I mean in Spanish [companies], small and medium or even large ones, the truth is that [the way these companies are run] leaves a lot to be desired. I mean…very authoritarian, very paternalistic (…). I think there were many shortcomings and I didn't want to follow that same school. I wanted to learn other styles of managing people, other styles of communicating.

Daniel's comment that the typical Spanish management style *"leaves a lot to be desired"* underlines his membership in something that could be referred to as a 'cosmopolitan transnational elite'. Due to his international experience he was in the position to criticise the prevailing management culture in Spain that he believed to be outdated (Cabrera & Carretero, 2005). What was noticeable about his main narrative was that he did not mention the economic crisis, giving the impression that it would not have had an effect on his career if he had stayed in Madrid. Indirectly, he thereby drew symbolic lines between himself and 'ordinary' Spanish migrants who left out of 'necessity' (Bygnes, 2017).[11] In contrast to Madga, Daniel's everyday work environment was very international as he had colleagues from all over the world. For people working in his field, gaining international work experiences seemed to be the norm rather than the exception (Nowicka, 2006).

VOLUNTARY WORK

After having discussed various forms of paid work experience, it is important to shift the discussion to voluntary engagements. This work often served as a source of important biographical meaning and had a significant impact on how my informants experienced their lives abroad. These civic engagements took on various forms, depending on the informants' objectives and biographical background. What the volunteers in my sample shared was an authentic commitment to making a difference in other people's lives whilst also perceiving it as an opportunity to learn new skills and feel useful.

Oscar, aged 29, is an engineer by training but had not had the opportunity to practise his profession. After moving to the UK, he struggled to find a job in his field of expertise. Since he was under pressure to pay his bills, he accepted a job as a cashier at a fast-food restaurant. Oscar expressed how detached (or alienated) he felt from his own labour at the fast-food chain (*"After a while you get tired of making hamburgers. I mean if you know inside that you are an engineer (…) you feel a bit (pause) not sad, but you feel a bit frustrated"*). Much like other participants, he struggled to reconcile his previous biographical achievements with his current ways of making a living. Furthermore, he sensed that his English was not improving rapidly enough, as his interactions with customers were reduced to taking orders. In this situation, he found an organisation that helped isolated elderly people in Britain. For Oscar, this volunteering opportunity seemed attractive because he could practise his English skills with native speakers. Furthermore, he could derive biographical meaning from these visits (*"Every time I visit, their eyes light up"*), a sense of purpose that he did not get from his daytime job at the fast-food chain. It seems that by diversifying his activities, he could attenuate this biographical rupture and maintain a positive self-image.

While Oscar was specifically looking for contact with native speakers, there were other participants who were civically engaged in the Spanish community. Tomas, aged 24, first arrived in Hamburg as an Erasmus student in 2012. Prior to his semester abroad, he was involved in the 15-M movement in Madrid and deeply identified as an activist. In Germany, he was looking for ways to continue this biographical project. Together with some friends, he founded an initiative to provide legal advice to migrants from Spain who were in vulnerable situations (Roca & Martín-Díaz, 2016; Ballaste-Isern, 2017). Throughout the interview, he voiced his discontent with the *"Spanish state"* that had seemingly failed young people in particular. In Hamburg, Tomas then continued to help people who belonged to this generation, an example that illustrates how different political and economic crises are not confined to national borders. In other words, even after arriving in Germany many Spanish migrants could not escape the cycle of precariousness: *"Okay, so here's the mini jobs option, which is a very precarious job, but if you're in the Spanish state, there's nothing."*

Tomas's consistent use of the term *"Spanish state"* instead of Spain reflects his critical stance towards the government. Tomas was also critical of the German state, giving various examples of Spanish friends in Hamburg who barely survived on their mini job income and were sometimes pushed into illegality. He made specific suggestions on how to improve the situation of low-paid workers in Germany by changing the legal framework. The interview with Tomas resembled an expert interview with a community organiser.

Despite not having any specific training as social workers, it seemed as if he and his fellow volunteers found an effective way of supporting co-nationals in need.

There were a few informants who chose to volunteer in ways that were somehow related to their academic training. In María's case, her unpaid work at the university library gave her a sense of purpose and biographical continuity (cf. case study). These needs were not met by her main job as a kitchen porter. These informants sometimes lacked the self-confidence to apply for jobs in their field of expertise due to their limited language skills. Volunteer work seemed like an accessible opportunity to reconnect with one's qualifications and long-term biographical projects without the pressure of a full-time paid position. Besides practising their language skills, they hoped to pick up some skills that could potentially become relevant when applying for a more formal job.

6. A WEB OF SOCIAL RELATIONSHIPS

My participants were integrated in a web of different social relationships, which had a major impact on how they evaluated their stay in the receiving society. Firstly, there are the relationships with those who stayed in Spain, including family members, friends and intimate partners who may or may not have supported one's decision to move abroad. The vast majority of participants made use of communication technology and cheap flights, trying (and sometimes failing) to maintain intimate bonds over a distance. To varying degrees, some people filtered what their loved ones at home saw of their lives abroad, which affected their communication both online and during return visits.

Secondly, there are the new relationships migrants make after arriving in the new country. In this discussion, I pay special attention to a) the role of social media in meeting new people and in alleviating feelings of isolation; b) tensions within the 'Spanish' community based on ascribed cultural differences and national identities; c) the transitory nature of social bonds made abroad and; d) my informants' relationships to members of the respective receiving society.

ON WORKING TO MAINTAIN PERSONAL TIES TO SPAIN

Advantages and limits of communication technology

The past two decades have witnessed significant advances in communication technology. As recently as the 1990s, international phone calls used to be expensive and were used only on special occasions. Letters sent by post would sometimes take days or even weeks to arrive in another country (Alpagu, 2019). Today, most people have access to cheap, instant and seemingly more 'three-dimensional' channels of communication such as video calls. Although migrants from previous generations might have envied inventions such as Skype or WhatsApp, the participants in my study often regarded contemporary communication technology as both a blessing and a curse.

The majority of participants were grateful for being able to contact friends and family anytime they wanted. They often set aside a specific time of their daily routine to call their loved ones at home (Gordano Peile & Ros Híjar, 2016). In this context, several interviewees mentioned young children in their families (e.g. nieces and nephews) who stayed in Spain. Being able to exchange pictures and video chat via WhatsApp or Skype seemed to ease feelings of 'missing out' on their development. Some of the older participants appreciated how easily their elderly parents could contact them in the case of an emergency. People at home were often curious about my informants' experiences abroad and expected regular updates. However, being constantly 'online' also had some disadvantages.

Jorge, aged 25, was working as a warehouse manager in a small town in England at the time of our interview. As a young teenager, he had watched a TV documentary about young people who started a *"new life abroad"*. The programme had left a lasting impression on him, as he recalled hoping that *"one day"* he would find the *"courage"* to do the same. At the time of our meeting, he had been in England for about a year. He critically reflected about how his childhood expectations and reality of living abroad diverged.

> *What happens is that there is one, the only change that I see is that when I was twelve years old and said that when I was older, I would leave, I wanted ... Well, I wanted to go abroad and live alone. At that time there was no Internet... no social media was used. So if you were going to contact a friend, a family, you would have to write*

a letter, or use the telephone, but I think that the telephone between countries was used less. Now with the problem of the Internet and social networks, it seems that I have never really left Spain. I always have to be talking to my friends there, I always have to be talking to my family and it's something I don't like very much because I don't like talking to people I can't see. If I talk to people, I want to see them. And if I can't, well…for me it's a bit annoying to have to do that.

Jorge's assessment, "*it seems that I have never left Spain*", contains an element of disappointment. As a child, he had envisioned himself going on an adventure alone. He intuitively sensed that constantly talking to his friends and family in Spain took time and energy that he could otherwise use to invest in building a new life (Komito, 2011). Even though he had a very close relationship with his parents, Jorge's migration project also seemed to be fuelled by trying to get some distance. Social media and other communication technologies appeared to undermine his desire to be independent, which frustrated him. His expression, "*I don't like talking to people I can't see*", underlines how he perceived video calls as a poor replacement for real life face-to-face interactions. For Jorge, seeing someone on a video screen did not count as actually seeing a person in real life, as the virtual barrier took the joy out of such conversations.

In contrast to Jorge, who was actively seeking distance from his friends and family, there were other participants who put high hopes into communication technology. This was especially prevalent among informants who were, or had been, in intimate relationships with partners who had stayed in Spain (Chien & Hassenzahl, 2017). Felipe, aged 23, was working as an au pair in Bristol at the time of our interview. After graduating from university in Spain, he felt that the only way he could become a physical education teacher was by improving his English.[1] Leaving Spain was a difficult decision, as it entailed a spatial separation from his long-term girlfriend. The couple took solace in the idea that "*it would only be for one year*". After arriving in Bristol, Felipe slowly realised that he had overestimated his ability to learn English perfectly within twelve months. He needed more time to fulfil the purpose of his stay and his migration project became 'open-ended'.

In the beginning, my girlfriend also supported me…but our relationship cooled down. She wanted to know when I would come back but I didn't know. I had two options basically. Trying to find a job in England, which is easier when you're in the field of education. There are actually a lot of job offers for sports teachers or teaching *assistants, so that could be a realistic goal. Or go back to Spain with an x-times better level of English, a C1 at least. But there it's really difficult. So yeah our relationship suffered a lot because of course you always have good and bad days…but if the other person is not there to share these experiences with you, you grow apart. There were long periods when we didn't get to see each other at all and in the end we <u>had</u> to break up. It was really hard.*

In this sequence, Felipe recalls the painful disintegration of his five-year relationship, which he considered to be a consequence of his migration project.[2] Even though Felipe spoke to his girlfriend every day (on WhatsApp), he sensed how their conversations became more distant. It is noticeable that he switched to a generalising pronoun ("*you grow apart*") when speaking about how their relationship slowly disintegrated as he strongly believed that this could happen to any couple after being separated for months at a time. The expression, "*in the end we <u>had</u> to break up*", underlines his difficulties with coming to terms with the separation that he attributed to structural forces outside of his control.

When comparing Jorge's and Felipe's experiences with communication technology, one can detect important differences but also similarities. Jorge was frustrated about feeling that he "*had never really left Spain*", as he longed to be alone. In contrast to that, Felipe and his girlfriend actively tried to maintain their intimate bond through communication technology, a makeshift solution that seemed to have worked for some time. The couple slowly realised that this 'virtual intimacy' could not replace face-to-face interactions. Their relationship "*cooled down*", as Felipe put it, due to the lack of shared experiences. Despite seeing each other on the computer screen every day, Felipe had indeed "*left Spain*", to use this expression. When his migration project became open-ended, the couple could no longer ignore his physical absence, ultimately leading to the relationship breakdown.

A filtered presentation of everyday life

Several interviewees chose not to inform their close family members about obstacles they encountered while living abroad, including precarious living and working conditions as well as personal problems such as loneliness (Feaster, 2010). The reasons for this were varied, but often had to do with not wanting to be a source of concern for loved ones in Spain.[3] Pablo, aged 52, had a university degree in theatre studies. He was working as a kitchen porter in Scotland at the time of our meeting. In the following data sequence, Pablo described how he maintained his relationship with his elderly mother and others who had stayed in Spain via phone calls and sporadic return visits.

> *Then I call her, before I called her every week, then with this bad period I called her less because I was not motivated to do so and also, with Spain I have a relationship in which (…) I feel obliged to contribute something positive because Spain is very depressed. When I was doing well, the first two years whenever I went on holiday… ehm… I would try and bring optimism and joy to people who care about me. I would say, 'I'm fine! Even though I'm washing dishes, I'm fine!'… But when I was doing badly…I had a hard time because it's…they have already enough on their plates, you know. And then, I contact them less until I start to feel better.*

Pablo carefully filtered what he shared about his life abroad with those who stayed at home. The physical distance allowed him to conceal negative experiences, including feelings of loneliness and isolation. Creating an idealised public persona of oneself often carries negative associations of inauthenticity and self-importance. However, Pablo's reasoning for acting happier than he truly felt involved a concern for others, especially for his 92-year-old mother. His decision to migrate at a later stage in life had triggered a certain sense of guilt about not living up to his responsibilities as a son, a problem constellation that he described as quite common among migrants of his age.

Pablo's habit of not telling the 'whole truth' about his life in the UK was not confined to how he communicated with his elderly mother. Instead he brought up how it affected his *"relationship with Spain"*, an umbrella term under which he seemingly subsumed all kinds of social relationships, including family members and old friends. Pablo sensed that many people in his social surroundings struggled with the repercussions of the economic crisis, both financially and emotionally (*"Spain is very depressed"*). His strategy of *"contributing"* to their wellbeing involved him assuming the role of an entertainer. During his return visits, he would frequently share funny stories of life abroad while purposefully omitting his personal problems. Keeping up this façade took a lot of effort, which is why he preferred to reduce contact in times of extreme hardship. This type of 'impression management' (Goffman, 1971) had its disadvantages.

> *The effect is that they say, 'Oh, you live well!' They treat me as if I were privileged. And then I say, 'No, I'm washing dishes!', 'Oh, you're so lucky in England!', and I*

don't know what. And I say, 'No, no England is fine, but would you really want that?' It's because sometimes I too feel very lonely.

His habit of playing a "*happy clown*" apparently backfired. Pablo, who was professionally trained as an actor, had seemingly crafted an alter ego that was so believable that it triggered feelings of envy in others. Attempts to reveal his true feelings ("*I too feel very lonely*") were thereby often ignored or not taken seriously. Pablo's case stood out in my sample due to his age and theatre background. His habit of glossing over difficult periods of his life abroad when communicating with his friends and family resonated to differing degrees with the experiences of other interviewees. Several participants engaged in 'information control' (Goffman, 1968a) by not telling their parents about their personal and work-related problems. The reasons underlying such communication practices varied. Some informants believed that they had to overcome difficulties on their own and felt too proud to ask for help. Due to the spatial distance, these migrants also believed that there was little their friends and family could do anyway to improve their situation.

THE EMERGENCE OF NEW SOCIAL RELATIONSHIPS IN THE RECEIVING SOCIETY

While some informants had a few close contacts in the new country before leaving Spain, others arrived without knowing anyone. For most participants, moving to a completely foreign environment was a daunting prospect. Although my participants' professional and personal circumstances differed widely, many shared a sense of vulnerability at the beginning of their migration experience and wondered how they would cope in a new environment without their social support network from home.

A note on social media

Social media, such as Facebook, have become a very popular form of communication among Spanish (and other) migrants living abroad (Davis, 2017). It seems that for almost all major and sometimes even smaller British and German cities, Spanish migrants have set up a Facebook group titled "Españoles en (…)" using it as a platform to discuss problems, socialise and exchange information about work opportunities, language courses etc. These types of Facebook groups often have several thousand members (e.g. "Españoles en Bristol" = 25,575 members in January 2022).[4] I had the chance to interview a man who was the founder of a popular social media platform for Spanish people in Exeter where he lived. Ignacio, aged 36, was working as a computer scientist for a mid-size company at the time of the interview. In his spare time, he had assumed the role of an informal community organiser and was happy to share his lay theories on the Spanish diaspora based on his observations.

> *It's complicated to start over in a new place. If that is interesting for your work, I'm telling you that the people who migrate kind of reset their lives. Reset... it's a word we use in computer science a lot. They reset their lives. They leave their friends and families in their home country and they come here without knowing anybody. They come here and start to form new relationships etc. This has to do a lot with Facebook groups like "Españoles en Exeter". Resetting your life takes up a lot of energy. (…) I can only tell you my theory. When people reset their lives, when you are in your mid-twenties or thirties, those who are looking for new friends are also in the same situation. It's the people who reset their lives, who leave their friends and families in Spain behind. Well, the English people are at home here. Here they have their friends from all their lives. (…) Therefore, we tend to socialise with people who also reset their lives: migrants usually. (…) When I was in Madrid, I didn't consciously go out to make new friends. I was busy enough maintaining the friendships I had all my life. That's why we end up socialising with people who have the same social needs… so we end up hanging out with each other.*

Ignacio's metaphor of *"resetting"* one's life is useful when trying to understand how migrants go about socialising in the new country. His observation that Spanish people tended to befriend mostly other migrants from Spain and other countries resonated with the data I collected both in Germany and the UK. Social media thereby facilitated the 'first move' so-to-speak, as migrants could easily access an already existing community. The biographical narratives revealed that social relationships with other foreigners often developed quite naturally (both online and offline), as they often coped with similar challenges (e.g. learning a new language) and were at the same time uniquely open to meeting new people (*"same social needs"*) (Askins, 2016).

Although most of the interviewees in my study were members of at least one of these Facebook groups for Spanish migrants, their approach on how to use these online platforms differed significantly. Whilst some people were quite inactive on social media, others seemed deeply appreciative of these websites as a tool to meet new people their own age. This was especially obvious among the informants who worked in quite *isolated* settings, such as for a family. In contrast to Erasmus students, the au pairs in my sample had to make a conscious effort to go out and *look* for new friends in their spare time. Going online was a convenient way to search for people with similar "*social needs*" in one's city (or town) of residence, including au pairs of other nationalities.

One of the recurring themes in the academic literature about virtual communities is the extent to which they can mimic 'real' communities. Whilst 'virtual' and 'real' communities cannot be strictly separated as some people use these electronic platforms to organise meetings in real life, the situation is less clear for individuals whose primary communication is electronic. Komito and Bates (2009) argue that, for these individuals, social media is a way to maintain an on-going *background awareness of others* who often share the same problems and experiences. The concept of 'virtual co-presence' or the 'background noise' of others resonated with my data material. María, who had never attended any of the social events organised over this forum, illustrated the meaning of these groups as follows.

> *It's just sometimes you miss certain things and it helps when you know that there are people feeling the same way. Sometimes these are very silly things… but these are things you grew up with all your life that don't exist here. Or sometimes you find some English attitudes and customs a bit strange… and then if you read a post from somebody on one of these websites, it's a bit of a relief because you suddenly realise, 'Ah, at least we are two people who think that'. It makes you feel less alone in some sense.*

Komito and Bates (2009) argue that this 'background noise' of 'shared histories' can enable and support a greater sense of community. This insight can be applied to a number of creative outlets in the Spanish community. One example is a YouTube channel called 'Spaniards', which covers themes and obstacles many Spanish migrants in the UK seem to struggle with. In a self-deprecating way, these videos address themes such as language barriers and cultural differences that can be a source of embarrassment. Other videos cover the phenomenon of having to work in a low-skilled job despite having "*two bachelor's and a master's degree*" or trying to maintain a long-distance relationship with a partner who stayed in Spain. One protagonist constantly highlights his Catalan identity by correcting British people who guess that he is from Spain based on his accent in English ("*No, my accent is not Spanish, it's Catalan! That's different!*"). The writers of the show exaggerated the characters and 'shared histories' on purpose in order to ease their viewers' sense of isolation. This supports what Komito and Bates called 'a greater sense of community' even if it is purely virtual.

Intra-group tensions in the Spanish community

Several informants revealed difficulties in identifying with the Spanish community in the receiving society. The reasons for 'keeping a distance' varied but often had to with socio-economic, educational and perceived cultural differences based on people's regional (and national) identities.

(a) A note on class distinctions

Some of the professionally successful migrants drew symbolic boundaries between themselves and their less successful counterparts, with whom they did not want to be associated (Bygnes, 2017). This tendency became especially visible in the narrative of 40-year-old Nicolas, who was working as a civil engineer in Germany at the time of the interview. Along with other participants in my study, he referred to a popular TV show in Spain to illustrate his point.

> *There is this program on TV, maybe that's interesting for you. It's called "Españoles por el mundo" and they only show you success stories. People with lower education think that all they need to do is buy a ticket to Munich, get off the train and then they are offered an excellent job. Furthermore, you are going to meet a hot German girl and have blonde kids. If that is your expectation, of course you're going to be disillusioned. You need to speak the language. The problem with this programme is that all the stories are stories of success. Many people think that if you go to another country without qualifications, you find work.*

In this commentary, Nicolas drew symbolic boundaries (Lamont & Molnár, 2002) between himself and seemingly less educated Spanish migrants who, he believed, were easily deceived by TV entertainment. According to his view, these people migrate with false expectations while lacking the necessary qualifications. What is interesting about Nicolas' line of argumentation is that he not only described them as 'naive' about their chances on the labour market but also as having 'bad taste' (Bourdieu, 1984): *"Furthermore you are going to meet a hot German girl and have blonde kids."* There is an element of tackiness in this portrayal of ordinary Spanish migrants, which also appeared in other interviews. Various informants vividly described feeling *"embarrassed"* when seeing a large group of Spaniards speaking loudly among each other in public places. My participants claimed that these people often showed little interest in improving their foreign language skills or learning about the new culture. Socialising *exclusively* with fellow Spanish migrants was thereby portrayed as a sign of ignorance and unwillingness to step out of one's comfort zone. Several informants expressed their concern that these people were ruining the reputation of Spanish migrants abroad and hoped that their participation in my research project would counter common stereotypes.

(b) Tendencies of division based on national heritage

Identity politics in Spain is a complicated matter. Under the Francoist regime, Catalan, Basque and Galician languages, along with other forms of cultural expression, were supressed as an attempt to achieve 'national homogeneity'. Andalusian traditions such as flamenco and bullfights were systematically promoted as part of a larger national identity, which was widely experienced as forced and artificial. These policies of cultural repression have left deep scars on the collective memory of millions of people across the country (Olivieri, 2015). Throughout the dictatorship and in the decades that followed after Franco's death, Spain has witnessed the rise of sub-nationalism and various independence movements as a counter-reaction to this type of subjugation.[5]

Against this historic background, it was not surprising that several interviewees felt uneasy about being put in one category with 'Spaniards'. Since our initial contact mostly happened via social media platforms specifically for *Spanish* migrants abroad, these participants made a conscious effort to distinguish themselves from these groups by emphasising their Catalan or Basque identity. They had joined these online communities out of convenience but felt uncomfortable about the prospect of officially being classified as e.g. an 'Español en Bristol' in my study.[6]

The intensity of sub-nationalist feelings differed throughout the sample. There were a few informants who had no problem identifying as Catalan and Spanish simultaneously, which often had to do with their family histories. In the interviews, they sometimes referred to their ancestors as *"immigrants from Spain"*, which they mentioned when contextualising their own migration projects to Germany or the UK. Others had an exclusive understanding of their national heritage and drew strict symbolic boundaries between themselves and "*Spaniards*" with whom they claimed to have nothing in common (see De la Calle & Miley, 2008).

What was noticeable is that the current political tensions in Spain affected everyday interactions among Spanish citizens abroad. Various participants from Barcelona reported how they kept being confronted with the question of Catalan independence when meeting new people. Sometimes, these questions came from a place of intellectual curiosity. On other occasions, they were posed in an antagonising and hostile way. My informants generally experienced the latter as tiring, especially since it rarely evolved into a balanced and fruitful discussion.

Some Catalan participants openly identified as separatists. Others were strictly against the movement, describing it as populist and misled. Regardless of their political stance towards the issue of independence, they agreed that there were certain cultural differences between themselves and people from more southern regions. Examples include distinguishing qualities, such as speaking in a "*calmer and more refined*" way than their Andalusian counterparts and allegedly having a different work ethic.

In the previous section, I referred to the narrative of Nicolas, who was working as a civil engineer in Aachen at the time of the interview. Throughout the interview, he drew a variety of symbolic boundaries between himself and others by referring not only to class differences but also to his cultural heritage. He stressed how he believed that his Catalan identity gave him an advantage when adapting to the German culture.

> *Hmm, the thing is that I am a Catalan from Barcelona. I have a Catalan identity, which is much more European than that of the people in the south. There are many cultural differences in character and how to understand life. On a cultural level and in terms of understanding life and work, I feel closer to a German than to somebody from Andalusia. On a cultural level, we are more serious. We understand when work begins and when you have Feierabend or Wochenende.*

One can detect a sense of superiority that Nicolas associated with his Catalan identity. His identification as '*European*' allowed him to construct a closer resemblance to the receiving society, which he backed up by pointing to alleged similarities in work ethic. It is not a coincidence that he chose the German expressions "*Feierabend*" ('after hours') and "*Wochenende*" ('weekend') to stress this point. He thereby portrayed himself as somewhat more worthy of being in Germany than people from the south of Spain who, he believed, lacked discipline.

Attempts to construct a special resemblance between the receiving society and one's national identity could also be found in interviews with people from different regions. Ander, aged 29, grew up in San Sebastián in the Basque country. He had spent six months in England before returning home to work as a business consultant.

> *(…) the difference between north and south, one of them, is that we have a more refined accent, we speak more dryly. And… then we have a very different way of life, very different from the…what I was going to explain to you, is that we Basques are very influenced by English culture because in the nineteenth century all our metal industry and commercial relations were with the English. And in fact, in Bilbao, there is an area called La Campa de los Ingleses. There was a British cemetery, we still have the British cemetery in another place, which belongs to the British crown. Our football team, which is called Athletic Club, was founded by the English. And with all the industrial fields, where there has always been and still is the most industry, it is here, in Euskadi, in the Basque country and in the area of Bilbao. We are very close to both the English and Germans. In Andalusia, when there has been a 30% unemployment rate, our unemployment rate has been 13%.*

Not unlike Nicolas, Ander distanced himself from his Andalusian counterparts while at the same time constructing resemblances to both the receiving society (UK) and me as a researcher (Germany). The historic ties between Britain and the Basque country seemingly gave him a unique sense of 'belonging', as he grew up with a background awareness of English culture. Throughout the interview, Ander portrayed Basque culture in a very positive light, engaging in contrastive comparisons to Andalusia. With much pride, he remembered how a Spanish friend whom he had met in England came to visit him in San Sebastián. According to Ander, his friend was astonished at how bar owners in the Basque Country trusted their customers to pay their bills later if they did not have enough cash, which his friend believed would be impossible in his hometown in Andalusia. In the interview, Ander presented this anecdote as supporting evidence for his belief in Basque moral superiority. That being said, it is important to mention that the majority of Ander's friends in the UK were from the south of Spain. Throughout his narrative, he affectionately referred to them as his *"Andalusian family"* who offered him much support during a personal crisis. The latter also introduced him to the woman who would later on become his girlfriend.

> *Since I only knew Andalusians, they said, 'Look, we're going to introduce you to a girl from the north like you', and they did. They introduced her to me. 'What's your name?', 'Amaia, what about you?', 'Well, Ander, ahh, ehm…and where are you from?', 'From Navarre, and you?', 'From San Sebastián! What are you saying? What are you saying? You are close to me!', 'And you to me! Yes man, yes yes yes!' We showed each other our IDs… wow…yes. And she gave me a hug, 'Man, at last a Basque from the north! I'm sick of so many Andalusians.' (laughs).*

This anecdote illustrates that Ander's gossip about Andalusia should be taken with a pinch of salt. It seems that in the 'Spanish' community abroad, some people playfully compete with each other, mocking others in a friendly way without wanting to cause harm. Ander's narrative revealed that it was only in England where he first got to know people from Andalusia on a more personal level. It seems that, by migrating to another country, his long-held prejudices were challenged (Luconi, 2003). It is, furthermore, quite telling that they decided to introduce him specifically to a woman who was also from the north of Spain. His *"Andalusian family"* apparently sensed that he and this woman would be a good match because they had a similar cultural background.

The aforementioned examples give a first impression of the heterogeneity of my sample and how some informants' were uneasy identifying with 'ordinary Spanish migrants'. Such tendencies of division were rooted in perceived differences in class, education, political affiliations and national identities. The narratives suggest that the concept of a European identity seemed to offer a cosmopolitan alternative to Spanish nationalism, since the former carried much less historic baggage than the latter.[7] It is important to stress that tensions based on national identities have the potential to escalate. As a reaction to the Catalan independence referendum of 2017, the Guardian reported how Spanish migrants in London launched a 'hunt for independence supporters' online. In the Facebook group "Españoles en Londres", various members threatened to remove Catalan flags and promised a "night of broken glass" (Glaister, 2017). Although there was no evidence of actual violence that night, the tone of these online debates was harsh and aggressive. The latter serves as an example of how on-going collective tensions are not confined to Spain's national borders and can overshadow social relations in the diaspora.

SPACES OF TRANSITION

As indicated before, most of my participants tended to socialise mainly with other migrants from Spain and other EU member states. Sometimes these were co-workers who had lived in the receiving society for longer and who could give them reassuring advice on how to overcome everyday obstacles. Meeting fellow migrants who struggled with the foreign language as much as they did appeared to be a source of relief for my informants, as they felt less isolated in their speechlessness. The combination of feeling vulnerable (e.g. due to imperfect language skills) and a unique openness to meeting new people provided a fertile ground for new and biographically significant social relationships to develop (Askins, 2016).

That being said, the majority of the informants also spoke about the frustrating experience of friends leaving the shared place of residence (see the case studies of Adam and María). Cities like Bristol or Berlin were thereby portrayed as spaces of transition, where people live for a limited amount of time before moving on with their lives. Either they returned to their home country or they moved to a third destination. The friendships they made abroad seemed *precious* but fleeting and transitory. Attempts to build up a stable and lasting social circle often ended in disappointment.

Nora, aged 29, had returned to Madrid by the time of the interview. She looked back at her time in Brighton fondly, but also remembered why she decided to return.

> *And then in Brighton, um… also in Brighton, what happens is that when you are in Brighton, it's like you're living in the world of Brighton, you're like in another sphere. For me, Brighton is not real, it is not real life because … I lived with my German friend and we had parties at home, 40 people came, so your life was carefree, you cared about partying, meeting people and so on. (…) I'm telling you, I was getting tired of meeting new people, and then people leave. I got to know new people, and then these new people are leaving.*

In retrospect, Nora evaluated her social life in Brighton as slightly surreal. She chose the pronoun *"you"* on purpose to illustrate that she believed her lifestyle to be somewhat representative of the lifestyles of other young people in her town (*"your life was carefree"*). The parties she and her friend organised bring to mind images commonly associated with Erasmus students, i.e., dozens of young people from different countries coming together to socialise in informal settings. While Erasmus schemes are by definition time-limited, Nora sensed that, for her, this type of lifestyle had become something permanent. Instead of spending a 'semester abroad', it had indeed become 'her life abroad', a set-up that she regarded as artificial and tiring in the long run. Nora's frustration about "*new people are leaving*" resonated with the rest of the data material. It seems that the community of young migrants could rarely offer my informants a lasting foundation upon which to build a new life.[8] The fear of close friends leaving the shared place of residence seemed to overshadow my informants' migration experience and often became a decisive factor in deciding to return to Spain.

PERCEIVED BARRIERS IN EVERYDAY INTERACTIONS

The discussion on 'new social relationships' would not be complete without a note on my informants' relationship to members of the host society. Many participants revealed ambivalent feelings when speaking about attempts to form close relationships with 'locals' (Meier & Daniels, 2013). In the following section, I will firstly discuss some examples of what can be subsumed under the category of constructing 'cultural differences'. Secondly, I offer some observations on the role of age and gender in everyday interactions, as they appeared in my data material.

(a) Reflecting on 'cultural differences'

The interview with León, aged 26, took place in Madrid in the summer of 2017. In the past six years, he had spent two prolonged periods of time in the UK, the first of which was as an Erasmus student at the University of Bristol during his undergraduate degree in history. A few years later, he followed his German girlfriend to Edinburgh in order to pursue a master's degree. After graduating, the couple returned to Spain where they were working as English teachers. León's narrative, which he told in English, was especially rich as it entailed detailed descriptions of situations that resembled ethnographic observations (in the style of Barley, 1989). In the interview, he recalled several culture shocks he experienced when he first arrived in the UK at the age of 20.

And I got into a small music band with two English friends. One of them had obsessive compulsive disorder (OCD) and the other one was autistic. He had Asperger's. And I became very good friends with them. (...) And at the moment I am more friends with the guy with OCD but when I was there I felt a lot of empathy towards the guy with Asperger's Syndrome. You know, autistic people have this disorder which means that they don't really understand social situations because there are a lot of unwritten laws and customs and norms that they don't teach you when you're a kid. So when you are foreign you are in the same kind of situation because you don't understand what's going on. You apply the standards of your country, not the… because you don't know the new country. So I understood only this guy with the…the boy with autism… with Asperger's Syndrome. I understood him very well because of that. I could see the things that he didn't understand were the same things I didn't understand. So I was a fool.

Without taking León's theory about his friend's 'autism' at face value, it highlights how he identified with him for not being able to pick up easily on social cues. In order to illustrate this point, he then gave the example of greeting women with two kisses on the cheek, which is a common courtesy in Spain. In the UK, he remembered, his female housemates felt deeply offended by this habit (*"they looked at me as if I was going to rape them or something."*). In the UK sample, several participants expressed their insecurity but also annoyance about what they defined as *"British politeness"*. In Spain, they argued people tended to be much more direct and express their opinions openly. León explained why this was a source of frustration for him and others.

Right, the second thing that shocked me a lot was that in this country we are very honest, at least here in the centre of Spain we are honest, we are direct. We say what we think. We may try to say it politely, but we are direct. And if we don't like something, we say it! But with English people that's not the case. So you never know when you are doing something that is not right. And when I had been there for five or six months I saw a small Internet meme. It said, 'What the British say, what they mean, what European people understand.' I am sure you have seen it. For example, 'it's interesting', 'it's interesting' means 'it's interesting', right. No, 'it's interesting' apparently means, 'I think you are saying nonsense.'

A lot of expressions like that. And my most hated expression was 'fair enough' because I couldn't understand it. And this was the heaviest cultural barrier I had. In Spain you either agree or disagree, you love or hate. (...) There is no space for compromise. And there is no space for indifference. Now, 'fair enough'. What's the meaning of 'fair enough'? It means 'I see your point, but I don't want to talk about it.' But for us, it feels like 'Shut up. I don't care.' For a Spanish person... and I talked about this with some friends, and they confirmed this feeling... 'Fair enough.' It's extremely offensive, it's like telling you to shut up.

This data extract illustrates how cultural clashes occur in a reciprocal manner. While his British housemates perceived his way of greeting women as disrespectful, León and his Spanish friends felt very offended by the seemingly innocuous phrase "*fair enough*". His claim that where he comes from "*there is no space for indifference*", clashes with seemingly polite attempts to avoid conflict. One can easily imagine how these cultural misunderstandings could be a source of conflict, as León's style of communication might come across as 'too direct'. At the same time, British people may not be aware that trying to end a discussion prematurely may cause offence to individuals who are not used to being 'cut-off' in conversations (Lorenzo-Dus & Bou-Franch, 2003).

This observation corresponds to socio-linguistic studies on different forms of politeness in Europe (Hickey & Stewart 2005). Hickey (2000) argues that Britain tends to be a 'negative-politeness' society whereas Spain tends towards 'positive politeness'. What this means is that British people regard it as polite to give each other space in personal interactions, avoid conflict and be generally quite indirect. In contrast to that, Hickey (2005, p. 317) writes, "Spaniards seldom leave each other alone to live quietly, neither do they like being left alone themselves: The average Spaniard's image of hell is close to others' 'peace and quiet'". Instead 'positive politeness', as it is seemingly more prevalent in Spain, focuses on direct interventions to make the hearer feel good about themselves (e.g. 'You look sad! Can I do anything?'). In other words, while British people value 'being polite' as a somewhat *passive* quality, Spanish people put more emphasis on 'doing politeness', so to speak. Hickey (2005) argues that the Spanish language has, furthermore, no single term corresponding to the English term 'politeness'. Instead, people refer to 'courtesy', 'friendliness', 'morality' and 'correct behaviour' in how to treat others. This is an important distinction that sheds light on why León and others felt irritated by British mannerisms, including calling an opinion 'interesting' while in reality disregarding it completely.

Hickey (2005, p. 317) argues that millions of British tourists "who visit Spain each year perceive Spaniards as friendly, outgoing, likeable, jolly people and thoughts of 'politeness' get lost in these warmly admired qualities."

While small breaches of unwritten rules of conduct can be easily overlooked or ignored on holiday, they are more likely to cause problems in everyday life (e.g. at the workplace). Although friendliness and politeness might appear to be interchangeable character traits, in fact they are *not*. In other words, a person can be warm and friendly while at the same time be breaking certain etiquette rules of 'negative politeness' by being too direct (*"And if we don't like something, we say it!"*). This is a potential source of irritation and embarrassment that several interviewees in my study could relate to. Furthermore, Hickey's (2005) claim that 'average' Spaniards do not like 'being left alone' sheds some light on why León was deeply irritated by the seemingly polite phrase "fair enough". Instead of appreciating the personal space British students intended to give him, he felt pushed aside and ignored.

One topic that often appeared in the context of 'cultural differences' is that of the role of alcohol. León vividly recalled being quite shocked when observing British students drinking excessively, which apparently differed from what he had been used to in Spain (Järvinen & Room, 2017).

> *A big difference I noticed was the drinking culture. I think British people have a serious problem with alcohol. So in this country, in Spain, for us drinking is like a marathon. (…) It starts, let's say, you start drinking at eight. And you are going to have dinner. You start with some wine and some beer. And what we do is that we try to drink as much as possible, [but slowly] in time. So the first person to be drunk is a loser. He didn't want to be drunk. He wanted to be tipsy. There are like… I didn't make a count … but it's funny that in English you only have one word – 'tipsy' – whereas you have one hundred expressions to say that you are 'drunk' or 'wasted'… blah blah blah. Whereas in this country (Spain) we have a lot of expressions to say that you are somewhere between being sober and being drunk because that's how we like to play. We drink little by little. We talk a lot. We drink with food. So when we start feeling funny, we eat a little bit. (…) And it's very slow. In England it's a one hundred meter race. It's all about speed. You win if you're the first person to be wasted… It's excessive.*

León sometimes intellectualised his opinions about *"the English"* in ways that resembled the argumentation style of cognitive anthropologists (Frake, 1968), backing up his claims by referring to apparent linguistic differences as 'evidence'. For him, having many English expressions for being drunk but only one expression for being *"tipsy"* had a deeper meaning. There is a judgemental undertone in how he described drinking habits among British students, as they seemingly breached rules of social conduct that he had grown up with.

León's examples gave the impression that he had discussed the topic of 'culture clashes' extensively with fellow exchange students. By using the personal pronoun 'we' and 'us', he underlined that he was not alone in his opinions. Although he recalled many memories in a humorous way, his anecdotes frequently revealed how foreign he had felt in certain situations. This was a feeling that he shared with many other participants both in Germany and the UK (Bagnoli, 2007).

When comparing my data, it was notable that certain lay theories about German and British people overlapped, e.g., that they are very reserved in everyday social interactions. There were, however, also important differences: my informants often described themselves as 'direct, but warm' and British people as 'polite, but cold'. In contrast to that, Germans were commonly portrayed as 'direct and cold', a combination that several interviewees found intimidating. According to House (2005, p. 25), German speakers tend to produce speech that is characterised by directness, including raw imperatives, when performing requests. Furthermore, "being polite in German is different from being polite in an English-speaking country. (…) It involves saying what one means and meaning what one says, as well as engaging more and sooner in 'serious talk' rather than carefully preparing the ground with 'small talk'." This insight from applied linguistics resonates with the experiences of several informants in my German sample, who spoke of co-workers and superiors they perceived as harsh and unfriendly. Much like León, other participants described themselves as 'direct' but they felt that they had the social skills to 'counter-balance' this type of forwardness, which meant that they were also warm and affectionate. In contrast, 'German directness' was generally experienced as much harsher towards the addressee.

Although befriending 'native' members of the receiving society often took time and effort, several participants described biographically significant social (including romantic) relationships with British or German people that had evolved during their stay abroad. Interestingly, the participants tended to befriend locals that they portrayed as quite 'alternative'. For my informants, these individuals stood out as they had often travelled extensively, sometimes spoke Spanish fluently, and/or had opinions and mannerisms[9] that they claimed differed from the average 'German' or 'Brit'. This became especially apparent in a group interview I conducted in a small town in Germany. Bruno, a 29-year-old mechanical engineer, described how he and his friends had created a 'social bubble' in a town that they otherwise found quite unattractive.

> *We have a group of eight to ten people. Us three, a Chilean guy with his wife – he is a colleague of mine – there are two Peruvians… but we are also friends with Germans. We formed a group with kind of a Latino flair, but it's multi-cultural. The Germans are kind of outsiders. They are a bit different from the average people here. They like to dance etc. and get along better with us.*

In this data sequence, Bruno drew lines between his social circle and "*the average people*" in the German town, which were not strictly based on nationality but on attitude or "*Latino flair*" as he put it. In his eyes, his local friends had diminished their average 'German-ness' by being open-minded and engaging in activities such as dancing.

(b) Observations on the role of age and gender

When reconstructing social barriers to form meaningful social relationships with 'native' members of the receiving society, one ought to look beyond alleged 'cultural differences'. For this purpose, I would like to share some thoughts on differences in everyday interaction patterns depending on migrants' 'generational location' (Mannheim, 1928) and gender roles.

While most informants in my sample were in their twenties, I interviewed a few people who had reached their late thirties, forties or even fifties by the time of the interview. Some of these informants had built up a relatively stable existence in Spain, but often lost their jobs in the context of the economic crisis. After arriving in the new country, they were faced with the challenge of building up a new social circle from scratch. When asked whether he had made any friends in Germany, 40-year-old Nicolas responded "*No… ehm, the truth is I'm quite shy so I haven't really made any attempts to socialise with my colleagues yet. It's difficult, also because my German is really bad and I sometimes feel embarrassed…*" He did not perceive the Spanish community in the German town where he was living as an appropriate alternative to making friends, not only because of the alleged class and cultural differences, but also because of his age.

> *Ah yeah well… I met a few but I could not really identify with them. Also there is this group in Facebook, "Españoles en Aachen", where you made this post. The thing*

is they mainly promote parties there… but I feel I'm too old for that. I mean I'm 40 years old and people who socialise in this network are all in their twenties. It would be weird to go out with them… and I also don't feel like going to discos anymore.

While younger informants had many opportunities to meet new people (e.g. at university), slightly older participants like Nicolas felt that going to parties was no longer age-appropriate. Socialising therefore became an active task that they had to pursue, which took a lot of effort. At work, their colleagues tended to be either much younger than them (particularly those who worked in menial labour) or they were married and had children. Furthermore, these participants took longer to learn the new language, which proved to be an additional obstacle to social integration ("*My German is really bad and I sometimes feel embarrassed.*"). Migrants in their late thirties or forties were often unsure how they fitted in, and sometimes refrained from attempting to deepen social relationships beyond work-related contexts. Their biographical narratives therefore revealed a greater risk to social isolation.

Apart from age, the data I collected pointed to a gendered dimension in social integration. Although I cannot make any quantitative claims based on my sample, I noticed certain differences between my male and female participants. Especially in the beginning phase of their migration experience, women tended to have more social contacts than men. The female participants were often 'welcomed' into existing social networks, e.g. as au pairs by their host families[10] or by friends and partners who already lived in the receiving society. Having local contacts upon arrival appeared to be an advantage, which several men in my sample did not have. These male participants described how they experienced their first period in Germany or the UK as quite isolating, for example when they struggled to overcome certain bureaucratic hurdles. Without speaking the language fluently, even seemingly simple tasks such as writing a job application proved to be quite challenging. In a variety of interviews, my male informants drew contrastive comparisons to the opposite sex, claiming that both locals and fellow migrants were more responsive to young women's need for help. Three weeks prior to his departure to England, Ander tried to find accommodation online without much success.

And well, a month before I came to Brighton, three weeks before, I went to look for a flat. Mission impossible. Ehm…before I came here, by chance I met a couple of Basque people who were coming to Brighton because I joined the Facebook group of Spaniards in Brighton, where you put up your comment. But then, people are still

> *very macho. If a boy asks for help for certain things, he doesn't get an answer, but a girl with a pretty face gets all the help she needs, which is very sad, because that's not equality (…)*

In this sequence, Ander expressed his frustration about not receiving any help in finding a flat whilst being under the impression that people are very responsive to similar posts by young women. Although he specifically referred to the Spanish community online, he also struggled and suffered setbacks on other websites open to other nationalities, including locals. Sensing some form of gender bias in being chosen (or not chosen) as a flatmate was a theme that appeared in other interviews as well (see case study of Adam). Several men I interviewed sensed that people expected them to take care of themselves, as their requests for help were often left unanswered – both online and in real life. Other examples included the relative *ease* with which Spanish women could befriend their female co-workers (British/German), as getting lunch or coffee together was not seen as something out of the ordinary. This was something several male participants like Nicolas shied away from (especially those in male-dominated professions such as engineering), as they sensed it would not be regarded as appropriate or professional.

Several female informants in my study criticised the "*machismo*" they had witnessed or experienced by their co-nationals in the receiving society. Laura, aged 25, brought up the example of being in a nightclub in Edinburgh and hearing sexist comments about her appearance. The men in question assumed that she would not understand Spanish and therefore felt free to express vulgar remarks without facing consequences. She found this attitude extremely off-putting and offensive. Laura mentioned this experience when explaining why she avoided the 'Spanish community' abroad and preferred to socialise within quite international social circles.

With regard to members of the receiving society, a few women described how they were confronted with the expectation of being "*spicy Latinas*". This is a sexist trope that is not only degrading and inaccurate, but also conflates stereotypes associated with Spain and Latin America. These informants were very frustrated about how some people in their surroundings (e.g. colleagues) apparently perceived them in a very one-dimensional and simplistic way, which had very little to do with their actual personalities and biographical backgrounds.

A final – more positive – observation on the topic of gender: in Scotland, I interviewed two women together, who portrayed their migration experience as a "*feminist awakening*". One of them, 38-year-old Liliana, grew up in a very conservative village in central Spain, where traditional gender roles were apparently still the norm (i.e. women being full-time homemakers and men working in agriculture). She experienced her move to Glasgow as very liberating, as she felt less judged for her status as an unmarried woman in her thirties without any children. In the village, where she had spent most of her life prior to her migration, feminism was apparently not a topic of everyday conversation and it was even scorned ("*They'd think you're crazy.*"). It was only in Scotland that she started to question the patriarchal structures that she had previously taken for granted. In Glasgow, Liliana and Magda founded a feminist reading group for Spanish women. They were very proud of this initiative. Even though both informants were planning to move back to Spain in the near future, they were intent on continuing this biographical line in future by becoming active in the women's movement.

7. ESTABLISHED-OUTSIDER RELATIONS IN TIMES OF BREXIT

More than half of my sample moved to the United Kingdom, where many were then confronted with Brexit, a new collective crisis that took almost all of them by surprise.[1] One of the most divisive issues raised by the United Kingdom's decision to leave the European Union is the 'question of belonging' (Cassidy et al., 2018), and more specifically, "who belonged and had rights (or should have rights) and who did not (and should not)" (Bhambra, 2017, p. 91). Advocates of the 'Leave' campaign underlined the importance of 'taking back control' of the UK's borders, promising voters to put an end to the 'free movement' of EU nationals to Britain. The public discourse surrounding the EU referendum of 2016 was characterised by a distinctive anti-immigrant rhetoric, as tabloid papers put forward claims that migrants were taking jobs away from British workers or putting a strain on public services (Rzepnikowska, 2019).[2]

For a long time, there was much confusion about if, when, and how Brexit would be implemented. The years that followed the EU referendum were marked by political chaos, which took the form of snap elections, mass demonstrations and seemingly never-ending negotiations in Westminster and Brussels. This uncertainty has cast a dark shadow over the lives of non-national EU citizens (Anderson & Wilson, 2018) whose status has been described as being 'in limbo' (Remigi, 2017). At the time of writing, the UK has officially left the European Union, which has had significant consequences for millions of EU nationals living in Britain as well as those who have been planning to come.

The case studies of Adam and María already revealed how the EU referendum and its repercussions have changed people's perception of the receiving society. Although Adam had returned to Spain shortly before the vote, he was deeply disappointed about the outcome. The idea of not being 'welcomed back' if he decided to re-migrate saddened him also because it entailed a loss of reciprocity (*"I paid taxes over there…"*). María was still living in the UK at the time of the EU referendum. Her reaction to Brexit was quite typical for my sample, as she started to make prolonged argumentative commentaries using the personal pronouns 'we', 'us' (i.e. EU nationals) and 'them' (i.e. British Brexit supporters). These opinions and folk theories had often emerged in discussions with others.

Spanish EU citizens' participation in the discourse on Brexit could also be observed in the rest of the data material that I collected after the referendum of 2016. My informants often spontaneously recounted the situation in which they had learned about the result of the vote (e.g. watching television with friends and colleagues). This was, however, not enough. They had the urge to take a stance on Brexit, which became visible in longer argumentative commentaries. Many participants took the result quite personally, as it symbolically undermined the legitimacy of their migration projects. Furthermore, it posed a diffuse, yet increasingly tangible, threat to their legal status in the UK.

Given the dominance of argumentation as the main scheme of communication when the issue of Brexit came up in the interviews, I opted for a different format in the presentation of my findings in this context. In contrast to the previous comparative chapters, I am focusing on the argumentative patterns in the interview with a single participant. As a nurse working for the National Health Service (NHS), Diego gained unique insights into British society as he worked with patients from various socio-economic and educational backgrounds. By zooming in on his presentation of daily interactions at the hospital, it becomes possible to study Brexit from 'below' and gain first insights that are relevant beyond the single case. In the following discussion, I draw on Elias's and Scotson's (1965) established-outsider figurations as a sensitising concept.[3] Their early observations on social divisions in balance of power struggles appeared particularly relevant in the context of Brexit. I paid special attention to the role of gossip, which they defined as "a weapon of defence as well as a weapon of attack" (p. 104). Rather than trying to test a hypothesis or to force concepts on my data, my aim is hereby to discover new insights about Spanish EU citizens' experiences of Brexit and how they make sense of them.

THE CASE OF DIEGO

I interviewed Diego, age 30, twice: the first time was in April 2014 in the context of my MPhil dissertation, and the second time was in November 2016. The interviews took place in two different cafes in Bristol. His NHS employers recruited him while he was still living in Spain. He chose England over other destinations because he wanted to stay within the European Union due to a specific point system for healthcare professionals, which would facilitate a future return migration to Spain. Since his girlfriend was interested in learning English, the UK seemed like an attractive option for the couple as it allowed both of them to pursue their individual goals. In Bristol, she found a job unrelated to her academic training. Diego was one of the informants who seemed very well integrated in England. In his free time, he played football on a semi-professional level and had a wide social network. About one year after our second interview, Diego informed me via email that he and his partner had moved to Madrid where both of them had found full-time positions.

Brexit as an everyday encounter

When I met Diego for the second time, five months after the EU referendum, I simply encouraged him to tell me how his life had developed since our first interview in 2014. He opened up to me quickly, describing a recurring pattern that had emerged in his daily interactions with patients.

> *I still work at the same hospital, in a different department, which is one of the biggest changes. And then there is this question that so many patients have… the ones with whom you may have established a little bit of a relationship, who come to the hospital often and who know me and so on. They always ask me, 'Hey, are you thinking of going back to Spain?' or 'How has Brexit affected you?'. So I always respond to them in more or less the same way. 'Yes, I want to go back to Spain, because you put everything in perspective, the best type of lifestyle, good friends, family etc., etc. I believe that it would be better to be in Spain. Well, I don't know. I would like to return to Spain. I don't know if it would be better because you never know that, but*

it would be good.' And… it is of course difficult to know when to leave when you're not in a bad place. Because when they ask me 'Are you unhappy in Bristol?', 'Are you unhappy, or do you have any problems?', the answer is no. I am comfortable, I have my job, my friends, my life… and I also travel a lot because from here everything is easier.

The beginning sequence of the second interview contains several themes that illustrate how Brexit has appeared in his everyday life and how he chose to position himself in response to it. Diego worked in a unit in the hospital that specialised in treating a rare chronic disease, which meant that he worked with patients from different regions of the country. As these patients would regularly spend several hours at the hospital, he had time to establish relationships that went beyond his physical care work. Diego thereby seemed to gain a unique first-hand insight into the host society, which differed from other participants who worked as cleaners in isolated settings.

In contrast to when we conducted our first interview in 2014, Diego was now confronted with the question of a possible return on a daily basis. His wording does not suggest that he experienced this question as malicious, but more as something that is asked out of a mixture of curiosity and concern. Some patients seemed worried that they might lose a nurse they have come to trust and like. His presence as a foreigner working in the UK had suddenly become a topic of everyday conversation, which is something he had probably not experienced in the same way when we first met in 2014. Regardless of the patients' political affiliations, the question of whether he intended to go back to Spain entailed a 'question of belonging' (Bhambra, 2017).

Despite being asked the same question of a possible return over and over again by different patients, Diego still remained open to talking about it. When taking a closer look at his routinized response, it is apparent that Diego did not refer to Brexit, instead emphasising his autonomy by telling his patients that he planned to return on his own terms. In such situations he visibly refused to let Brexit define his status or dictate his decisions. He also emphasised how he felt fully integrated in Britain, as he had a stable job, a close-knit group of friends and an ability to travel. By sharing his achievements of having built up a successful life in the UK, he was able to re-position himself to a level equal to his patients. Diego did not want to be victimised or pitied.

Later in the interview, when I asked him to tell me "*a little bit more*" about his work, Diego underlined his belief in the meritocracy at his workplace. He told me about an attractive job opening at his hospital for which he had applied. In the end, a Portuguese co-worker was chosen for the position over several British applicants. Diego was visibly impressed by his NHS employers' sense of fairness and professionalism. If a similar situation had happened in Spain, he argued, the chances of a foreign applicant would have been quite low, regardless of his/her credentials. Diego emphasised twice that even in times of Brexit, the hiring procedures at this hospital were purely based on merit. It makes sense to refer to his workplace as a protective space of recognition.

After Diego portrayed his NHS employers in such a positive light, I asked him, "*So Brexit doesn't affect you, right?*", a premature presumption that he vehemently denied. Taking this question as a starting point, Diego engaged in a spontaneous and lengthy argumentation sequence about how he is dealing with Brexit.

> *Brexit affects me, it has affected me. Now I have already forgotten a bit about it, but… What affected me most is the moral aspect of it… it's in my mind. For me, it's a question of dignity or like… to feel comfortable. This is much more important than any type of politics or bureaucracy. Like if they put hurdles in front of me to get a visa, or if I have to leave because I can't work here anymore. Yeah no, this is not the case, this is not <u>my</u> case. I don't care about all that, if I don't feel comfortable. I thought about it a few times, whether I will feel comfortable in a place where 54% of the population, well I don't remember the exact percentage, have voted for Brexit.*

The decisiveness in how Diego rejected my assumption illustrates that he took the outcome of the vote quite personally. He was aware of his privileged position as a nurse, whose chances of getting a work permit would remain high even after Brexit ("*this is not my case*"). This fact, however, did not shield him from sensing a societal shift that made him feel uncomfortable. Overnight, it seems as if the temperature had dropped by a few degrees. The UK had become a colder and less welcoming place for non-national EU citizens. It made Diego question whether he could see his future in the UK regardless of his personal employment situation and legal status. In his day-to-day life, Diego sometimes encountered patients who expressed anti-immigration views. In this context, he remembered one situation that occurred briefly before the EU referendum, which contained elements of teasing.[4]

I remember one patient in particular. I said, I knew already, or like… sometimes when people come in you already know like… 'Are you gonna vote for Brexit then?', 'Yes, yes, yes…', 'But c'mon man, don't vote for that…', I told him that as a little joke, right? 'Don't vote for it, they are gonna kick me out of the country and I don't want to go yet.', 'No, no, no, no… I am going to vote for it, but that is not to say, I mean… You, you stay here!' I don't know… they told me, they always started telling me about Poles, about Bulgarians, about such and such… and I said, 'Well, and what about the Spanish?' … a bit like a joke, right? And he said, 'No, no, no… it's because I don't know who is coming in and that is why I am in favour of it.' Or like… 'I don't want you to leave, like you are here, one of us…. But I don't want that one because of so and so…'

This anecdote reveals a certain established-outsider dynamic that Elias and Scotson (1965) explicated in their study on Winston Parva. The patient in question very much thinks in hierarchical categories of 'us' versus 'them'. By portraying Poles and Bulgarians as the unknown and undesirable 'other' *("I don't know who is coming in")*, this man implicitly distinguishes himself as being a superior, 'established' member of society who claims his house rules. There is an element of absurdity in the situation, as the patient openly voices his anti-immigration sentiments while being cared for by a foreign nurse. In contrast to being served coffee by a migrant, being treated for a serious disease involves a different level of trust. The patient, who is ill and in a vulnerable position, has to rely on Diego and others to take their work seriously. Furthermore, Brexit poses a tangible, objective threat to the legal status of all EU citizens, including Diego, which is comparable to a 'social boundary' as defined by Lamont and Molnár (2002). The patient, however, did not see the immediate link between his support for the 'Leave' campaign and the Spanish nurse who was treating him at the time.

Diego, who recognised these contradictions, used self-deprecating humour to challenge the patient's view on Brexit. According to the narrator, the patient did not change his mind on voting for 'Leave' but instead symbolically tried to 'adopt' Diego as an honorary member of his 'we-group'. In the words of Elias and Scotson (1965), he had 'earned' the special 'group charisma' of the 'established' by being a good nurse. His response could be compared to what they described as the 'established' group's habit of 'praising' individuals they identified with – often with patronising undertones. The data extract also reveals something about the emergence of an ascribed ethnic hierarchy, as the patient preferred some EU nationalities to others (e.g. Spanish over

Bulgarian). Diego strongly disliked this attitude and refused to be drawn into a 'we-coalition' against central and eastern European migrants.

> *One of the best surgeons in my hospital is Italian and another is Greek. For these two people, they will probably move everything in the world to make them stay. These are the people who interest them. They want them. It's the kind of migration they want. They are selective. It's like in the United States and Australia, they are selective. 'We need you, but not you', but I don't like that because the Polish girl, who cleans the operating room after that person operates, has the same ehm…the same right to make a living, as the surgeon…as the surgeon who operates on an open heart and is an eminence in Europe. But they don't want them, they don't want the Bulgarian boy who replenishes Tesco so that they can go shopping the next day, but they want the Spanish nurse when people are not able to put a venous catheter in him, the Spaniard comes because, well, maybe he has some skills that are a little more refined and he is nice and so on. So that's what they want. Now the Pole who cleans the floor of the hospital, so that it's clean wherever he steps on it, he doesn't want that one. Well, no, I can't accept that. I don't like that, I don't like living in a country where there is this kind of… sectarianism, or bias…sectarianism. Of course, I didn't notice any kind of racism, not even in the slightest bit, towards me. Not even in the least, not from the patients, nothing, and I do not want to be arrogant, but everyone loves me. Now, what I did notice is some kind of, when I talk to them, some kind of racism towards other people.*

This argumentative sequence reveals how Diego was visibly annoyed about the patient not valuing the contributions of seemingly low-skilled workers without whom the hospital would not function either. Even though he took pride in his own achievements of possessing skills that other nurses do not have (inserting a venous catheter), he rejected the notion that this makes him more deserving of being in the UK. In his view, this was very much a question of principle. Diego purposefully used the metaphor of the hospital floor to comment on how the patient in question *"steps on"* the Polish cleaner's work while at the same time dismissing his/her right to be there.

The data extract conveys Diego's basic sense of solidarity with other Europeans. Lamont (1992, p. 12) argues that "boundary work is also a way of developing a sense of group membership, it creates bonds based on shared emotions, similar conceptions of the sacred and the profane, and similar reactions toward symbolic violators". When looking at Diego's line of argumentation, he invokes a European identity or new 'we-group' emerging in resistance to Brexit.

The interviews that I collected for this project suggest that participants experienced some uniquely European spaces in Britain, where people from different EU member states work together and sometimes form biographically significant relationships. Examples include work environments such as restaurants, hotels and factories where the vast majority of employees are from countries such as Poland, Romania, Italy and Spain. Diego's hospital is no exception as he estimated that two thirds of the employees were from different EU member states. It seems that in this way, work and personal relationships emerge between people he would have never met if it had not been for their common migration to the UK. In this context, Brexit appears as a common threat affecting all EU nationalities alike. Despite claiming that he had not been personally targeted (*"everyone loves me"*), Diego felt offended by the discrimination he had witnessed against his Polish co-workers.[5] He took issue with the imagery of essentially strange migrants who take away 'our' jobs and live off 'our' benefits. Whilst such 'othering' tendencies have existed for many years, it seems as if the outcome of the EU referendum had given such stereotypes more weight and legitimacy.

Forms of resistance

Elias and Scotson (1965) emphasised that in situations marked by volatile power disparities, the outsiders tended to retaliate by resorting to counter-stigmatisations. This is an observation that resonates with my data material. Much like other interviewees in my study, Diego presented the 'Leave' platform, including the supporters he had encountered, as ignorant.

> *And I... I... I was angry to learn that 95% of the people who voted for Brexit were not able to put forward one rational reason that they had thought through in their heads. I talked to the patients, I was sometimes happy to hear someone openly say to me, 'I'm going to vote for Brexit, for this, for this and for this reason', not to be told, 'No, no, I'm not going to vote for Brexit' and then they go vote for Brexit anyway. That is to say that first they should be sincere and clear about their reasons. But unfortunately, in this country, the people who voted for Brexit, I tell you in more than 90% of the cases, they simply let themselves be carried away a little by television propaganda, by radios, by 'They are stealing our jobs!' That was a very clear reflection of British society, you who studied sociology surely love these things.*

In this argumentative sequence, Diego brought up how he had felt deceived by patients who, he believed, were secretly in favour of Brexit while not admitting it openly. He was visibly irritated by this perceived lack of transparency, which made the situation worse in his opinion. Diego thereby drew moral boundaries between himself and secret 'Leave' supporters, underlining the importance of being honest. In his perception, many voters bought into xenophobic news coverage propagating simplistic slogans such as *"They are stealing our jobs"*. This example illustrates how he regards Brexit as something not only ignorant but also immoral and rooted in 'bad taste' (Lamont, 1992; Bourdieu, 1984). When asked about his immediate reaction to the result, he responded:

> *I was talking to a patient about it [Brexit] yesterday. 'If you have no access to a job, and someone who doesn't speak English gets the job instead, you have to look at yourself. Perhaps you aren't doing something right.' Do you understand? Yes, rather a feeling of anger at the rejection received by the majority of English society… Or like a feeling of pride, we are not too many here, if I'm the fifth wheel, well I'm leaving. Or like, I'm stronger, I am bigger than this, I don't care because I don't have to be here, you know? I also, I got angry in the sense that… I thought it was funny in the beginning. I took it very sarcastically in the sense of how can you be so, excuse the word, be idiotic enough to vote for Brexit? Or like, 'Look at these idiots.'*

When thinking in terms of established-outsider dynamics, it seems as if Diego (and his friends) resorted to 'blame-gossip' as a 'weapon of defence' (Elias and Scotson, 1965, p. 104). In this example, Diego used the personal pronoun "we" as in *"we are not too many here"*, defending not only himself but also other migrants who may be in more vulnerable positions (e.g. the Polish cleaners at his hospital). His emphasis on feeling *"bigger than this"* and *"I don't have to be here"* sheds light on his refusal to be victimised by Brexit. Much like other participants in my study, he constructed Brexit as something 'ignorant' as the supporters he had encountered appeared unable to explain how they had arrived at their decision. Diego appeared to create some distance to Brexit by intellectualising the phenomenon, aligning himself with the intellectual elites in the UK.

> *To be honest, I really like sociology, if I could choose again perhaps I would have studied sociology instead of nursing. I see this city as very polarised, there are poles. Do you understand? It's a spectrum… People, let's not talk about their economic*

> *level or level of lifestyle because here a normal employee can afford a certain living standard, a house, a car and so on, and so on. A plumber lives well in this country, better than in Spain. But let's talk about the intellectual level of people. That's how I would explain it. When you look at 100% of the population, there is a percentage of people, people who are highly educated, a very high intellectual level, perhaps higher than in other parts of Europe. But at the same time, the percentage of people who are ignorant is also very high. That's why there is a big societal divide. So the class, let's call it that, perhaps it's not politically correct, the intellectual middle class is very small. In Spain, in Portugal I believe that the intellectual middle class represents the majority of the people.*

In this part of the interview Diego addressed me much like a fellow social scientist (*"I really like sociology"*), sharing his own theories about British society, which he apparently based on his own 'participant observations' from the hospital. My co-membership in the category of EU citizens (i.e. being German) in the UK was, of course, also relevant in this context. If I had been a British researcher, Diego might not have shared his thoughts on the subject so openly.

This data extract illustrates how Diego shifts the power balance created by Brexit by bringing up a different form of 'group charisma' that is based on cultural capital (Bourdieu, 1984). From that standpoint, the intellectual elites in Britain, which he identifies with, remain the 'established' group with regard to their sense of 'cultural superiority'. His claim that the majority of people in Spain and Portugal belonged to what he defined as *"the intellectual middle class"* is also interesting as he indirectly elevated them above the average British 'Leave' supporter. He felt that he was part of large 'we-groups' that he believed to be superior in cultural terms, referring both to the intellectual elites in Britain and *"the majority of people"* in his home country. According to this logic, Brexit voters may be legally above but at the same time morally and intellectually below EU non-nationals – an interpretative strategy that allowed him to create some distance to the result and maintain a positive self-image.

Apart from his spontaneous moral argumentation about Brexit and how the referendum affected relationships, Diego also mentioned some practical consequences that he believed could impede some work-related projects in the future. As he had explained to me in our first interview, one of the main reasons why he chose the United Kingdom in the first place was its membership in the EU. For him, and many of his co-workers, it was important to be integrated in a special EU point system for healthcare workers in public hospitals because it would facilitate a return migration in the future (Buchan et al., 2014). In our second interview, he stressed how Brexit could impede the NHS's efforts to recruit staff from abroad.

> *So for all the Spanish nurses, and we are many working in this country, and we are working here for many different reasons, but one of them is to earn these points so if we want to go back to Spain one day we can take the exam to become a state employee. In Spain, the more points you have, the more possibilities you get to qualify to enter this competition. (…) If Brexit goes ahead, it will be much more difficult to convince a Spanish nurse to choose England over Ireland or France, Germany, because we won't get these points. That is to say that, if someone wants to go back to Spain, his options of getting work will be smaller than those of people who went elsewhere.*

His British employers had headhunted Diego while he was still living in Spain.[6] According to him, it would become more "*difficult to convince a Spanish nurse to choose England*" in the future. He thereby highlighted the reciprocity of intra-European migration flows, as the NHS is in competition with other countries to attract qualified healthcare workers from abroad (Baird & McKenna, 2019). From this perspective, the power balance between xenophobic 'Leave' supporters and EU nurses (and other hospital staff) is skewed towards the latter. Rather than being outsiders who are dependent on the established group's mercy to allow them to stay in Britain, as many doors across Europe remain wide-open,[7] the vast majority of interviewees in my study expressed their desire to return to Spain eventually because it was important for them to be close to their families. Given the current labour shortage in the NHS, Diego's concerns about no longer being integrated in this EU programme should be taken seriously (Buchan et al., 2014).

Bhambra (2017) compares Brexit to an act of "turning citizens into immigrants", thereby drawing parallels to legislations that restricted the rights of 'Commonwealth citizens' in the 1980s. Whilst Brexit had been quite a diffuse threat for a long time, its official implications are becoming increasingly tangible. My informants' attempts to present Brexit as something 'idiotic' and 'Leave' supporters as lacking cultural capital could therefore also be compared to gallows humour, which helps EU citizens cope with the depressing reality of having been made 'legal outsiders'.

LOOKING BEYOND THE SINGLE CASE

A close scrutiny of Diego's interview leads to the discovery of certain phenomena, which are also visible in other data that I collected. On a macro-level, Brexit has often been compared to the UK's 'divorce' from the EU. When analysing my participants' experiences and memories of everyday encounters, it seems as if the result of the EU referendum triggered similar feelings to a personal break-up – including anger, disappointment, indifference, but also feelings of sadness, disillusionment and rejection. It seems that Brexit had become something like a 'litmus test' for social relationships: are you for or against me?

Sara, a 25-year-old journalism graduate who had recently moved to Edinburgh from Bristol, where she had spent about two years working at a restaurant on a boat, shared these memories.

> *I was living in Bristol at the time of the referendum. And the people in my house… you know in the first flat I was living with a family, and this family voted to leave Europe. (…) For me, that was weird. They told me… well they told me that it wasn't because of the immigrants… 'It's because of all the money we're sending to Europe'. And then one week later, I was on the boat and two of my co-workers, one English and one Spanish guy, got into this big argument and I believe they started beating each other up because the Spanish guy had found out that the English guy had voted to leave Europe. So my Spanish co-worker got so angry with the English guy because he told him, 'You're voting so that they'll throw me out'. In the end the English guy had to leave because this conflict got so intense that one of them had to quit this job.*

This data extract coveys an atmosphere of distrust and high tensions in the immediate aftermath of the referendum, which could be compared to an awareness context of suspicion (Glaser & Strauss, 1965). Brexit had become the elephant in almost every room. The family seemed intent on avoiding tensions in their household by assuring Sara that their decision to vote in favour of Brexit had nothing to do with immigration (and her). Instead, they put emphasis on the seemingly more neutral economic arguments. The question whether this was an authentic explanation, or rather an ancillary motive (Mills, 1940) to avoid offending their guest, remained open at this point. Metaphorically speaking, it seemed as if the topic of Brexit had become a Pandora's box. Opening it could cause irreparable damage to social relationships (e.g. with tenants, co-workers), which became visible in Sara's second example. Brexit was not treated like any other political topic with which one may 'agree to disagree'. The fact that the conflict took place "*one week later*" indicates that the English co-worker had not openly spoken about his intention to vote for Brexit at work. Instead, Sara's Spanish colleague heard it through the grapevine ("*had found out*"), which possibly exacerbated his feelings of personal betrayal and anger.

Several other informants also expressed their personal disappointment about British co-workers, friends and acquaintances, who turned out to be in favour of leaving the European Union. Brexit seemed to have triggered what could be described as a *collective disenchantment* with the UK. The autobiographical narratives revealed how Europe as a space to pursue biographical projects had given many participants a future perspective in sometimes seemingly hopeless situations. Britain had, furthermore, a special place in this open European space, as it was known as quite a multicultural and cosmopolitan society. That being said, Brexit was experienced as a 'rude awakening', as it symbolically devalued their migration projects.

It was noticeable that my interviewees resorted to different forms of spontaneous argumentation when speaking about Brexit. In other words, rather than merely narrating or describing how they experienced the EU referendum, they started to argue fiercely and took a stance on the negative portrayal of migrants both in the media as well as in everyday conversations (see Diego's encounter with the patient). The political debates had become very personal. The notion of Brexit being something 'idiotic', which British people will come to regret in the future, appeared in almost every interview that I have conducted in the UK since 2016. As discussed in the case study, intellectualising Brexit appeared like an interpretative strategy to distance oneself from feelings of rejection.

A great number of the informants in this study worked in menial jobs that were unrelated to their academic training. Some people were subordinate to managers who openly expressed xenophobic attitudes, e.g. by making fun about their lack of English skills. These informants were directly exposed to anti-immigrant sentiments and therefore took Brexit much more personally than those who worked in more sheltered environments such as Diego. While being clearly disappointed about the result, many participants found solace in what could be categorised as *geographic, professional and personal spaces of recognition*. They stressed how 'their' city or region did not vote to leave the

EU, emphasising local forms of belonging (*"Cambridge didn't want Brexit!"*).[8] Furthermore, in the aftermath of the EU referendum, some informants received messages and phone calls from British friends and colleagues who 'apologised' for the result and expressed their support. Similar to Diego, other participants also commonly used the personal pronoun 'we' when speaking about the topic, referring to Spaniards and other EU nationals. Being a member of a large 'we-group' seemed to give my participants confidence, indicating the emergence of a special European solidarity in resistance to Brexit.

Finally, it is important to point out that Brexit not only affected the participants who were currently residing in the UK but also those who had returned to Spain at the time of our interview. Many people were nostalgic about their stay abroad, especially because they often found themselves alienated from their old surroundings after their homecoming (Schütz, 1945). Several returnees had thought about re-migrating to the UK, as they encountered difficulties in finding a full-time job. The prospect of potentially not being 'welcomed back' was therefore experienced as a breach of reciprocity (see the case study of Adam). As mentioned, intra-European migration flows have been described as 'liquid' (Engbersen & Snel, 2013) as many people seem to move effortlessly from one member state to another. While this term does not always capture the biographical complexity of how my participants made the decision to migrate, there was something fluid about how they had thought about their migration, return and/or re-migration prior to the EU referendum. Metaphorically speaking, Brexit could be interpreted as a 'dam' that slows down or stops these types of transnational migration flows into the UK.[9]

A NOTE ON THE RECENT POLITICAL DEVELOPMENTS

At the time of writing, the UK has officially left the European Union. This has had significant consequences for the 3.5 million EU citizens living in Britain (Office of National Statistics, 2021), as well as many others still living in mainland Europe. The process of applying for the 'EU Settlement Scheme' has repeatedly been criticised as bureaucratic, inefficient, arbitrary and confusing. Whilst the official deadline (30 June 2021) has already passed, the Home Office indicated that it would take many months to process the high number of applications it had received, putting many people in a state of legal limbo (O'Carroll & Gentleman, 2021).

The situation for EU citizens, who are currently thinking about (or planning) to move to Britain, is even more complicated. Since January 2021, free movement to the UK has officially been replaced by a strict points-based system, which requires newcomers to apply for working visas. The Home Office (2020) published an official policy brief on the issue, stating:

> For too long, distorted by European free movement rights, the immigration system has been failing to meet the needs of the British people. (…)
>
> From 1 January 2021, EU and non-EU citizens will be treated equally. We will reduce overall levels of migration and give top priority to those with the highest skills and the greatest talents: scientists, engineers, academics and other highly skilled workers. (…)
>
> We will replace free movement with the UK's points-based system to cater for the most highly skilled workers, skilled workers, students and a range of other specialist work routes including routes for global leaders and innovators.
>
> We will not introduce a general low-skilled or temporary work route. We need to shift the focus of our economy away from a reliance on cheap labour from Europe and instead concentrate on investment in technology and automation. Employers will need to adjust.

The tone of this policy statement is unequivocally harsh towards EU migrants. The principle of free movement is hereby constructed as a negative development that has "distorted" the UK immigration system for "too long". According to the new system, visa applications from EU citizens will be treated as equal to those coming from overseas. This is a gradual restriction of rights that has been referred to as "turning citizens into immigrants" (Bhambra, 2017). Furthermore, the UK government makes a very clear distinction between who they consider welcome and who they do not. There is a dismissive undertone in reducing the contributions of thousands – if not millions – of EU citizens (e.g. working in manual jobs) to "cheap labour from Europe". For a working visa, applicants need to qualify for at least 70 points on a rigid scale, designed to assess migrants on, e.g., their academic qualifications, English skills, and salary levels (table 1).

Characteristics	Essential	Points
Offer of job by approved sponsor	✓	20
Job at appropriate skill level	✓	20
Speaks English at required level	✓	10
Salary of £20,480 (min) – £23,480	✗	0
Salary of £23,040 – £25,599	✗	10
Salary of £25,600 and above	✗	20
Job in a designated shortage occupation	✗	20
Education qualification: PhD in subject relevant to job	✗	10
Education qualification: PhD in a Stem subject relevant to the job	✗	20

Table 1: UK Points-Based Immigration System, Home Office (2020)

This list defines which characteristics the UK government considers as 'essential', thereby symbolically devaluing EU citizens' contributions to British society that cannot be pressed into this narrow form. When evaluating this list in the light of this study, I realised that only a handful of my informants would have qualified for a working visa if these criteria had already existed at the time of their migration to the UK. The implementation of Brexit is still ongoing, and it will take time to see whether this new points-based immigration system is feasible long-term. That said, the time when EU citizens could effortlessly travel in and out of the UK to explore work and life opportunities is definitely over. There have been media reports of, e.g., Spanish travellers being detained at British airports and held against their will in immigration removal centres (Tremlett & O'Carroll, 2021). This would have been unimaginable in 2014 when I first started my fieldwork in the UK. In the light of the recent political changes, the biographical narratives I collected in this country may soon be regarded as historic documents of migration processes that are no longer possible.

In retrospect, Diego was quite on point with his political predictions *("It's like in the United States and Australia, they are selective. 'We need you, but not you.'")*. On paper, Diego would perhaps be considered one of the 'lucky ones'. Due to the labour shortage in the healthcare sector, his chances of getting a working visa are still very high. That being said, one ought to ask a different question: what are the UK's chances of attracting nurses like him in the future? Diego's biographical narrative revealed that he chose Britain over other destinations primarily because it made a permanent reunion with his girlfriend easier. Furthermore, it was important for him to stay in the European Union due to the point system that would facilitate a future re-integration into the Spanish labour market. With the new points-based immigration system, these two pull factors no longer apply. Against the backdrop of the NHS's reliance on EU citizens for its staff (many of whom have left since the referendum), this is quite a worrying observation (cf. Rodriguez-Arrastia et al., 2021).

I would like to emphasise that single case studies, such as that of Diego, should not be reduced to merely a micro-sociological exercise. By paying close attention to his experiences at the hospital, one could learn something about the societal impact of Brexit that goes beyond the single case (e.g. the ascription of ethnic hierarchies by established members of society, the meaning of Brexit as a litmus test for the trustworthiness of others, etc.). It also serves as a basis for developing new research questions about the emergence of new European identities in resistance to Brexit versus tendencies of division (Mazzilli & King, 2019).

8. AN UNEASY HOMECOMING

Although most people regarded the time they had spent abroad as a valuable chapter in their lives, only a very small number of participants expressed the desire to stay in the receiving society forever. Throughout different stages of their migration experience, the question of *whether*, *how* and *when* to go home remained at the back of their minds (Bagnoli, 2007). The biographical processes behind the wish to return differed and had to do both with personal and collective developments in the receiving society as well as in Spain. The ultimate decision to move back was rarely made in an isolated context, but rather evolved in conversations with others. In many cases, the lived experience of 'coming home' differed from my informants' expectations, as it turned out to be a more complicated process than originally anticipated (Vathi & King, 2017).

The following chapter is mainly based on the interviews I conducted with returnees who had moved back to Spain by the time of our meeting. I begin by discussing how different voices in my informants' minds overlapped when deciding whether to return 'home'. Building on this discussion, I then compare the real-life experiences of those who had moved back by the time of the interview. I am thereby drawing on Alfred Schütz's 'The Homecomer' (1945/1971), identifying similarities and differences between my participants and returnees of earlier generations.

RETURNING AS AN ANSWER TO WHAT?

(a) The fear of 'missing out'

Almost every participant in my sample brought up the topic of the warmer climate in Spain as one incentive to return eventually. Throughout different stages of their migration experience, they struggled to adapt to colder temperatures, rain and shorter days. While common phrases such as *"el español necesita sol"* ("a Spaniard needs sun") may sound light-hearted, they encapsulate important qualitative differences in everyday life. Such comments about the Spanish climate or sunshine, which are shared and confirmed by fellow migrants, refer to more than just the temperature and light conditions. They express a deep longing for a whole way of life that 'we' miss (Bolognani, 2016). In contrast to this, several informants portrayed Germany and the UK as 'colder' countries, thereby not only referring to the weather but also to how 'locals' seemed much more reserved in social interactions (King & Christou, 2014, p. 90).

Nora, aged 29, recalled difficulties adjusting to life in the UK.

> *When you see that your friends here in Madrid are at the swimming pool, at the beach, barbecue, and I'm alone in London, with an umbrella ... well ... I did not want to live that life. I want to enjoy myself, go out until 10pm, here is the Spanish life, it's like you have time to do everything. You work, but you go to the gym and do the shopping, and everything is in one day, and you go to see your friends. In Brighton, I didn't have time for anything, it was... I left work, I went grocery shopping, gym if anything, and then I went to bed because it was already dark.*

The contrasting image Nora painted between herself *"alone in London, with an umbrella"*, while seeing pictures of her friends enjoying life in the sun underlines a certain fear of 'missing out'. She and other participants associated the rainy weather and lack of daylight with a generally more isolated and joyless way of life that was very different from what they had been used to. Several informants expressed the belief that the warmer climate also had an impact on people's mentalities, making them more open and sociable than their British or German counterparts.

Many migrants were at first shocked, briefly fascinated but ultimately frustrated by the rougher climate in the host country. The narratives revealed that it was above all the lack of light that took a toll on their wellbeing. During the winter months, some informants went to work in the dark and left work in the dark, which was something that they had never experienced before. Everyday life in Britain and Germany was portrayed as much less eventful in comparison to what they had been used to, revolving mainly around work and being at home.

Some participants, especially in my UK sample, expressed some discomfort about having to mainly socialise in pubs with their colleagues after work. This was especially apparent in interviews with people who did not drink alcohol, as they felt like outsiders in these settings. Since days in Spain tend to be longer, these informants claimed that there were more ways to spend their free time that did not involve drinking.

Several informants were keen to show me that their praise for this type of lifestyle was rooted in certain objective criteria rather than simply patriotism. For this purpose, they brought up the phenomenon of British (and to a lesser degree German) people retiring on the Andalusian coastline (Benson & O'Reilly, 2016) as 'evidence' of the superiority of the 'Spanish way of life'. If English people do not want to stay in the UK when given a choice, why should we?

(b) Mission accomplished?

For many people I interviewed, the step to move to another country was tied to a specific purpose such as learning a new language (Bagnoli, 2009). Once the 'mission' was completed, the question of 'return' became imminent. This was especially apparent in the interviews with those who took part in institutionalised exchange programmes, such as Erasmus or time-limited au pair schemes. Others worked in menial jobs but perceived their stay abroad as a 'gap year' (Vogt, 2017). These participants had arrived in Germany or the UK with the clear intention of moving back to Spain after a predefined period of time (e.g. six months) and had sometimes already bought a return ticket prior to departure. Some participants adhered to their original date of return, while others prolonged their stay due to unforeseen developments, such as attractive job/study opportunities in the receiving society and/or weakened personal ties to Spain (i.e. dissolution of long-distance relationships). Various informants kept postponing their planned date of return due to a promotion they got at work. In some cases, people who originally planned to stay for a few months (or even weeks) ended up spending several years in the receiving society. This is a phenomenon that has been well documented in migration literature on the life of 'guest workers' in Germany (Yahirun, 2012).

Several participants contemplated returning to Spain in situations where they had reached some level of stability in the receiving society. They knew the city they lived in very well, they were fluent in the new language and had become confident in their ability to manage their tasks at work. After the initial excitement about experiencing a new culture had worn off, people seemed to become more aware of the disadvantages of living abroad. In this situation, they often started to wonder whether it was 'time to go', as they were seemingly not getting 'anything new' out of the experience.

(c) 'Maturing out' of one's migration experience

A number of participants stressed how they perceived their way of life in the receiving society as no longer age-appropriate. This was especially prevalent in interviews with people who had reached their thirties and above. Although these informants were grateful for the experiences they had had abroad, they felt increasingly 'trapped' in a certain stage of their youth. What they feared was a sense of biographical stagnation, as they felt unable to make significant progress in the receiving society both in a work-related and personal context (Cuzzocrea, 2019).

Sources of frustration included poor housing quality (e.g. mice, vermin, lack of hygiene) and having to live with many housemates, which they deemed tolerable for a short period of time but not long-term. At work, these informants often drew contrastive comparisons between themselves and their younger co-workers. Being in one's early twenties is often thought to be a stage in life when people go on adventures, travel, make new friends and focus on getting to know themselves. A concept that is useful in this context is that of a 'psychosocial moratorium' (Erikson, 1968), which allows a young person to 'postpone' adulthood for some time to indulge in self-experimentation. For a limited period of time, this is socially acceptable because it is considered a normal stage in one's development. Cuzzocrea (2019, p. 570) writes that during this stage "commitments are not completely absent, but not felt as urgent either. The motto is 'yes, but not yet.'"

This was different for slightly older migrants, who faced institutional expectation patterns with regard to their careers, marriage and family planning. Many people sensed that in contrast to their younger co-workers, they had less 'time to waste' in pursuing important biographical goals. Their 'license to postpone' was rapidly expiring. After spending sometimes years working in menial jobs, these informants worried about losing touch with their academic qualifications. This became especially apparent after 'learning a new language' could no longer provide a legitimate pretext for their ways of making a living, as they had already become fluent in English or German by the time of our interview.

(d) Family obligations

There were several informants in my sample who moved back to Spain due to family obligations (Ni Laoire, 2008). The circumstances of these types of return migrations differed widely. A few participants had to prematurely return home in order to care for a family member in Spain who had fallen seriously ill. In cases of emergency, these migrants tended to prioritise family-related responsibilities over their own personal projects. These decisions were not taken lightly, as various informants expressed their concern about what was expected of them and doubted whether they would be capable of living up to such tasks.

However, family-related return migration processes did not always revolve around emergencies. Many interviewees brought up different types of future scenarios that they took as an incentive to move back, for example having parents or grandparents who might eventually need their support. This was, however, not the only family tie that pulled my informants back to Spain. One topic that appeared throughout my sample was that of children. Many people lamented the fact that they were missing out on their younger siblings', cousins', nephews', and nieces' development. Quite a few participants also brought up their wish to become parents one day, drawing contrasting comparisons between the child-rearing conditions in Spain and the UK or Germany. They argued that Spanish culture was generally more child-friendly, in comparison to the seemingly 'cold' receiving society, and that children had more opportunities to play outside due to the warmer climate. The most important reason why most people seemed to prefer the idea of their future children growing up in Spain was the proximity to their extended family.

This theme became especially apparent in the narrative of Irene, aged 28, who had been working as a nurse in a village close to Frankfurt. She had given birth to her first child six months prior to our interview and was on maternity leave. Irene and her partner were planning to return to Spain within the following year.

> *(…) now that I've had a baby, I come from a family that has always been very close, with cousins, uncles, grandparents, all together, and for me it's very sad that [my daughter] doesn't have that. Here she only has a mother and a father. She has no grandparents, no uncles, no cousins, no one. And I feel sorry for her. Because I really enjoyed growing up in a very close family and I would like her to live that way too. And apart from that, I want to leave when she's very small, because if not, her country will be Germany, and my country will be Spain, then we're going to throw each one to one side. You know, I don't want her to start school here because then she would start to put down roots here. And she will always want to come back. And I'll want to go back there, so we'll always be destined to be separated.*

What is interesting about Irene's argumentation is that she drew contrasting comparisons between herself and her daughter. She strongly believed that if she decided to stay in Germany, her child would be deprived of what could be called an 'innocent Spanish childhood', i.e., being surrounded by extended family members and having many opportunities to play outside (cf. Ni Laoire, 2011). She deemed this experience invaluable in her own biography, which is why she expressed much concern for her daughter (*"I feel sorry for her"*).

Irene strongly thought of herself as part of a wider family unit, making decisions based on what is best for everyone involved instead of focusing solely on her own career. Later in the interview, she also spoke extensively about her family in Spain, including her mother and sister, who had children of her own. Irene believed that by staying in Germany she would not only deprive her daughter of her grandparents, but also her own mother of her grandchild, which was something that she also felt guilty about.

In the second part of Irene's commentary, she expressed her fear of growing distant from her child. If her daughter started to have *"her own life"* in Germany (i.e. by starting school), Irene believed that a return migration might become much more complicated (Tyrrell et al., 2018). This fear is especially visible in her prediction that *"her country will be Germany, and my country will be Spain, then we're going to throw each one to one side"*.

Although Irene's situation was unique, as she was the only participant who had a baby, similar thought processes could be found in many other interviews. When asked about whether they could see themselves living in Germany or the UK forever, many people pointed out that they would not want to raise their future children abroad. There were, however, also a few exceptions to this rule. The informants, who explicitly stated that they did not intend to move back, also brought up the topic of future children. By staying in Germany or the UK, these participants wanted to prevent future scenarios involving their children having to go through the same struggles they had to overcome in Spain (e.g. dealing with economic hardships).

(e) Trajectories of suffering

There were a few interviewees in my sample who got caught up in extremely difficult situations in the receiving society and were simply looking for 'a way out'. In their narratives, they often recalled situations in which they felt 'desperate' and isolated. During my fieldwork, I was contacted by a woman whose adult son had recently returned from working as a waiter in Germany. As a teenager, Martina's son had developed a serious eating disorder that almost cost him his life at age 17. After receiving specialised treatment, his condition had stabilised but his health condition was still frail. In the context of the economic crisis, Martina struggled to provide for the family as a single mother. She recalled how they had to survive several months without water and electricity, even reaching a point where they had no money left to buy food. Out of necessity, her son decided to move to Germany to work as a waiter, hoping to support his mother financially. He did, however, encounter many obstacles as superiors were harsh and unfair. According to his mother, his health-related disposition of vulnerability exacerbated the situation.

> *And another problem this year, which was in Germany when he went to work, is that he paid for his food in the restaurant where he worked. But he was not allowed to choose, he could only eat pork and chips. And that created a serious problem for him because he paid for the food but he couldn't choose the food. And he got fat and that really bothered him psychologically. (...) He did not want to fail me for that, for four months he never told me that something was wrong. It went on and on and on and on and on and on. After four months he told me 'I'm coming back', 'What happened?' When he started to tell me, I mean, for my son to come back, it has to be hard and he must have had a lot of problems because he is a boy who likes to work, he never fails, he is very, very hardworking and does whatever it takes. Well, he came back completely disillusioned.*

This sequence captures how Martina's son got caught up in a serious trajectory of suffering while living abroad. According to her, his employers in Germany had reacted indifferently to his request to choose his own food, which put his health and mental wellbeing at risk. While the majority of my participants came from middle, and sometimes upper-class backgrounds, Martina and her son literally struggled to survive. If it had not been out of economic necessity, her son would probably not have decided to go abroad due to his past struggles with anorexia.

Her son's unwillingness to admit his problems to his mother during the first four months points to a certain level of pride and commitment to family responsibilities. There is something tragic about the combination of him not wanting to 'fail her' and his ultimate decision to return prematurely. His homecoming could be described as an action scheme of escape from a serious trajectory of suffering. In the interview, Martina described how her son had still not recovered from the experiences he had had abroad, carrying a certain sense of shame and defeat about not having succeeded ("*he came back completely disillusioned*"). She recounted how, since his return, he had become very reclusive. While Martina's case stood out due to her son's past with eating disorders, there were several migrants in my study who got caught up in extremely difficult situations from which they wanted to escape. Examples include workplace bullying, the threat of homelessness and isolation. These informants struggled to cope with such challenges also due to a lack of language skills and weak social networks in the receiving society, which also undermined their self-esteem.

Although intra-European movements, such as travelling from Spain to Germany, are often regarded as a privileged form of migration, there are nevertheless serious risks involved for the individual. While Martina's son's decision to move back to Spain would officially be qualified as 'voluntary', he felt forced to take this decision due to factors outside of his control. His failed attempt to prove himself abroad apparently triggered a deep sense of shame and resignation. His mother told me that he had stopped speaking for a few months at a time. Instead of a strict dichotomy between forced and voluntary return migration (Vathi & King, 2017)[1], it is therefore important to take a closer look at the complexity of biographical processes.

MOVING 'BACK': EXPECTATIONS VS. REALITY

Alfred Schütz's view on the 'homecomer'

The obstacles that returnees face have long been of social scientific interest. The social phenomenologist Alfred Schütz (1945/1971, p. 106)[2] observed that "to the homecomer home shows – at least in the beginning – an unaccustomed face". In contrast to a complete stranger, who may anticipate a lack of orientation when entering a new community, the homecomer "expects to return to an environment of which he always had and – so he thinks – still has intimate knowledge and which he has just to take for granted in order to find his bearings within it" (pp. 106-107). But instead of simply picking up his social life where he had left it prior to going away, he is likely to experience difficulties in understanding others and making himself understood.[3]

According to Schütz, in face-to-face relationships, people share the physical space and time as long as the connection lasts. This includes seeing each other's facial expressions and gestures that are instantly observable as signs of thought processes. Furthermore, "the same things are within reach, within sight, within hearing, and so on. Within this common horizon there are objects of common interest and common relevance; things to work with or upon, actually or potentially" (p. 109). Face-to-face relationships also enable partners to participate in the "onrolling inner life of the Other" (p. 110), following the other's thought processes as they develop.

After an emigrant leaves home, his or her social relationships become somewhat fragmented. Schütz observed that "there is no longer the total experience of the beloved person, his gestures, his way of walking and of speaking, of listening and of doing things; what remains are recollections, a photograph, some handwritten lines" (p. 112). After departure, memories replace vivid experiences with others and "these memories preserve merely what home life meant up to the moment he left it behind." While there were letters as a form of 'keeping in touch', Schütz noted that correspondents often communicated with the presumption that their significant others remained the same people to whom they had said goodbye.

However, being exposed to a foreign environment for a prolonged period of time often has a transformative effect on individuals. Due to new experiences, the returnee's horizon widened and his priorities and interests may have shifted. The 'homecomer' is therefore unlikely to be a static copy of his younger self, especially due to the 'irreversibility of inner time' (p. 114). Even if he wanted to, he cannot undo or unlearn what he has experienced abroad. Trying to rekindle 'old' social relationships therefore takes a lot of effort, not only from him but also from his 'old' peers. How do we deal with a person who we presume we have intimate knowledge of, but who thinks differently, acts differently, and seems to be interested in things that are unfamiliar to us?

Staying connected?

Alfred Schütz published the article on the 'homecomer' over 75 years ago. One may ask whether modern communication technology can facilitate one's re-integration into 'old' social circles. If a migrant had consistently kept 'in touch' with her friends from home while living abroad, would it not make sense that she could 'pick up' her social life where she had left it?

Remaining 'virtually' integrated in social circles at home (via communication technology) is something that sets my informants apart from migrants of earlier generations (Gordano Peile & Ros Híjar, 2016).[4] Until the 1990s, migrants often had to rely on letters that would delay communication by days and sometimes weeks. International phone calls used to be expensive and were often only used on special occasions. Once a person left home to work in a foreign country, the separation from those at home appeared more rigid and permanent in comparison to their contemporary counterparts.

While my informants' social relationships with those at home still appeared fragmented, they had almost unlimited access to the 'fragments' of their significant others. Many participants often spoke to their friends, partners and family at home on a daily basis via WhatsApp, Skype or Facebook Messenger. They could, and were sometimes expected to, share their new experiences instantly by posting photographs and videos on social media. Since these communication patterns were reciprocal, my informants were also immediately informed about what had been going on in their hometowns by receiving pictures of the latest social gathering. This phenomenon is part of the virtually mediated 'background noise' of one's migration experience (Komito, 2011).

In contrast to handwritten letter exchanges, video chats enable people to see each other's facial expressions during conversations, a technical feature that makes their interactions seemingly more three-dimensional. The narratives revealed that this constant stream of information could sometimes 'dilute' my informants' feelings of isolation, as they felt that they were still somehow taking part in their friends' and family's everyday lives.

As Schütz remarked, the level of perceived connectedness depended very much on the level of intimate knowledge one has of a place or a person. The homecomers' image of home is based mainly on their experience up to the point of their departure. One can ask whether the contemporary counterparts of Schütz's 'homecomer' have a somewhat easier time re-integrating into their 'old' social environments due to the increased level of contact they had in between.

Interestingly, many returnees in my sample still struggled with the same problem constellations that Schütz had identified in 1945. This points to a somewhat 'illusionary' layer of mediated communication. While the quantity of the 'fragments' (i.e. pictures, chat conversations) has increased in comparison to earlier times, they still remain 'fragments'. Each party can filter the part of their lives the other person gets to see, often presenting themselves in an idealised light. The latter habit could be compared to taking 'perennial selfies', thereby creating the illusion of constant cheerfulness. Much like an Instagram or Photoshop filter, a migrant may artificially add 'colour' to how she presents her daily life to loved ones at home while keeping personal problems to herself (Schwartz & Halegoua, 2014; Feaster, 2010).

Furthermore, sending photographs of new places to friends and family back home does not translate into real life shared experiences and memories and vice versa. Simply because a migrant is still virtually integrated in WhatsApp groups with her friends from home does not mean she has truly taken part in shared activities. These shared experiences are, however, necessary to maintain the same level of intimacy. Although communication technology may absorb or soften the initial "shock" that Schütz described, the basic social processes underlying the return experience remain the same. Several returnees initially experienced their 'homecoming' as disappointing, as their expectations both concerning their professional and social re-integration rarely aligned with reality.

Re-connecting pieces of 'home'

For the majority of the returnees in my sample, returning to Spain was a surprisingly disorienting experience, surprising in the sense that people knew their way around yet were somehow unsure how to fit in. When trying to reconstruct my informants' actual return experience, one may think of the metaphor of a 'jigsaw puzzle'. 'Home' was no longer accessible as a unified familiar entity, but instead felt somewhat fragmented. The returnees in my sample were in some ways picking up the pieces of what they had left behind, some of which they were still familiar with and some of which they did not recognise.

These 'pieces of home' took on various shapes. Since their departure, some informants noticed new shops in their hometowns while old stores had closed. While this observation appears insignificant at first sight, it captures a sense of disorientation. They still recognised the streets, but the city had changed since they had left. This image is helpful when trying to reconstruct how they felt after returning home, also with regard to their social relationships.

Attempts to reconnect with childhood friends often failed, as my informants sensed how they no longer shared the same worldview. Metaphorically speaking, my informants could themselves be compared to 'pieces of a puzzle' that had expanded and developed new edges while living abroad. After moving back to Spain, my informants sensed that they no longer fitted the 'hole' that they had left behind prior to their migration. This was a source of frustration, as attempts to join 'the puzzle pieces' did not go as smoothly as imagined. This was especially apparent after sensing that others were only superficially interested in, or even indifferent about, the experiences they had had abroad and which informants felt were worth telling. Furthermore, some participants felt that others tried to 'push' them back into the 'hole' they had left behind (i.e. old friendship dynamics), as they were unable or perhaps unwilling to accept how much their friends had changed while living abroad.

Several interviewees reported that in the beginning everybody wanted to see them, but that this initial excitement tended to wear off very quickly. Their childhood friends, so it seemed, had quite 'settled lives' (e.g. living with their partners) in which my informants no longer played a major role. This was sometimes a painful realisation, as the returnees felt somewhat 'left behind'. It seemed as if the migration experience pushed my participants to re-evaluate their social relationships in Spain critically and sometimes they realised that the quality of their old friendships had deteriorated significantly or perhaps was never there in the first place. Their narratives painted a picture of a somewhat distant reception, involving incidences of miscommunication. In this context, they drew contrasting comparisons between their childhood friends and the connections they had made while living abroad. Interestingly, several people emphasised how their *"real friends"* were still *"over there"* (UK/Germany) – an image that served as a source of solace in moments of loneliness.

The emergence of new social relationships

What several returnees had in common is that they initially felt impatient to build a new social circle, almost as if they were trying to fill a void that the migration experience had left in their lives. There was, furthermore, a somewhat suffocating quality of being back in seemingly familiar structures. Several people pointed out how they had the urge to experience *"something new"*. The biographical narratives revealed that many were mourning the loss (or rather spatial unavailability) of the friendships they had made abroad, especially after realising that their childhood friendships had changed. Much like after a personal break-up, several participants found themselves in what could be compared to short-term 'rebound' relationships with people with whom they did not have much in common.

One example is the case of Rocio, aged 25. After returning from her au pair year in England, she felt sad and disoriented. When her friend started a relationship with a local football hooligan, she briefly found herself falling into his social circles.

> *Hooligans who support the football team here, but in a very aggressive way. I couldn't stand it. (…) Some of my friends… from what I know, it's like the feeling that I had in the beginning… You know that I didn't feel like I fitted in and I was sad and needed something new… that happened to everyone!! For some of my friends it was worse! You know that crazy time I had with the hooligans? I was strong enough to break out of this.*

Rocio contextualised her *"crazy time"* with the football hooligans as part of her homecoming from the UK. In her view, it was a combination of not fitting in, sadness and a need to experience *"something new"*, which made her susceptible to these types of social influences. Furthermore, Rocio saw parallels with what she observed in the lives of other returnees, whom she described as similarly disoriented and depressed after moving back home (*"that happened to everyone!!"*). Without taking her theory at face value, she sensed that there was a destabilising dimension to returning to seemingly familiar structures. She backed this claim up by bringing up examples of other returnees she knew who suffered from anxiety attacks and depression (Vathi & King, 2017).

After being back in Spain for a while, most informants seemed to eventually 'calm down' and approach socialising with a more relaxed attitude. Although they were very interested in meeting new people, they expressed their belief that this should happen more naturally and that one ought to give it time. In retrospect, many returnees missed the relative ease with which one could meet new people (mostly fellow migrants) in cities like Cambridge or Berlin. It seemed as if being part of the Spanish diaspora abroad already provided my informants with some kind of informal membership to a larger community, which they used to varying degrees.

In contrast to that, it seemed as if looking for new friends in one's hometown in Spain seemed to be somehow less socially acceptable. Several informants shied away from publicly admitting that they felt lonely, as they did not want to be regarded as outsiders. Furthermore, they believed that their new colleagues were already quite settled (i.e. married with children) and did not have much time or energy to make new friends. The fear of 'bothering others' seemed to hold some of my informants back from widening their social circles.

Returning to one's family of origin

After returning to Spain, most informants moved back in at least temporarily with their parents or other family members. Since none of the returnees had an attractive job offer lined up prior to their departure, they often regarded it as a makeshift solution to save money and not worry about accommodation. This set-up turned out to be a source of frustration, especially when the job hunt took much longer than originally anticipated. The informants' descriptions of life back home resembled a second 'waithood' (Singerman, 2007).

The interviewees complained that their family members almost automatically reverted back to old patterns by asking well-meaning but nevertheless frustrating questions about their whereabouts ('What are you doing? Where are you going, and with whom are you going?'). This was a frustrating experience, especially due to what Schütz had defined as the 'irreversibility of inner time'. The returnees could not 'reverse' the personal development they had undergone abroad, yet some of them felt that they were treated in the same way as prior to their migration. It seemed as if the problem constellations that led my informants to migrate in the first place had not been solved while they were away. In retrospect, their migration projects seemed almost like a 'time out' from their problems at home. It was a break or escape from a prolonged period of dependency without offering a proper 'solution' (Cuzzocrea, 2019).

Hoping and waiting

Finding a stable job that could secure an independent existence turned out to be a much longer process than originally anticipated. Several participants returned to Spain with an increased sense of self-worth, as they took pride in what they had achieved in a foreign environment. These informants were cautiously optimistic that their new language skills and work experiences would give them a competitive advantage on the Spanish labour market. Furthermore, many people put faith in rumours, such as that "the crisis was already disappearing", a topic that they discussed both with people within the Spanish community abroad as well as with friends and family from home.[5] Despite clear signs of economic recovery, the climate on the labour market was still extremely competitive. After moving back to Spain, several informants described how they spent months at home sending out hundreds of applications without getting any replies. Furthermore, the job offers they did receive appeared very unattractive, especially in comparison to what they had been used to in Germany or the UK.

Nora, aged 29, moved back to Madrid after her father was diagnosed with cancer. Prior to her departure, she had an attractive position in a tourist company in Brighton, a job she received after earning a master's degree from a British university. Her work experience and academic qualifications in England served as a source of confidence and she was fairly optimistic about finding a similar position at home. Her self-perception as a competent young professional was, however, at first not reflected in her attempts to reintegrate into the Spanish labour market.

> *I was looking for work. And the only things they offered me in Spain were internships of €300. And it was like, again? Because I've already done an internship, and I was like, 'My God, I'm 28 years old, I don't want to earn €300 again!' I don't live in the centre, so I already spend €70 on transportation and if they pay me €300, it doesn't compensate me. Then, in one of the interviews, I told them thank you, but that I considered that my experience did not fit the €300, that I had already been in England, I had a master's degree, I speak English and whatnot. I do not think it's*

> *fair that you pay a 28-year-old person with experience that little. Then nothing, they told me that it's okay, they understood, and nothing. I had a hard time looking for a job. During three months, I couldn't find anything. They didn't call me. All this, with the routine of getting up, looking for a job, they don't hire you. It's more like a vicious circle. What did I do wrong?*

This data extract conveys a certain fear of biographical stagnation, especially after her first attempts to find a stable job failed. At 28, she was unwilling to accept low-paid internships. For her, this was not simply an issue of money but also of recognition. Accepting an internship position at this stage in her life would have felt like a step back or even a devaluation of her previous biographical achievements. At the same time, her attempts to find a full-time position seemed to go nowhere, which put her in a catch-22 situation. She could either lower her expectations and risk having to start her career from zero again or she could keep on waiting and hoping for a more attractive job offer to come along.

Nora's self-directed question, "*What did I do wrong?*", captures a sense of hopelessness and loss of orientation, which she shared with other returnees. Several participants described moments when they started to think that their decision to move back to Spain had been a mistake. They were gradually losing hope of being able to build up a stable existence, which was often the most important factor in their decision to return in the first place. Instead of finally being able to live a life they deemed more age-appropriate (e.g. living in a separate flat, higher income), these informants felt stuck in their parents' (or other family members') homes. In this situation, even factors that had attracted my participants back to Spain quickly lost their appeal when faced with the depressing prospect of prolonged periods of unemployment or precarious labour ("*Good weather. How wonderful.*" (sarcastic)). The returnees differed in how they 'filled' this 'waiting period'. Some people decided to continue their education, somewhat aimlessly, as a makeshift solution to avoid unemployment. Others took on unattractive jobs in call centres, which they experienced as alienating and depressing.

Finding modest stability

Although the initial phase of reintegration proved to be very difficult for the returnees, several informants eventually found a position that could provide them with some form of modest stability. Whilst their language skills did play a role in eventually finding a job they were content with, English (or to a lesser extent German) did not guarantee a smooth reintegration into the Spanish labour market. Instead my informants stressed the importance of having the "right connections" – commonly referred to as *"enchufe"* ("plug") – to land a job in Spain (Vono de Vilhena & Vidal-Coso, 2012, Adler & Ayala-Hurtado, 2021). In some instances, my informants received a job offer from people they had gone to university with and who were now in charge of hiring new employees. In other cases, the 'right connection' was even further removed from my participants (*"My cousin had a friend who was looking for a receptionist who spoke English"*) but nevertheless effective. In hindsight, several interviewees described their first attempts to find a job by sending out hundreds of applications as a *"waste of time"*. They argued that, without knowing somebody in the company, the chances of getting invited for an interview were very slim (Ponzo & Scoppa, 2009).

It is important to point out that several informants earned *"just enough"* to sustain themselves, but not much more. After graduating with a master's degree in education, Rocio eventually found a position as a course leader at a language school that organised trips to the UK for high schoolers. Her employers had recently promoted her to the position of manager. At the time of our interview, she had just returned from the UK where she was in charge of organising a month-long summer school.

> *I… it has been my first time as a manager and it was hard in the beginning because I didn't know how to manage people. Now I was the boss of all the Spanish leaders and I had 19 groups at the same time. Nineteen groups! So people asked me if I enjoyed my job and I was like, 'Well, I don't know. Last time, I enjoyed it a lot because I was with my group and I would do all these activities with them. But now, it was different because I was in the office all the time and the children hated me! Because I was the bad cop you know! 'You drank alcohol, you go home!', 'You are punished!' I was like the manager, so it's very different. (…) I am quite surprised that I could resolve all the problems by myself and I know, I know how to work under pressure. In these situations… but anyway, it was really hard of course. I had a girl who suffered an epileptic seizure. I had a girl who was very, very drunk. Highly intoxicated, so she went to the hospital. I had another boy who was very disrespectful. It's normal when you work with teenagers. Everything can happen in a second. Even though it was very stressful, I really liked this job.*

Rocio's job at the language school entailed many responsibilities. Managing 19 groups of 30 students not only involved organisational skills but also disciplinary tasks. Given that she was only 25 at the time of our follow-up interview, she had to adjust to this new role very quickly. When asked whether she was adequately compensated for her efforts, Rocio responded:

> *Anyone who knows that job knows that it's not enough and that you don't do it for the money. It's not enough and I don't do it because of the money... because I work 24 hours. I always work 24 hours, if something happens I need to be on call. It was okay, for me it was okay. I can tell you, it was €1200 for the whole month. The transport is included, the accommodation is included... but anyway, when you think that you never have a day off at all, you work from 7am to 11pm. I had to be in the hospital until 4am with one girl for example. It's okay, I love it, but it's not enough. I have never done this because of the money. It's a lot of work, a lot of responsibility. Of course, it's very different from my job now.[6] I had to control everyone, keep an overview of everyone. If you are a course leader, you also have a lot of responsibility for your students. You also work 24 hours. You need to be there for your students all the time. You don't get a day off... and you get €200 a week! It's nothing.*

Although living costs in the town where Rocio lived were lower than in the UK, a salary of €1200 did not allow her to save much. Furthermore, her work was seasonal, as this language school only operated during the summer months. Despite her low salary and inconsistent work schedule, Rocio took much pride in what she had achieved since moving back from England. Being able to manage quite demanding tasks served as a source of confidence in her skills as a competent educator. This illustrates how she saw an intrinsic value in her work regardless of the financial compensation. That being said, Rocio was also aware that her job at the language school did not provide her with enough stability to plan ahead with regard to buying a house or starting a family. At the time of the interview, she was therefore studying for a competitive exam to become a high school teacher at a state school, which was her long-term biographical project.

Rocio's working conditions at the language school were somewhat typical for that of other returnees. With a few exceptions, many people seemed to receive a salary that allowed them to pay rent and maintenance costs (food, electricity, water) but not much more (ca. €800-€1200/ monthly). Despite carrying many responsibilities, my informants sensed that their negotiating power was somewhat limited due to the job scarcity on the Spanish labour market (see the phenomenon of 'mileuristas' (Gentile, 2014, p. 126)).

A new perspective

The returnees I interviewed differed in terms of how long they had been back and also how much time they had spent abroad. Much like their migration experience, the reintegration processes also appeared to evolve in different stages. Some interviewees had returned only very recently from having spent several years in Germany or the UK. These informants appeared somewhat disoriented, as they were still trying to find out how they 'fitted into' their 'old' yet unfamiliar environments. For others, their stay abroad had only been a short-term episode that already dated back a few years by the time of the interview. Since their return, several of these informants managed to build up a relatively stable existence, both in work-related contexts and their personal lives.

The majority of returnees intended to stay in Spain. In particular, those who had managed to find a stable job by the time of the interview regarded their migration as a closed chapter. There were, however, a few participants who also contemplated emigrating again. In this context, they often mentioned how their city in the UK or Germany had become a 'second home', which served as a safety net in case their plans in Spain did not materialise. This is the phenomenon of 'circular migration' (Vertovec, 2013). As discussed previously, those who had previously lived in the UK expressed deep disappointment about the result of the 2016 EU referendum. They deemed the prospect of possibly not being 'welcomed back' despite having paid taxes in Britain as deeply unfair.

Apart from the idea of returning to the same place again, some informants also expressed their wish to explore new destinations in Europe and overseas (e.g. Latin America), a pattern referred to as 'onward migration' (Ortensi & Barbiano di Belgioso, 2018). After having proven themselves abroad (e.g. by learning a new language fluently, making new friends, etc.), my participants had high self-esteem with regard to their ability to adapt to foreign environments. The prospect of starting from zero again somewhere else did not appear as daunting as it might have been prior to their migration. Furthermore, several participants had built up quite international social networks and were planning to join their friends or partners who were living in other European countries.

I decided to end my discussion on this note to illustrate the somewhat circular nature of how my informants thought about moving in and out of different European countries. The notion of 'home' was no longer confined to the geographic space where they had grown up. Instead they had also made a 'second home' while living abroad. This was a foreign town or city that they had grown familiar with and associated with both positive and negative memories. Some participants were even willing to explore a third, or perhaps even a fourth, destination after realising how much they had gained from this chapter in their lives.

Almost all the participants in my sample shared a certain openness to new experiences and different cultures, a mind-set that many attributed to their migration experience. This finding became especially apparent in my interviews with returnees who were confronted with their 'old' selves when realising that they no longer had anything in common with their childhood friends who had not struggled in a foreign environment.

9. CONCLUSION

This study has been a collaborative project and would not have been complete without my 58 informants' extraordinary openness and willingness to cooperate. Before turning to a discussion on the relevance of this study for different audiences, I would like to recall how I proceeded and provide a brief summary of each chapter. This outline serves as a basis for contextualising what I see as the contribution of this research project.

A BRIEF OVERVIEW OF MY FINDINGS

I started my analysis by developing biographical case studies of three informants, who I named Adam Sanchez, María Navarro and Mateo López. The three informants differed in important aspects, including their age, generational locations (Mannheim, 1928), gender, education, work experiences and general biographical circumstances. The purpose of these case studies was to gain some initial analytical distance from the field to provide the reader with insights into my way of analysing data (Riemann, 2018) and to engage in contrasting comparisons in the sense of Grounded Theory (Glaser & Strauss, 1967). These case studies and their contrasting comparisons served as a basis for developing sensitising research questions and concepts. These research questions were subsequently addressed in five comparative theoretical and empirical chapters in which I drew on the whole data. The sequence of my chapters reflects the stages of the unfolding biographical and other social processes (including non-anticipated collective events) as they became visible in the interviews. In the following, I would like to give a brief overview of these five comparative chapters.

a) Time to Go?

Taking the question 'Migration as an answer to what?' as a starting point, I explicated various biographical patterns: a) 'going abroad' in the context of one's academic training, b) withstanding a collective mood of demoralisation, c) trying to overcome a prolonged period of dependency and stagnation, d) trying to cope with or escape from a trajectory of suffering, e) searching for professional recognition and adequate pay, and f) acquiring foreign language skills as a competitive advantage. These patterns, which sometimes overlapped, illustrate the diversity in biographical conditions and processes through which the decision to migrate evolved.

For some informants the economic crisis impeded their transition to an independent adulthood. They struggled to find stable full-time employment after graduating from university, which meant that they could not move out of their parents' home. Others who had entered the labour market prior to the economic crisis experienced a gradual deterioration of working conditions, job security and pay. Several participants became trapped in deep trajectories of suffering (Schütze, 1995) in Spain, which often emerged out of a combination of personal and financial problems in the context of the collective crisis. Moving abroad appeared like a way to gain control over a situation that they had experienced as quite threatening. There were also people who remained employed throughout the recession but experienced a gradual deterioration of their working conditions and a loss of recognition. They were aware of more attractive opportunities abroad (e.g. in the healthcare sector). A few informants decided to temporarily move to the UK (more so than to Germany) to learn English in the hope of gaining a competitive advantage in the Spanish labour market.

b) On Studying and Working abroad

While the majority of the informants arrived in the new country with the intention of immediately starting work, some people took part in exchange programmes at university at first. These were temporary stays that eventually developed into more permanent migration projects. These (former) exchange students experienced 'moving abroad' as deeply liberating. In Spain, they had lived with their families, which they experienced as tiring, they perceived their academic environment as suffocating, and they were sometimes exhausted by their activist involvement in the 15-M movement. The decision to stay abroad often also had to do with positive experiences with academic mentors and employment prospects in the receiving societies.

Quite a few informants planned a 'transition period' in the new country in order to learn English or German properly before trying to enter the 'real world'. Many young migrants perceived au pair work as an attractive option to 'ease' themselves into the labour market. They could learn the language and become familiar with the new culture without the pressure of having to pay rent. Working for a family, however, involved a number of challenges, including navigating one's own role somewhere between a 'family member' and a 'domestic servant'. Apart from au pair work, there were also a few examples of migrants engaging in alternative economic practices that did not involve any money (i.e. exchange labour for food and accommodation).

After moving to Germany or the UK, the majority of my informants started to work in jobs that were unrelated to their academic training. In this context, I considered various aspects of the experience of unskilled labour, including coping with biographical rupture, dispositions of vulnerability, and attempts at resistance. Furthermore, I discussed the biographical meaning of menial work and the seeming oxymoron of taking pride in – what I referred to as – 'unskilled skillsets'.

The phenomenon of migrants working below their academic qualifications (and work experiences) is well known and commonly framed as a very unfortunate case of unrealised potential. It is true that many of my informants suffered from feelings of alienation, physical exhaustion and difficulties reconciling their current ways of making a living with their academic background and previous biographical achievements. That being said, it was very important to stay sensitive to the nuances of their everyday work experiences, which sometimes included unexpected sources of pride and fulfilment. For quite a few participants, this was their first 'real' job, which allowed them to live as independent adults. That in itself was commonly regarded as an important biographical milestone.

There were a number of informants who could immediately work in their field of expertise after arriving in the new country. These interviewees stood out, as they were usually trained in occupations that were highly sought after in the receiving societies (i.e. nursing, engineering etc.). Although these participants were frequently considered the 'lucky ones' in migrant circles, they dealt with unique challenges such as carrying greater responsibilities despite limited language skills. Their narratives revealed, furthermore, that there are important national differences in some occupational profiles. In Germany, nurses do not have a university degree and many medical tasks are reserved for physicians. This was a source of frustration for some interviewees, who felt irritated by the fact that they were not allowed to make use of skills they had trained for in Spain. I also included a note on the case of 'transnational mobiles' who worked for multinational firms. For these highly successful individuals, gaining international work experience was regarded as normal rather than exceptional.

I concluded this chapter with observations on the experience of voluntary work. Examples included participation in projects supporting isolated elderly people, children, and fellow migrants (co-nationals and refugees). The informants enjoyed this type of work because it also served as an alternative source of meaning and sometimes provided them with a sense of biographical continuity. This was especially important for participants who had jobs that were far below their academic qualifications.

c) A Web of Social Relationships

In this chapter, I discussed my informants' experiences of both maintaining their social ties to Spain as well as the emergence of new friendships in the receiving society. In contrast to earlier generations of migrants, my informants had access to unlimited communication technology and cheap flights. In theory, these greatly facilitate the maintenance of long-distance relationships with partners who stayed in Spain. In practice, however, there appears to be a somewhat illusionary layer to this form of 'virtual intimacy'. Some informants spoke about a gradual estrangement from their significant others, which they retraced to a lack of common experiences and physical contact. The physical distance to Spain also allowed informants to present themselves to their relatives and friends back home in a somewhat idealised light. Some participants shared only their positive experiences while keeping their problems to themselves.

Apart from these types of 'transnational practices', I also discussed my informants' ways of socialising in the receiving societies. The biographical narratives I collected sometimes included sequences where informants drew 'symbolic boundaries' (Lamont, 1992) between themselves and 'ordinary Spanish migrants'. Sometimes these self-distinctions were made on the basis of class and access to cultural capital (Bourdieu, 1984). Several of my Basque and Catalan participants emphasised cultural differences between themselves and migrants from Andalusia, who they sometimes portrayed as less capable of adapting to the new country. Interestingly, these informants commonly underlined historic connections between their region of origin and the receiving society (e.g. British influence in the Basque country), which they perceived as a source of special belonging.

Even though the friendships my informants built in Germany or the UK were described as deep and meaningful, they were also somewhat 'fleeting' and 'transitory' in character. Many informants reported how they eventually grew tired of new people (mostly other EU migrants) coming in and out of their lives all the time. Whilst 'living abroad' was regarded as an interesting chapter in their lives, they eventually longed for more stability, a theme that would also become important in their plans to eventually return to Spain.

I also included observations on my informants' perception of the host societies. In this discussion, I paid special attention to cultural differences in what is perceived to be 'polite' in Spain and the respective destination country. My participants often described themselves as *warm* but *direct*, in contrast to British people who they perceived as *polite* but *cold*. In this context, German co-workers and superiors were sometimes portrayed as *cold* and *direct*, a combination that several informants experienced as intimidating.

d) Established-Outsider Relations in Times of Brexit

In the chapter on the collective crisis of Brexit, I decided to focus on the experiences of a single participant whose argumentative oral presentation appeared especially rich in this context. Diego, who worked as a nurse in a public hospital in Bristol, encountered the topic of Brexit on an everyday basis because patients kept confronting him with the issue. Drawing on Elias's and Scotson's (1965) 'established-outsider' figurations, it was possible to identify the emergence of new 'we' groups, forms of solidarity and attempts at resistance. Some Brexit-supporting patients were sympathetic to Diego (trying to adopt him symbolically as 'one of us'), while at the same time gossiping about other 'undesirable' EU migrants from central and eastern Europe. Diego felt uncomfortable with this type of preferential treatment, highlighting the important contributions of Polish cleaners in the hospital. Along with other informants in my study, Diego 'intellectualised' the phenomenon by framing Brexit as an ignorant decision that British people would eventually come to regret. Such phenomena could also be detected in other interviews. The topic of Brexit permeated the relationships and everyday encounters with British interaction partners. Assessing the other person's stance on this issue served as a litmus test for deciding *are you for me or against me?*

e) An Uneasy Homecoming

My last empirical chapter dealt with the experiences of returnees who moved back to Spain after spending a (prolonged) period of time working or studying abroad. Drawing on Alfred Schütz's 'The Homecomer' (1945), I discussed the fragmented nature of my informants' relationships with their old, yet somehow unfamiliar, social environments. Their expectations of 'moving home' rarely aligned with reality, which was sometimes quite a disorienting process. Despite clear signs of economic recovery in Spain, most of the returnees found it quite difficult to get a full-time job that could secure them a stable, independent existence. Some people eventually found modest stability in the form of jobs that paid enough to cover their bills but not much more, which has been referred to as the situation of the so-called 'mileuristas' (Holleran, 2019). While their newly acquired language skills (mostly English) did play a role in getting hired, these informants often had to rely on their personal networks to get an interview in the first place. Without any personal connections, finding an attractive position in Spain still appeared to be very difficult as some informants recalled sending out hundreds of applications without getting any response.

ADDRESSING DIFFERENT AUDIENCES

When thinking about the possible relevancies, uses and implications of this study, different audiences come to mind. In the following, I will share some thoughts on what I would like potential readers to take away from this book.

a) Migrant communities and returnees

When writing up my chapters, I tried to present my findings in a way that is accessible to readers without a social science background. I wanted, for example, 'new' Spanish migrants to be able to recognise themselves in the biographical processes of others or to find this research project useful for reflecting on how their own experiences differ. I imagine that some people may see themselves in the narratives of others when they read about certain difficult experiences that are usually not talked about openly. Gaining a certain background awareness of others in similar situations may offer some individuals a way to break out of their own isolation.

Spontaneous, biographical narration without the fear of being judged can be quite an empowering act. It is a form of communication that is not reserved for academic purposes only. Some migrants may use this form of storytelling as a way to organise self-help initiatives and build communities of people in similar situations. One example that comes to my mind in this context is the case of the returnees. The reality of 'moving home' rarely aligned with what my informants had expected. Their experiences abroad were often met with disinterest in their old, yet somewhat unfamiliar, social circles. Not being able to properly share (and sometimes 'work through') these experiences with anyone can be quite a numbing and isolating process.

There are already a few organisations in Spain that support returnees e.g. in their re-integration into the Spanish labour market and society ('Volvemos')[1]. Perhaps the organisers may recognise the potential of this form of biographical storytelling in empowering individuals and generate new insights and perspectives among (former) migrants. In a protected space (under the rules of confidentiality), it may be possible to arrange for some kind of self-help communication, which encourages people to learn about themselves and to discover things they have in common by listening to others. This is simply one idea for how to raise awareness about certain problem constellations and provide some form of relief for people in difficult situations (e.g. in overcoming feelings of shame and stagnation). I could also imagine some forms of cultural expression using biographical narration (e.g. in the form of documentary films, art projects etc.) when dealing with the experiences of migration and returning.

b) Members of the receiving societies

Apart from Spanish migrants, I also hope to reach readers who are 'native' members of the receiving societies. As discussed before, the current political climate in many European countries is marked by a harsh anti-immigration rhetoric. In the case of the UK, the current Conservative government has targeted Europeans specifically.[2] Campaigning for the last House of Commons election, Prime Minister Boris Johnson suggested that EU migrants had gotten ahead of themselves by feeling 'at home' in Britain (O'Carroll, 2019), a cynical statement that touched a sensitive nerve in migrant communities. Although there appears to be less prejudice against Spanish migrants than against their central and eastern European counterparts, some informants spoke about experiences of discrimination. Ethnocentric stereotypes entail oversimplified, one-dimensional visions of the unknown 'other'. When thinking about the relevance of this study beyond academia, I hope it serves as somewhat of a corrective to the anti-immigration rhetoric that is currently displayed by those in positions of power. In a modest way, I hope to have made some of my informants' *invisible* contributions to their destination countries more *visible* (e.g. their voluntary work with children, elderly people and refugees). I believe that this area deserves more attention in the public discourse.

Another (lay) audience that may take an interest in this study is German or British employers. Some informants were trained in occupations that are highly sought after in the receiving societies. The significant labour shortages in healthcare sectors across Europe serve as one example. There are thousands of open positions, which hospitals (and care homes, for example) currently struggle to fill. This is a serious problem that is exacerbated by the current coronavirus pandemic. Therefore, employers have a strong interest in not only recruiting but also *keeping* their foreign staff. Both in the UK and Germany, quite a few Spanish healthcare workers have prematurely decided to go home albeit for different reasons. Learning more about the nurses' biographical background and specific needs could thereby be an important tool to tackle this issue.

c) Implications for professional work and policymaking

By narrating 'how one thing led to another' in their lives, many informants shared painful experiences of suffering and losing control but also revealed important sources of meaning and skills. This insight deserves attention in the context of professional counselling of migrants. By listening to people's 'whole story', counsellors gain access to more resources that can be useful for understanding their complex life circumstances.

This may involve 'picking up' on earlier biographical interests, which individuals may have almost forgotten. In this study one can discover many problem constellations in which my informants might have needed professional support. Examples include coping with unemployment, personal crises, the decision to migrate, difficult work experiences abroad, as well as complications associated with returning to Spain.

The European Union has an interest in facilitating the free labour movement of its citizens. The situation of university graduates working in low-skilled jobs in different EU member states constitutes a problem, not only because it is a source of personal frustration, but also because the scale of the phenomenon adds up to significant macro-economic costs that are to some extent avoidable. Whilst there have been a few programmes aimed at e.g. recruiting young people from southern Europe for apprenticeships in Germany (MobiPro)[3], the success of these initiatives has been quite meagre (cf. Schryro, 2018). Many participants dropped out prematurely and returned to their home countries. In newspaper articles on this topic, journalists commonly cited very general themes and truisms such as language barriers and homesickness. When designing future programmes, it may be useful to engage in 'biographical policy evaluations'. Apitzsch et al. (2019) have done such evaluations in order to discover the relevance of policies and legal frameworks for biographical developments (e.g. in the context of evaluating migration policies in different EU member states). This line of research might be helpful in designing labour market integration programmes for different groups of migrants, including refugees.

d) A note for social scientists

Although my general research interest emerged in the context of the economic crisis in Spain, I did not simply presume that my informants had left their home country *because* of it. Instead, I gave each informant the space to share his/her unique life history, always remaining open to the discovery of new insights (Glaser & Strauss, 1967). The careful sequential analysis of their narratives revealed that their decision to leave Spain was a response to complicated biographical circumstances in the context of structural conditions and a collective crisis. This is quite different to asking informants 'why' they had decided to migrate. The latter approach often provokes responses that are primarily argumentative in character because interviewees feel under pressure to justify their decision by listing reasonable and sound motives. This can be problematic, as they may leave out important – yet somewhat disorderly – experiences and biographical processes, which cannot be reduced to a short and simple answer.

In the introduction, I referred to antagonistic patterns of interpretation with regard to young people's motivations to migrate that have emerged in the public discourse in Spain. My informants' migration projects, however, cannot be neatly pushed into either a positive ('spirit of adventure') or negative ('economic exile') frame. That is not to say, of course, that the biographical narratives I collected were apolitical in any way. In fact, many interviewees expressed how deeply frustrated they were about Spanish politics and institutions, which they believed had failed them[4]. I simply chose a bottom-up approach and kept some distance from these politically charged interpretations. Following the principles of Grounded Theory, I wanted to listen to my interviewees' biographical narratives with as few preconceptions as possible. My aim was to understand what they had gone through and how they made sense of their experiences in retrospect.

I would like to add a note on the type of analysis that I used. As indicated in the literature review, the majority of social scientists working on the 'new' Spanish migration have so far focused on very specific aspects and phases of migration experiences. Although traces of the informants' life histories and their biographical work of reflecting on their lives[5] could sometimes be found in data extracts used to illustrate such findings, their biographies themselves were not the focus of these studies. When reviewing existing publications on the 'new' Spanish migration, I often had the impression that biographical processes as such were not regarded as a proper and legitimate object of social scientific inquiry. The authors seemed less interested in the minute details or putative chaos of biographical developments than they were in their interviewees' evaluative and argumentative generalisations about collective circumstances and developments (about the widespread corruption and nepotism in Spain). For the reader, it was then difficult to put these quite general statements into a biographical context and to assess their functions for the respective interviewee.

The research approach I chose for this study is somewhat different. I have paid close attention to my informants' (often seemingly disorderly) narrative presentation of their experiences and what such details could reveal about biographical processes and the biographical meaning of their migration projects. I am not alone in these interests, as this form of biographical research has become quite well known in German-speaking countries and Poland. In the analysis of my data, which was informed by Schütze's (2008) socio-linguistically based analysis of social processes, I avoided taking my informants' self-representation and their own theorising at face value. Instead,

I carefully differentiated between different schemes of communication such as narration, argumentation and description. I paid attention to formal as well as substantive features of the texts and engaged in a careful sequential analysis in order to discover what the structure of their narratives revealed about what they had gone through – and how they made sense of it in retrospect (in argumentative commentaries). Sometimes, these analyses detected painful experiences that the informants found difficult to come to terms with and had "faded out" of their awareness (Schütze, 1992). In such cases, these experiences only became visible in symptomatic (i.e. non-intentional) textual indicators, such as self-corrective background constructions (Schütze, 2008; Riemann 2018), complex argumentative sequences (e.g. before a coda)[6], and conspicuous intonation patterns. The intensive consideration of formal textual features distinguishes this socio-linguistically based analysis of social processes from other ways of doing qualitative research. I also hope to have shown that a detailed sequential analysis of single cases can already lead to first insights on societal conditions and biographical developments. These insights can be further refined by contrastive comparisons.

I aimed to provide a holistic view on the experiences of 'new' Spanish migrants in the context of the economic crisis. I did not restrict my focus to what happened exclusively in Spain or the receiving societies in Germany and the UK. Instead, I shifted my attention towards the inner form of my interviewees' biographies and how the different phases in their lives are interconnected. I was thereby particularly intent on reconstructing the structural processes of their life courses (biographical action schemes, trajectories of suffering, institutional expectation patterns and creative metamorphoses) and other social processes, which sometimes developed over the course of several years.

Taking on a life history perspective was a way to 'follow my informants around' closely wherever they were – regardless of national borders. The study at hand serves as an example of how to gain a deeper understanding of the effect of different (yet interrelated) European crises on the lives of individuals, on their suffering and also their attempts to regain control. Analysing people's biographies in-depth should therefore not be confused with a mere micro-sociological exercise. Instead, it offers a way to overcome the micro-macro divide in the social sciences. In other words, I aimed to provide a 'high resolution' picture of how structural changes unfold in the lives of individuals. It is my belief that by paying close attention to such minute details in individual life histories, one can learn a lot about what is happening in society at large. A careful interpretation of spontaneous autobiographical storytelling allows for a reconstruction of how macro conditions, collective crises and participation in collective movements leave their mark in people's life histories. This basic insight is applicable to quite a wide range of topics, which could be the subject of future studies. I regard my study as a contribution to biographical research in the field of migration studies and as just one example of how to study Europe 'from below'.

I would like to address a few points of potential criticism.

For readers unfamiliar with biographical research, the detailed analysis of single narratives might be irritating. What is the point of zooming in on quite personal details in people's biographies, including inner thought processes about *how* they arrived at certain decisions? If it is not generalisable, why include it in the analysis? Is this even proper sociology?

I strongly disagree with this notion. As I explicate in the methodological appendix, there has been a long sociological tradition of doing research on written and oral autobiographical narratives, which can be retraced to the Chicago School of Sociology. When collecting this type of data, one cannot avoid interpreting them. They do not speak for themselves. I also do not think that it is fruitful to skip the analysis of a specific text and to formulate quick generalisations based on impressions of many data. I have tried to make my interpretive procedures and my interpretation of texts as visible as possible. I think it is always rewarding to enter into a discussion about different readings of a specific text. I invite readers to present alternative interpretations if they do not agree with what I offer as my analysis of certain sequences from interviews.

I have been reluctant in my use of concepts that have become influential in research and theorising on migration. This preference for a selective use or sometimes avoidance of such concepts has to do with my general commitment to Grounded Theory (Glaser & Strauss, 1967). During the analysis, I was very careful never to 'force concepts on my data'. Let me briefly illustrate my approach to two concepts.

I did not have any problems referring to *'transnationalism'* (Vertovec, 2009; Bartram et al., 2014, pp. 140-144) and *'transnational practices'* when I detected such phenomena in my data. I agree with Bartram et al. (2014, p. 143), who write that "some components of transnationalism seem genuinely new, or at least so much more prevalent as to constitute a qualitative change", but that it is also important that the transnationalism perspective "has helped us

(…) to see that earlier arguments about assimilation had overlooked patterns of transnationalism in earlier migration streams."[7] Early examples are the transnational spaces of the Polish Chicago of Thomas and Znaniecki (1918-1920) or the Russian Berlin of the 1920s and early 1930s (Schlögel, 2019).

In explicating new phenomena of transnationalism, researchers refer to the radical changes in global technology and transportation. Vertovec (2009, p. 15) states that "the speed and intensity of communication between home and away has created in many contexts a 'normative transnationalism' in which migrants abroad are ever more closely aware of what is happening in the sending context and vice-versa." My informants fit this profile, as they had access to mobile phones, Skype and cheap flights that made it easy to stay in touch with friends and family in Spain. The findings of this study, however, point to a certain 'illusionary layer' of communication technology, which became visible at different points in this book. One example was the difficulties of maintaining intimate bonds over a distance.

The difficulties (if not the impossibility) of organising one's lives in two different countries became especially apparent in my chapter on 'homecoming'. Even though all of the returnees I interviewed had access to communication technology and cheap flights, they encountered the same problems Alfred Schütz identified in his essay on "The Homecomer" back in 1945. Despite having kept 'in touch' with their friends and family whilst they were abroad, they felt deeply estranged from their old yet somehow unfamiliar social environment. None of them could simply pick up their social life where they had left it. This was a painful experience that most interviewees had not anticipated before moving back to Spain. I think such tensions do not fit easily with Bartram's et al. (2014, p. 141) designation of "a key element of transnationalism: emigrants often continue to be members of the communities they have left behind". I encountered something like a weakening membership (and a fragility of long-distance relationships) without denying the relevance of the new historical phenomena, which are discussed in the research on transnationalism.

There is one theoretical concept that has often been used in research on EU mobility (including studies on the 'new' Spanish migration), which I find quite problematic. The concept of *'liquid migration'* (Engbersen & Snel, 2013), which is influenced by Bauman's work on 'liquid modernity', suggests that EU movers today consciously choose to keep their options open concerning where to live long-term. In the light of the often quite painful biographical processes that were revealed at different points of this study, I felt that it would be inappropriate to ascribe my informants "a specific *migratory habitus* of intentional unpredictability" (Engbersen & Snel, 2013, p. 35), one of their six dimensions of liquid migration.[8] Many of my participants felt that the option of a stable and predictable career path in Spain had been taken away from them due to structural conditions outside of their control. Most of them had a clear idea of their long-term professional and personal goals, including where to live. Even the younger informants in my study were often frustrated by having to work under precarious conditions that did not allow for long-term planning and stability. Whilst the term 'liquid migration' may apply to a few migration projects in my sample, I did not want to subsume the majority or even a larger part of my interviewees under this concept, as it would not have done justice to the complexity of the life histories I collected.

Readers might miss some themes that I have chosen not to discuss in depth. My sample is quite large for a biographical study of this kind. Writing up my findings, I often had to make quite pragmatic editing choices when deciding which topics to focus on in my empirical chapters. I could have easily set some other accents in the presentation of my findings or gone into different directions during my fieldwork (i.e. by making other theoretical sampling decisions). At some point, I simply had to come to terms with the sample as it is, including its strengths and limitations. This study was never designed as a country comparison between the two receiving societies, which is why I did not explicitly compare the experiences of my informants in Germany and in the UK. Instead, I discussed them in a joint manner.

That being said – there are, of course, important economic, legal, administrative, cultural and linguistic differences between these two field sites. Some readers might have wished for a more explicit discussion of the latter. I tried to deal with such issues when they came up in the data (see my chapter on "established-outsider relations in times of Brexit", my reference to British zero-hour contracts and German mini jobs, my discussion of the experiences of Spanish nurses with the German division of labour in hospitals, and the section on different forms of politeness in Europe), but of course, a more systematic discussion of the respective national labour markets and administrative procedures could have been possible. I also referred to gender aspects when they appeared relevant in my data analysis, but I did not devote a whole chapter to this topic. These are simply a few limitations in this study, which underline the potential for future research in this area.

One reader criticised that I did not do more with the category of generation in theoretical terms. I referred to generational experiences when interviewees explicitly referred to them in the interviews, often by using the personal pronoun "we". Examples include comparisons between their life chances and those of their parents' generation, and/or references to other Spanish migrants in terms of a generational membership (e.g. when describing their involvement in the 15-M movement). Some informants used the term "generación ni ni" in a pejorative sense to draw symbolic boundaries between themselves and others who apparently *"neither work nor study"*.

I have explicated specific features of generational experiences in several chapters, e.g., in the distinction between different biographical contexts in which migration projects emerged. That being said, I think that it is possible to attempt a more explicit re-analysis of the data in terms of a generational analysis (employing Mannheim's (1928) theory, which entails distinctions such as "generational location", "generational context" and "generational unit"). For this book, I simply decided not to go in this direction. This had to do with my attempt to keep a certain distance from terms that are invoked in Spanish public discourse, such as "lost generation", a category that also appears in academic writings (Holleran, 2019). Since my interviewees did not use this term when speaking about their personal experiences, I decided not to use it in the analysis.

LOOKING BACK AND LOOKING AHEAD

I am very grateful for my informants' trust in me and I hope to have done justice to their biographical narratives. This is not an exhaustive study on the 'new' Spanish migration, as there are still areas that have not been studied sufficiently. This holds especially true against the background of the recent political, economic and health-related developments.

The Covid-19 pandemic has brought about extreme societal changes that would have formerly been unimaginable. At the time of writing, the coronavirus has already claimed over 5.6 million lives worldwide. There have been over 359 million reported cases of people contracting the virus (WHO, 2022). The on-going vaccination rollout is a silver lining in what can only be described as one of the darkest chapters in recent history. Throughout the past one and a half years, governments in Europe and overseas have taken unprecedented measures in an attempt to control the virus. Such policies included economic lockdowns, the resurrection of national borders, travel bans, and invasive restrictions of people's personal mobility. Apart from the devastating human costs, the economic impact of this unprecedented crisis has been substantial. Several industries that had previously been thought of as quite stable (e.g. air travel and hospitality) collapsed within a very short period of time. As a consequence, millions of people have already lost their jobs, homes and at times, means of existence. It may take many years to recover from this unprecedented crisis, which is a daunting prospect for millions – if not billions – of people across the globe.

In an attempt to make sense of what is happening at the moment, several commentators have already drawn parallels to the last global financial crisis that started fourteen years ago. There has been a worldwide concern for the 'class of 2020'[9], who have graduated from university in the midst of the pandemic. Instead of moving to bigger cities and starting their careers, countless recent graduates have found themselves back in their parents' home with no clear perspective on how to proceed with their lives (Jones, 2020).[10] Journalists and policy makers have expressed concern about the potential emergence of a 'coronavirus lost generation' (Privitera, 2020). Is this 2008 all over again or will it be even worse this time?

Whilst the informants in this study were able to pack their bags and move elsewhere in the European Union, this process has become much more complicated since 2020. The new obstacles to this form of labour mobility are multi-layered. Apart from the obvious health risks and travel restrictions, it has become much more difficult to find a job, even in EU member states formerly deemed economically stable. After arriving in the new country, a significant number of my informants worked in the hospitality sector, e.g., as kitchen porters, waiters, or cleaners in restaurants and hotels. This is an industry that has been affected especially hard by the pandemic. Countless businesses have either significantly reduced their number of staff, filed for bankruptcy and/or are entirely dependent on state subsidies. Taking into account how many people have become redundant during the pandemic, the competition for informal jobs has become fiercer. The prospect of having to compete with native speakers for jobs, which were formerly regarded as quite unattractive, may send discouraging signals to those who are contemplating migration.

Brexit, another on-going crisis, further complicates this matter. As indicated in chapter seven, EU nationals living in the UK have been undergoing a process that has been referred to as 'turning citizens into immigrants' (Bhambra, 2017) by gradually restricting their rights. Millions of people have applied for the 'settled status' scheme but are yet to be informed about the final outcome. The treatment of 'new arrivals' from Europe has been even harsher, as there have been cases of unlawful detentions at British airports and forced deportations (Tremlett & O'Carroll, 2021, May 13). These incidences would have been unimaginable in 2014 when I first started collecting data for this study in the UK. In many ways, Brexit has been a painful collective experience, which I, as a German citizen, have shared with my informants for the majority of my graduate studies in Cambridge.

The long-term repercussions of Brexit remain an open question at this stage.[11] EU migration to Britain will certainly continue but some of it will be criminalised. For many of my informants, their right to free movement had offered them a 'way out' of difficult biographical circumstances that often (but not always) had to do with the economic crisis in Spain. Moving to the UK was often experienced as an act of emancipation to take control and give their lives a new direction. This door is now rapidly closing.

What I documented in this study covers only the initial stages of the Brexit process. There are (and will be) many open research questions in this context. This study has shown that there are unique benefits to biographical research (on the basis of narrative interviews) in studying collective developments in different European countries and how they are reflected in the lifelines of individuals. I hope that other social scientists find it useful when designing future studies on other intra-European movements.

While this research project relied almost exclusively on biographical narratives, there is also much potential to combine it with other research methods. Take, for instance, my data that points to the emergence of uniquely European spaces in the UK, where individuals from different EU member states work together (e.g. hotels, hospitals, restaurants etc.) and sometimes form relationships that become biographically significant. When trying to gain a deeper understanding of the emerging 'established-outsider relations in times of Brexit', it might be sensible to conduct ethnographic research or group discussions.

I am inviting my academic and non-academic readers to assess my findings critically. Perhaps they will discover points in my data that I have overlooked. For me, an exhaustive interpretation of the narratives has not been as important as presenting my informants' life histories in a way that makes such critical assessment possible (Riemann, 2018). I hope to have provided the reader with a deep sense of who my participants are and what they went through at different stages in their lives. These biographies were marked by structural conditions outside of the individual's control but also entailed many experiences of actively coping with difficult challenges and finding creative solutions. My informants' stories are a stories of vulnerability, but also ones of human endurance and resistance.

10. METHODOLOGICAL APPENDIX

Before turning to my own field research, I will give a short overview of the history of biographical research and will provide some background about the analytical procedures and their theoretical underpinnings on which my study is based.

A NOTE ON BIOGRAPHICAL RESEARCH

The interest in the collection and analysis of life histories and other 'personal documents' has not just been confined to sociology but has marked the development of other social scientific disciplines as well (Allport, 1942; Gottschalk et al., 1945). But, of course, this has been a chequered history. While an interest in such data declined, such as in the mainstream of psychology, the situation has been quite different in parts of anthropology.

The beginning of a sociological interest in life histories and 'personal documents' is usually located in the early Chicago sociology of the 1920s and 1930s, when students often wrote their empirical theses under the supervision of Robert Park and Ernest Burgess (Bulmer, 1984). The best known example of early Chicago biographical research is Thomas and Znaniecki's (1918/1920) "The Polish Peasant in Europe and America". Bulmer (1984) argues that the study "marked a shift in sociology away from abstract theory and library research toward a more intimate acquaintance with the empirical world, studied nevertheless in terms of a theoretical frame" (p. 45). The authors succeeded in providing a more sensitive and subtle account of the experience of migration and life in America than would have been possible without the extensive qualitative data they collected – including a series of letters that relatives sent to and from Poland, newspaper accounts and records of social agencies and courts. The systematic use of letters as sociological data was original at the time and so was the use of a second type of data, namely written life histories – in this case, the life history that Polish immigrant Wladek Wisniewski had written down and which appeared in the third volume of the five-volume publication of 1918-1920. Even a century after its original publication, sociologists keep revisiting this piece of research by offering detailed re-interpretations of what Wisniewski had written about his life (cf. Waniek, 2019). It has also been noted that there are strong affinities between Thomas and Znaniecki's perspectives on Polish migration and current theorising on transnationalism (Sinatti, 2008).

Quite a few Chicago studies of the 1920s and 1930s made use of "personal documents" such as letters, diaries and written life-histories (besides ethnographic fieldnotes, social work files and many other data), which allowed insights into biographical processes, personal relationships and intimate experiences. Students were encouraged to collect life-histories of immigrants, and it is still worth considering the suggestions they were given by the Chicago sociologist Vivien Palmer, who compiled an interesting manual on the basis of her experience as a supervisor of students' research projects (Palmer, 1928, pp. 149-150).

> The life-history may be secured by conversing with the person or by having him write his autobiography. (…) If the data are obtained entirely through conversation it will be advisable to have the person narrate the story of his life with as few interruptions as possible and to discuss specific points with him later. The appeal for co-operation can usually be made on the basis of securing the history of the experience of people of his group in America, and the interest evinced in the narrative opens the way for more intimate confidences.

This sounds very similar to my own interviewing for this study, except that Vivien Palmer and her students could not use portable audio-recorders, which had not yet been invented at the time of their research.

There were other fields of sociological interest in which life histories were collected and co-produced with the assistance of sociologists who also provided analytical commentaries in the publications, especially in the field of juvenile delinquency. The most well-known of these documents is Clifford Shaw's "The Jack-Roller: A Delinquent Boy's Own Story", originally published in 1930 and republished in 1966 with an introduction by Howard Becker. Becker's (1966) introductory comments suggest that at the time of the re-publication of "The Jack-Roller" such texts still fascinated sociologists, especially symbolic interactionists who studied deviance (Rubington & Weinberg, 1968), even though the relevance and appreciation of such data had declined since the proliferation of survey research during the 1930s and the dominance of structural functionalism in American sociology after the Second World War. Procedures for an intersubjectively controllable analysis of written life-histories and other personal documents were not yet available, and doing research on such a basis lacked the impressive rigour of quantitative investigations.

Biographical research never totally disappeared in the post WW2 period (see for example, Oscar Lewis' "The Children of Sanchez" (1961) and other writings of anthropologists). It led a niche existence in the social sciences – except in Polish sociology (Szczepanski, 1962) where 'the biographical method' flourished even under state socialism, partially due to the lasting influence of Znaniecki. But in the late 1970s and early 1980s, sociological biographical research re-emerged on an international level when Daniel Bertaux, Paul Thompson and other European social scientists coordinated their activities (especially in the International Sociological Association) and started joint projects, including the journal "Life Stories/Récits de Vie" (Inowlocki, 2018). In this period several influential publications appeared that gave an impression of diverse thematic interests, attracting researchers to this field in different countries (Bertaux, 1981; Thompson, 1978; Thompson with Bornat, 2017; Plummer, 1983, 2001b; Kohli, 1978; Kohli & Robert, 1984). These included interests in:

- Understanding societal processes which led to the de-standardisation of the normal life-course regime and new forms of "individualisation" (Kohli, 1986) (and the need to overcome traditional sociological ways of separately studying phases of the life-cycle);
- Developing new and less restrictive forms of research communication in which participants, often members of underprivileged communities and stigmatised minorities, were given a voice and were encouraged to share their biographical experiences by freely narrating them (an

interest which has been shared with researchers in the field of oral history);
- Devising innovative and disciplined procedures of analysing oral narratives (which have also proved useful for the interpretation of written autobiographies); and
- Understanding the impact of authoritarian and totalitarian forms of government, collective crises and catastrophes (such as wars and genocides) on life histories (a self-reflexive research interest which is very visible in biographical research in Germany and central and eastern Europe).

At this point it is not possible to give an overview of the differentiation and ramification of biographical research in sociology and other social sciences in the last four decades. There are distinct differences between the styles of biographical research and related fields in countries like France (Bertaux, 2016), the UK (and other countries in which English is used) and Germany. The situation in the UK (see Nurse & O'Neill, 2018) is very much marked by the dynamic and innovative potential of the oral history movement with a strong egalitarian appeal to appropriating history 'from below' (Thompson & Bornat, 2017; Perks & Thomson, 2016) and making it useful for different practical purposes. Several oral historians have argued that the alleged 'unreliability of memory' can also be seen as a strength of the approach rather than a weakness. They argued that oral histories provide researchers with "clues not only about the meanings of historic experiences, but also between the relationship between past and present, between memory and personal identity, and between individual and collective memory" (Thomson, 2007, p. 54).

Recent handbooks on narrative and life history (Goodson et al., 2017) and biographical research (Lutz et al., 2018) reveal the diversity of theoretical and substantive interests and the ways in which researchers reflect about the types of oral narratives they collected, such as political narratives (see Goodson et al., 2017, pp. 271-402). Similar to the early (Chicago) phase of biographical research the study of migrants' lives (Apitzsch & Siouti, 2007; Siouti, 2017) has been an especially dynamic field. There have been numerous biographical studies on the generation of the 'guest workers' and their children (e.g., Juhasz & Mey, 2003), care workers from eastern Europe (e.g., Karakayali, 2010; Satola, 2015) and many other countries (Lutz, 2011), new forms of intra-European mobility (e.g., Waniek, 2012; Domecka, 2019) and patterns of transmigration (e.g., Siouti, 2013, 2019) and forced and 'illegalised' migration (e.g., Rosenthal & Bogner, 2017; Worm, 2019). A well-known example of biographical migration research is Catherine Delcroix's (2013) single case study on the Nour family, a Moroccan immigrant family in France. There has been a lively transnational cooperation in biographical migration studies between doctoral students from Strasbourg and Frankfurt (see Apitzsch et al., 2014). Ideas on how to use biographical single case studies for the evaluation of migration policies in different countries (Apitzsch et al. 2019) have also been generated in this context.

Getting an overview of the different analytical approaches, which have developed in biographical research and oral history in different countries (see Thompson with Bornat, 2017, pp. 351-391) is a challenge. It is also not easy to get a sense of the actual work practices, including how researchers go about understanding and analysing the data in front of them (Riemann, 2018). One approach, which has received a lot of attention in the English-speaking world, is Chamberlayne's and Wengraf's biographic-narrative-interpretive method or BNIM (Wengraf, 2001), which is strongly influenced by the research strategies of Fischer and Rosenthal (Fischer-Rosenthal & Rosenthal, 1997; Rosenthal, 2004). Their work is partially rooted in the sociological approach on which my study is based, but they use and combine other resources as well for their differentiation between the experienced and the narrated life history, especially Aron Gurwitsch's phenomenology and Ulrich Oevermann's Objective Hermeneutics (cf. Oevermann, 2002). I will now turn to the sociological approach on which my study is based. This approach is still not very well known in the social sciences outside of German speaking countries and Poland[1]. Therefore, I will provide some background on how it emerged and developed.

THE AUTOBIOGRAPHICAL NARRATIVE INTERVIEW AND PROCEDURES OF SEQUENTIAL ANALYSIS

a) A note on the development of the research approach[2]

This study is based on research strategies developed by the German sociologist Fritz Schütze in the 1970s and early 1980s. Schütze, who had done intensive theoretical studies in the sociology of language. He was under the impression that there was a deep gap between interesting sociological insights (e.g. with regard to phenomena such as 'non-decision making', etc.) and their convincing detectability in empirical data. While the criticism of standard sociological research had remained on a very abstract and theoretical level in the German dispute on positivism (in 1968), he was interested in using interpretive sociological approaches (especially ethnomethodological conversational analysis and Symbolic Interactionism) and sociolinguistics for the development of new forms of data collection and analysis. His idea was that new methods should systematically be based on communicative competencies of members of society, such as on people's ability to narrate, to argue and to describe in an orderly fashion. This orderliness had to be discovered and respected in the various phases of the research process. Qualitative researchers such as the aforementioned Vivien Palmer (1928) had certainly intuitively oriented themselves to such orderliness, but Schütze's idea was that the intersubjective controllability of the research process could be improved by taking the activities and constraints of different schemes of communication (see Kallmeyer & Schütze, 1977) into account in a more systematic manner.

The form of interviewing which became known as the 'narrative interview' (Schütze, 1977) did not originate in biographical research but in a research project on community power which Schütze conducted at the University of Bielefeld in the 1970s. Local politicians were asked to narrate their involvement in a certain political crisis, and while they told their story the interviewers did not interrupt them. Questions were asked after the coda (Labov & Waletzky, 1967), the final formulation of the narrative. This format worked surprisingly well, the spontaneous narratives revealed much (about politicians' involvement in political backstage events), which the interviewees would have otherwise kept to themselves in standardised interviews.

In studying these narratives, Schütze discovered and explicated a phenomenon which became quite important for the reconstructive analysis of the experiences of an interviewee: off-the-cuff-storytelling about personal experiences (not just in interviews, but also in encounters in everyday life) was marked by certain narrative constraints. (Of course, it is possible to circumvent such constraints by carefully planning or rehearsing one's story.) These three constraints were already mentioned in the first paper on the narrative interview (Schütze, 1977), the following quote (in which he also added the noun 'drive') is taken from a more recent publication, which appeared in English (Schütze, 2014, p. 236).

There are three of them: (1) the drive and constraint to condense, (2) the drive and constraint to go into details, (3) and the drive and constraint to close the textual forms (Schütze, 1982). The narrative drive and constraint to condense entails the narrator's being driven to tell only what is relevant in terms of central "knots" of the overall happenings in the story to be told. Single events and situations have to be evaluated and weighed permanently in terms of the announced overall thematic meaning and moral of the story to be told. The narrative drive and constraint to go into details has the following effect: if the narrator has told event A, then she or he has to go on and has to tell also event B related to event A as the next link in the chain of experienced events – these events are concatenated formally in temporal succession, causality, finality, et cetera. In case of implausibility of the envisaged narrative proceeding from event A to event B, there has to be a "background search," a checking of the details of the supposed link between events A and B. The narrative constraint to close the forms (*Gestalten*) has the following impact: the narrator is driven to finish the depiction of an experiential pattern (such as an episode in the unfolding of events, an interaction situation, a chapter in one's own life history, etc.). This implies the closing up of embedded experiential patterns. In off-the-cuff storytelling, there is always an undecided competition between these three narrative drives and constraints, whereas in written storytelling the competition between the drives resp. constraints becomes re-harmonized and disguised under the polished surface of a literary make-up.

When studying the interviews with the politicians, Schütze noticed that there were many traces of the interviewees' biographies, which he found difficult to fully grasp and analyse. Therefore, he decided to try out interviews in which interaction partners were asked to tell their whole life history – a form of interviewing (the autobiographical narrative interview) on which my study is based.

In sequentially analysing these interviews (in a style informed by conversational analysis) Schütze noticed a certain regularity in which similar formulations reappeared in order to announce a decisive shift in the character of one's experiences. He used the linguistic term 'suprasegmental markers' for these formulations because they marked the beginning of longer sequences which extended over more than one narrative segment. This discovery became important for categorising certain structural processes of the life course (Schütze, 1981; 2008) – concepts that became quite influential in biographical research, especially in German speaking countries and Poland

(I made use of them in the analysis of my narratives, e.g., in my three case studies and in other chapters):

- Biographical action schemes by which persons actively shape their life course (e.g. biographical projects in choosing a certain occupation or joining a social movement, projects of migration, but also schemes of regaining control in difficult life situations or escaping from them etc.);
- Trajectories of suffering and losing control "in which persons are not capable of actively shaping their own life anymore, since they can only react to overwhelming outer events; in the course of their suffering they become strange to themselves" (Schütze, 2008, p. 11)[3];
- Institutional expectation patterns, in which people are orienting to normative and institutional expectations, e.g., with regard to what is expected from them in certain stages of the lifecycle or in phases of an occupational career;
- Creative metamorphoses of biographical identity – the emergence of various kinds of creativity, a development that is often surprising and puzzling for the person.

Carefully using such concepts, which should not be misunderstood as 'ideal types', is always based on the detection of pertinent textual indicators.[4] It would be a misunderstanding and contrary to basic assumptions of grounded theory if one applied them (top down) as fixed terms from a vocabulary book. It is always possible to refine such concepts and to discover something new.

Before turning to the interview format and the steps of analysis I will conclude this section by shortly referring to six textual phenomena which according to Schütze empirically reveal the 'epistemic force' of extempore storytelling[5] about one's own experiences (Schütze, 1987, pp. 94-97). In an article (Riemann, 2018) I illustrated these phenomena by using a narrative interview with a young Spanish migrant (Felipe). I will use quotation marks for a rather free translation of small parts of Schütze's text:

1. "The natural segmentation and focusing of the presentation express phases and lines of attention of the narrator's sedimentation of experiences, which correspond with her or his former process of acting and suffering." One can distinguish between single narrative segments and the aforementioned supra-segmental larger units.

2. "The narrative does not just report about exterior sequences of events, but also presents the inner world of the narrator as the protagonist or participant in the events which she or he talks about."
3. "The non-narrative parts which are embedded in the narrative at expectable locations reveal the current and, in part, the former theoretical and evaluative attitude of the narrator." Locations for argumentative commentaries are very common at the end of narrative segments or in pre-coda sequences, once in a while in the preamble of narratives, too. Narrative and non-narrative (argumentative and descriptive) parts "can be intuitively and clearly distinguished".
4. "The narrative does not just present the content of experiences of events; its presentational mode also expresses experiential values which the narrator senses but cannot explicitly formulate." This is visible in the emotional "colouring" of speech: breaks, intonation patterns and elements of style.
5. "The dynamics of the spontaneous presentation also indirectly reveal experiences of the narrator, which had been half forgotten, faded out of awareness or partially repressed: difficult experiences of the narrator as former actor in situations of failing, being hurt, being entangled in compromising events, feeling guilt or shame or compassion with fellow human beings." These experiences are often revealed in background constructions (see Schütze 2014, pp. 236-239) through self-corrective insertions of experiences that had been left out before. Background constructions clearly illustrate the effectiveness of the aforementioned narrative constraints. In my study, I have referred to this phenomenon in different parts (e.g. in the case study of Mateo and in the discussions of trajectories of suffering in chapter 4).[6]
6. It is also possible that the narrative "indirectly expresses events and their structural conditions, which the narrator had not (totally or partially) experienced herself or himself". But the consequences had determined, impeded or changed her or his actions, which can be discovered in discrepancies in narrative presentations.

b) The interview format

The design of the autobiographical narrative interview has remained quite stable over previous decades. It starts with the researcher conveying a genuine interest in learning 'how one thing led to another' in the life of the interviewee. It is thereby important to avoid confusing the participant by mixing narrative and argumentative elements in formulating the request to the interviewee to tell her or his life-history. Questions such as "I'm interested in *how* one thing led to another in your life. *Why* did you decide to migrate?" are likely to cause confusion, as the informant is unsure whether s/he should 'remember' or 'explain'. It would be a misunderstanding to assume that I have a general preference for narrative over argumentative questions. There are many research problems that suggest, e.g., initial argumentative questions for generating a group discussion. What is problematic is the diffusion of the schemes of narration and argumentation, as already discussed at the end of my second chapter.

When the interviewee has agreed to participate, the introductory narrative unfolds. The researcher should not interrupt this narrative, as long as s/he is able to understand the story. There are, of course, non-verbal ways to signal interest and encouragement to the narrator, including nodding, smiling and laughter. In practice, it is sometimes necessary to ask some questions in order to understand what the narrator is talking about (especially when faced with language barriers). That being said, interruptions should be kept to a minimum and should never disrupt the free flow of the narrative.

After the narrator finishes his/her introductory narrative with a coda (e.g. "*That's it. This is where I am now.*"), it is possible to ask narrative, descriptive and argumentative questions. These questions should initially be based on the introductory narrative. In this second part of the interview, the researcher has the opportunity to explore more narrative potential, but also focus on what appears to be a 'lack of plausibility'. It is, of course, also possible afterwards to bring up topics that did not appear in the informant's introductory narrative but have emerged in the course of the whole research project.

c) The steps of analysis

The central proposition of Schütze's narrative theory is "that to a considerable extent, extempore narratives retrieve currently ongoing experiences during past phases of life. But, since extempore narratives express some important aspects of former life experiences only indirectly – and that means through allusions, style, or even partially unintended and unnoticed paraverbal symptoms of speech – research has to start with the sequential analysis of the formal structures of narrative presentation" (Schütze, 2014, p. 267). By now it should have become clear that his approach is marked by a rejection of two widespread assumptions: the naïve assumption of an "unproblematic 'mirror' depiction of reality through autobiographical narrative renderings" and the assumption "of the freewheeling and suitable making up of autobiographical stories according to functional requirements of social situations" (Schütze, 2008, pp. 12, 14).

Schütze has developed a type of analysis, which combines the use of single in-depth case studies with a comparative approach. His work was influenced by insights from sociolinguistics, ethnomethodological conversational analysis, and Grounded Theory (Glaser & Strauss, 1967). The impact of the latter is visible in Schütze's use of theoretical sampling, contrastive comparisons and the notion of theoretical saturation. Glaser (1978, p. 36) defines theoretical sampling as "the process of data collection for generating theory whereby the analyst jointly collects, codes and analyses his data and decides which data to collect next and where to find them in order to develop his theory as it emerges". The aim of theoretical sampling is not the same as that of probabilistic sampling. The researcher's objective is not to arrive at conclusions with regard to quantitative distributions.

The research process usually starts with the collection of a few narrative interviews on the basis of theoretical sampling (if possible). The researcher then selects a first interview for an in-depth single case analysis. This narrative should entail biographical and other social processes that appear especially relevant in the thematic context of the study. The first step of this single case analysis consists of a specific critique of the interview and a differentiation between narrative, argumentative and descriptive sequences in the text in order to understand their functions for the interview. The second step is a sequential structural (formal and substantive) description of the unfolding of the narrative segments of the text. The purpose of this step is to carefully reconstruct the central structural processes of the life course, other social processes and the ways in which the narrator makes sense of his/her life in retrospect. A narrator's former and current perspectives have to be differentiated. And by doing so it is important to make careful use of all kinds of textual phenomena, including background constructions, extended argumentative sequences, and conspicuous vagueness, and to spell out how one uses them as analytical resources for understanding the narrator's past experiences and current perspectives (see Riemann, 2018). It is also possible to thereby arrive at insights about other persons who are mentioned in the narrative. The process of doing structural descriptions has similarities with 'open coding' as described by Strauss (1987), but in contrast to classic Grounded Theory, it involves a careful distinction between different schemes of communication and a special focus on linguistic and paraverbal phenomena.

The third step of the single case analysis is the analytical abstraction, which explicates the essential insights of the structural description: (a) insights into the central structural processes of a life course and their relationship with other social processes (e.g. an economic crisis), and (b) insights into the theorising of the narrator as it is visible in argumentative and evaluative commentaries. What can be learned by relating steps (a) and (b) to each other? Through careful textual analysis it is also possible to discover tendencies to fade out of awareness (Schütze, 1992) and self-deception. In any case, it is important to avoid general and condescending statements that are not sufficiently empirically founded. It should be made clear which features of the narrative seem to be case-specific to the individual and which appear to be quite general. There are different ways of presenting such biographical case studies. In order to enable readers to follow, assess and control their interpretation of the narratives rigorously, some authors include longer narrative sequences that consist of different segments (Riemann, 2018). Due to practical restrictions such as word limitations (of articles and dissertations), researchers often include only excerpts of a narrative and their structural description. That being said, the analytical procedures should be as transparent as possible.

After finishing a first single case analysis it is useful to repeat the process with a few of the other interviews. These narratives should be quite different from the first case study in order to detect as much theoretical variation as possible. A contrastive comparison between these cases enables the researcher to generate the first outlines of a theoretical process model (e.g. on different phases of migration projects). This first version of the model is then confronted with other interviews, which had not been selected for in-depth case analyses. The purpose of this step is to reconsider, refine and condense the emerging categories and their relationships. In order to make this work of grounded theorising visible, some excerpts from the rest of the data material should also be included in the text. The sequence of research steps is also mirrored in the presentation of empirical findings in this monograph.

10. Methodological Appendix

THE HISTORY OF MY FIELD RESEARCH[7]

A long-term perspective

This book is based on a line of research that I started as an undergraduate student and continued throughout my MPhil and PhD research (Riemann, 2013, 2014, 2020). As shown in my data overview, I conducted over 60 interviews (58 autobiographical narrative interviews and four follow-up interviews) during this time period. For a biographical study of this kind, this is quite a sizable sample. Some readers may wonder why I decided to continue this line of research over the course of several years in the context of various degrees. In the following section, I would therefore like to share some thoughts on how my research journey evolved throughout the years.

The 'new' Spanish migration caught my attention as both a 'macro' and 'micro' phenomenon at the beginning of 2013. I was in my final year of my undergraduate degree at the University College Maastricht. The collective economic crisis affected millions of people across Spain and other parts of southern Europe and had complex and devastating implications for their living conditions and life histories. Biographical projects had to be given up or postponed. Quite a few (mostly young) Spanish citizens decided to leave their country in these circumstances. I could relate to the young people whom I read about in the news, as we were about the same age, shared a middle-class upbringing and had gone to university. But I also sensed that there were vast differences in our experiences and perspectives.

At the time, I knew little about Spain, which I had visited only once on holiday. However, there was a linguistic connection as I spoke Spanish fluently. As a high school student, I had participated in a twelve month exchange programme in Argentina. I decided that it should be possible to do empirical research on the 'new' Spanish migration because I could communicate with migrants in their own language. Given that I was interested in the complexity of the relationship between the macro crisis and people's personal sphere, as well as in long-term biographical and other social processes in migrants' lives, I soon realised that an effective and sensible way to study such phenomena was biographical research.

I was aware of Schütze's socio-linguistically based analysis of social processes and had read studies that made use of the biographical narrative interview. I had little experience with qualitative research at the time but wanted to do something original for my undergraduate thesis and make 'a contribution' to the field – however small it might be. At the time, there was furthermore hardly any academic literature on the 'new' Spanish migration, which encouraged me to follow through with the idea of doing a biographical study on Spanish people who had gone to Germany in the context of the crisis. In the end, I interviewed six people for this first research project, all of them living in Germany close to the Dutch border. Due to my lack of experience, I was quite nervous in the beginning of my fieldwork. When comparing the *first* interviews I conducted as an undergraduate student with those I collected later on (especially in the context of my PhD), it is apparent that the latter went much more smoothly, an aspect that I will discuss later on in this chapter.

The structure of my bachelor programme did not reserve additional time for our 'capstone' project since we were expected to complete it alongside our coursework. Given the small sample and its short length, I therefore regard my undergraduate thesis as an exploratory study. Nevertheless, it helped me to practise forming structural descriptions of oral narratives. I included one case study of the narrative of a middle-aged Catalan engineer, Nicolas, who had been unemployed for two years before finding a job in Germany. This in-depth analysis helped me identify certain themes and biographical processes, which I could later refine and build on. One aspect of my bachelor study – which I did not explore in-depth in my MPhil and PhD dissertations – was a focus on the gender dimension of my interviewees' experiences of unemployment and migration. Of course, I was sensitised in this regard in the interpretation of my data in my doctoral thesis, but I did not devote a whole chapter to this issue because of simple pragmatic reasons (having to make difficult editing choices due to word limits). My undergraduate thesis was well received and had tapped into a line of research that was worth exploring further.

When applying for the master programme in Cambridge I submitted a proposal for doing field research on young unemployed people in Spain who had *not* gone abroad. My MPhil supervisor, however, suggested that I conduct a complementary study to the one I had done in Maastricht, i.e., a biographical study focusing on the 'new' Spanish migration to the UK. Much like Germany, the UK had become a major recipient of 'new' southern Europeans who headed north in the context of the economic crisis. Given the research focus of this MPhil programme, I was given more time for the fieldwork and writing up process than during my bachelor programme.

This resulted in a slightly larger sample, as I was able to interview fifteen people for this project. The design of the study consisted of (1) three single case analyses (or 'portrait chapters' as they are sometimes called in German biographical research) which were subjected to a contrastive comparison so that (2) a sequential model of the migration experience emerged which was further substantiated in chapters in which the other interviews were selectively used, i.e. the interviews, which had not provided the basis for the aforementioned 'portrait chapters'. This is the basic structure that I built and expanded on in my PhD dissertation. For readers unfamiliar with the system in Cambridge, it is worth mentioning that the MPhil programme is partly designed for students to explore whether or not a topic has the potential for further doctoral research. The path that I took with these successive studies is therefore not that uncommon.

When asked how my MPhil thesis differed from my PhD dissertation, I would like to point out a few things. Firstly, the scale of the study was much smaller and focused exclusively on the UK. Secondly, I included three case studies that were extremely abbreviated for this type of biographical research. Given the word restrictions of the master thesis, I could not make my form of data analysis as visible as in this doctoral dissertation. I used an interview with one participant, María, for a case study in my MPhil thesis and interviewed her again twice (in England and then after her return to Spain) during my doctoral research. These three interviews were also the basis for a single case study or 'portrait chapter'. That being said, this case still 'informs' the analysis of the empirical chapters. Thirdly, my MPhil sample did not yet include any 'returnees' who had moved back to Spain by the time of the interview. And, last but not least, the political circumstances of Spanish migrants (along with all other EU movers) in the UK were radically different in 2014, a time when the EU referendum had not even been announced. The broad database of my doctoral research allowed me (1) to take other biographical phases (in the case of the 'returnees') and the experience of unforeseen and far-reaching new collective crises (especially 'Brexit') into account and (2) to develop much more differentiated and denser comparative chapters than in my previous studies in order to get closer to 'theoretical saturation' (Glaser & Strauss, 1967).

The feedback I received for my MPhil thesis was very positive and I was informed that it had 'potential for outstanding PhD work'. After my MPhil, I took a gap year from academia as I was still somewhat unsure whether I wanted to continue to do a PhD. The positive feedback on my previous work, however, stuck with me and I decided to continue with what I had started. I mention this to give my readers the opportunity to reconstruct my decision making process for why I decided to continue with this line of research. It is important to mention that at the time (2014), the number of conclusive studies on the 'new' Spanish migration was still limited.

After returning to Cambridge, I was encouraged to build systematically on my previous findings and think about how I could expand on them. Incorporating previous data from my earlier studies was not considered a problem as long as I was transparent about *whom* I interviewed *when*. This is why I created a table of all my informants, which can be found at the end of this chapter. I thought that this would be the most convenient way for readers to look up the interviewees that I quoted in the empirical chapters. The interviews from 2013 were conducted as part of my BA thesis and those from 2014 as part of my MPhil thesis.

Being able to compare 'older' with more 'recent' data has made this study stronger. This is especially visible in relation to Brexit, a topic to which I have dedicated one chapter. I conducted a few follow-up interviews with key participants with whom I had initially become acquainted in the context of my MPhil project. It was astonishing to see how much their relationship to the receiving society had changed within the course of a year and a half. Whilst I did include some data sequences from my undergraduate and MPhil research in this PhD thesis, I revised my interpretation of these interviews in light of the much larger sample. My current reading of some of the earlier interviews is quite different from how I interpreted them as an undergraduate student.

Linguistic challenges

The vast majority of interviews were conducted in Spanish, which is my third language after German and English. Four participants insisted on speaking English and German respectively, as they perceived it as an opportunity to practise their foreign language skills. Even though I speak Spanish fluently, this form of data collection was quite an ambitious undertaking. Peninsular Spanish differs significantly from Argentine Castilian not only in terms of pronunciation, but also with respect to its speech rate, colloquial expressions and even grammar. Furthermore, quite a few of my informants had strong regional accents (e.g. from Andalusia), which created an additional challenge.

Since I am not a native Spanish speaker, the transcription of my data would have been extremely time-consuming if I had done everything by myself. Since the methodology I chose for this research project pays very close attention to linguistic details and textual phenomena, it was therefore important to get the transcription right and avoid inaccuracies. This is why I asked a Chilean friend of mine, a native Spanish speaker, to assist me with this task. Alba's support greatly facilitated this part of the research process, as she could easily pick up on Spanish expressions with which I was unfamiliar. She was, furthermore, very experienced at transcribing, which she had practised as a freelancer for several years. Alba was not only quick, but also showed great sensitivity in documenting my informants' emotional reactions during the interview (i.e. laughter, tears, moments of silences, changes in intonation patterns etc.). After receiving the transcripts, I could then translate the transcripts to English (sometimes with the help of online dictionaries and translation programmes without uncritically relying on their accuracy).[8] When translating the data from Spanish to English, I was very intent on keeping certain linguistic features (e.g. self-interruptions, changing levels of detail, anacolutha, argumentative commentaries etc.) as accurate as possible. Of course, the work of translating is a delicate process which deserves special scrutiny and self-reflection since meanings can be distorted or lost, but I think I am in good company. Members of transnational biographical research projects and research workshops with participants from different countries (Inowlocki, 2018) have learned that it is quite feasible for all practical purposes to analyse carefully translated data by taking formal textual features into account.

Finding participants

At the beginning of my fieldwork, I did not have any contacts in Spanish communities abroad (neither in Germany nor the UK). I could recruit a handful of participants via snowball sampling, as friends and acquaintances referred me to Spanish migrants in their social circles. (I also sometimes used snowball sampling in later phases of my fieldwork, such as during my stay in Spain when I interviewed 'returnees'.) As a first step to finding more informants, I turned to social media. On Facebook, I discovered the popularity of groups with titles such as 'Españoles en Berlin' for cities, and sometimes even smaller towns, across Europe and overseas.

Throughout different stages of my fieldwork (i.e. BA, MPhil, PhD), these social media platforms proved to be very helpful in getting in touch with prospective informants in different locations. Following the principle of theoretical sampling (Glaser & Strauss, 1967), I was intent on interviewing people from quite diverse socio-economic backgrounds, age groups, gender, education levels, current occupation and other biographical circumstances – as such criteria flexibly emerged and appeared relevant in the course of my field work and analysis. Social media helped in this context, as people reached out to me with whom I would otherwise never have crossed paths.

The basic idea of theoretical sampling is to collect, code and analyse data in a way that does not rigidly pre-determine the order of activities of data collection and analysis. This process involves critically evaluating one's sample and deciding which data to collect next in order to develop theory as it emerges (cf. Glaser, 1978). When I first started my doctoral research in 2015, I could not have foreseen the emergence of Brexit, a collective crisis that has had a significant impact on the daily lives of millions of EU movers in the UK. After the EU referendum of 2016, I spontaneously decided to contact a few of my MPhil informants, as I was interested in how their relationship to the receiving society had changed since 2014. Even though I had not originally planned to re-interview the same participants, this data turned out to be very insightful. Another example of theoretical sampling was my decision to conduct fieldwork in Scotland, a region to which I had previously not paid much attention. In the aftermath of Brexit, I became interested in the experiences of Spanish citizens in another national and decisively pro-European context.

Finally, I would like to mention that narrative biographical interviews have the potential to become analytically interesting in quite unexpected ways. I did not know any of the informants before the interview and each of them had a unique life history. I interviewed a few participants, who – on paper – seemed like typical cases, as they were young and had migrated after graduating from university. A close look at their narratives revealed very unique problem constellations that I had not considered before (e.g. the topic of adoption). I arrived at such unexpected insights not because of a specific sampling choice I took prior to the interview. Instead, I simply tried to remain open to the unique biographical experiences of every new informant and allowed myself to be surprised.

The way I recruited informants online has remained quite stable over the years. Firstly, I would publish a public post in one of the Facebook groups for Spanish people living abroad (e.g. "Españoles en Bristol"), informing members about my research project.[9] I phrased the description of my study in a way that also reflected my critical stance towards the somewhat simplistic media coverage of the topic. I made clear that I was interested in people's 'whole' life histories (i.e. "*how one thing led to another*" in their lives) as opposed to only focusing on their migration. Furthermore, I assured anyone who was interested in participating complete confidentiality.

Secondly, I would wait to see how people reacted to my post. The responses would mostly exceed the number of participants I could realistically interview. At the beginning of my fieldwork, I remember receiving over 40 messages within two hours after publishing my request for informants online. The open biographical approach appeared to have struck a chord with the audience, as many people expressed enthusiasm about wanting to share their personal life history. On a few rare occasions, I did encounter a so-called 'internet troll' who enjoyed ridiculing my project. Although I only very occasionally received a negative or even aggressive comment, it did remind me of the downsides of social media. The public nature of my posts also meant that I had no control over who would get to see my contact details.

Thirdly, I would choose whom to interview. Given that the number of replies usually exceeded the scope of my fieldwork, I sometimes had to make quite practical choices. I made it a habit to respond politely to each person who expressed an interest in participating, asking when they would be available for a meeting. Since I would often only spend a few days in one city, a number of respondents could not participate, as they had made other commitments during that time. Scheduling issues already reduced the number of prospective participants I could realistically meet and interview. A second criterion was the content of the introductory messages I received. Whilst many people wrote quite short emails indicating their willingness to participate, a few people took the time to engage a bit more deeply with the description of my research post and how it related to their story. Examples included allusions to a 'sad love story' that one informant perceived as the cost of his migration, and/or other experiences that people deemed could be interesting to include. When selecting interviewees, I would commonly pick those who had sent me slightly longer and more personal messages, as I interpreted it as a sign of their seriousness and willingness to open up. I also kept the criteria of theoretical sampling in mind as they had become relevant at this specific moment in the research process. For example, after having interviewed many participants who were in their early to mid-twenties, I consciously decided to choose respondents who were at a different stage of their lives. This diversity is also reflected in the empirical chapters of this book.

Fourthly, I would arrange a meeting. The experience of being heckled online made me aware that I could never be completely certain about a prospective participant's intention. Meeting strangers from the Internet always carries some risks, especially for a female researcher. I therefore avoided meeting new informants at their homes despite being invited a few times. Instead, I suggested public places, typically cafes. For the most part, this seemed like an appropriate environment for the interviews as it provided quite a relaxed and casual atmosphere. I also conducted a handful of interviews over Skype. These were informants who lived quite far away (e.g. returnees who lived in different regions in Spain), but still wanted to participate in my research project. This video-chat set up worked very well for all practical purposes. I did not have the impression that the quality of this data differed from the face-to-face interviews as long as the technical connection was stable.

The work of interviewing

The steps of the autobiographical narrative interview (Schütze, 2008) are clearly defined. In the beginning it is necessary to develop a basis of trust by thoroughly informing the participant about the structure, purpose and conditions of the interview. After the informant signed the consent form, the researcher should formulate the original question so that a spontaneous and detailed narrative can be generated. An interviewer should ideally only ask further questions (as long as (s)he can follow the story) in the second part of the interview after the informant has finished his/her introductory narrative with a coda (e.g. "That's my life."). The participants in this study differed quite significantly in how they reacted to this initial stimulus. Whilst some people immediately understood the concept and launched into in-depth explanations about how their lives developed, others started their narratives by quickly summarising their biography (much like in a CV) and then waited for me to ask more questions.

This also had to do with my (initial lack of) skills in communicating my request. When re-reading some of my first interviews, I realised that my skills as an interviewer had improved since then. I needed some time to develop a relaxed style to formulate my generative question in the beginning before giving the floor to my interaction partner. I sometimes interrupted participants in their narration and brought up unrelated topics quite abruptly. Furthermore, I was much more nervous than during the later stages of my fieldwork, which affected the extent to which my informants opened up to me. In other words, if I felt tense and nervous, so did my participants. If I was relaxed and gave off the impression that I knew exactly what I was doing, they were relaxed and felt free to narrate. Furthermore, I had to learn how to trust the natural flow of a narration (due to the aforementioned narrative constraints), which means accepting moments of silence during the interview. Starting to ask questions too early could sometimes divert informants from their memories and prevent them from closing the form (Gestalt) of their narrative presentation.

In the beginning of my fieldwork, I also underestimated the importance of introducing myself properly to establish a level of trust. If I spent 10 to 15 minutes narrating about myself – for example, about my own migration background (my mother is originally from Vietnam), where I learnt Spanish, what I studied, and how my interest in the topic and my interaction partner's very personal life history developed – my informants would open up quite easily. In a few cases, I made the mistake of rushing through this initial stage. This hastiness 'backfired' as the participants in turn also 'rushed through' their biographical narrative and quickly expected further questions.

In the interview situation, I had to focus on a few tasks simultaneously including understanding my informants properly (despite some linguistic barriers), identifying important biographical and other social processes and experiences, and then spontaneously formulating questions in Spanish based on their introductory narrative. Whilst I do believe that I have succeeded in managing these tasks for the most part, I also think that some interviews might have developed more smoothly if the participant and I had shared the same native language. If I had conducted the interviews in German or English (which I practise much more often than Spanish), it would have been easier to formulate refined questions in a more spontaneous manner. When reading the transcriptions, I discovered that I often tended to formulate summary statements (expressing how I understood what the interviewee had said) where a clear and open question would have been more helpful to generate further narrative sequences. But such summary statements were probably necessary at that time in order to make sure that I had understood my interaction partner correctly.

A few interviewees appeared to be a bit intimidated by my association with the University of Cambridge due to its elitist reputation. As indicated in the data overview, many people were engaged in low-paid manual labour at the time of the interview. My imperfect Spanish skills helped level out this perceived power imbalance and made me more relatable as a researcher. Most informants arrived in the new country with limited (in some cases non-existent) foreign language skills, which they improved over time. Whenever I struggled to find a word in Spanish, they reacted very sympathetically by reassuring me that they knew exactly how I felt. Being an outsider to the Spanish community had, furthermore, some advantages as participants took time to explain and describe how 'things work' in Spain. This is information they might have omitted otherwise (i.e. if the researcher was a co-national). In the UK context it also mattered that I was a non-British co-European as interviewees invited me to share impressions about our host-country – a way of establishing solidarity. I made it a habit to send each of the participants an email afterwards to thank them for their participation. I stayed in touch with a few key informants, which served as the basis for a small number of follow-up interviews.

Reflections on the meaning of telling one's life history

I was often astonished by the openness of my informants, who sometimes shared very personal experiences with me, a perfect stranger. I believe it was this distance to me as a researcher that quite a few participants experienced as liberating. Some informants were in difficult personal or work situations and they appreciated being given the opportunity to talk about it to 'someone' outside their immediate social circles. In a few cases, people confided in me secrets and doubts which they kept hidden from friends and family for fear of damaging relationships.

There were several informants who were, at the time of the interview, experiencing a deep trajectory of suffering and/or recovering from a personal crisis. They were among those participants who especially appreciated telling – and also arguing – about their life histories, as it allowed them to put certain experiences into perspective. These participants seemed in special need of doing what has been referred to as 'biographical work' (Betts et al., 2008, pp. 26-31; Corbin & Strauss, 1988) to reflect upon their past experiences, make sense of them, and develop a perspective for the future. They were trying to create order in experiences of disorder.

Most interviewees seemed to appreciate me as a researcher (or simply as an outsider) taking an interest in their biographies. By being given the time and space to recount how *one thing led to another* in their lives, these informants sensed that their experiences were taken seriously by someone outside their social circles. In other words, what they had gone through mattered and was of social scientific interest. The interview format gave them space to narrate freely about what had happened in their lives. When recounting how their decision to leave Spain developed, the informants could include details about coincidences, unexpected biographical developments and the significance of social relationships. These long-term biographical processes (and complex experiences) would have been difficult to capture in standardised interviews, or even in open interviews that primarily or exclusively focus on special themes (e.g. migration).

Notes on the analysis and presentation of my findings

In my study phases during which I collected data, the processes of data transcription and analysis were intertwined (similar to other inquiries influenced by Glaser's and Strauss's (1967) Grounded Theory). I mostly interpreted transcriptions of my interviews by formulating informal and abbreviated (formal and substantive) structural descriptions and analytical abstractions. Such notes or memos, which also contained keywords and comments that summarised especially interesting aspects of a specific interview became important in my work on the comparative chapters when I drew on the whole data corpus.

During my field research I selected a few interviews for in-depth case studies or 'portrait chapters'. This decision was based on *formal* and *substantive* aspects. The interviews were selected not only because of the degree of narrative detail and interesting textual phenomena (such as background constructions or pre-coda argumentation), but also on the basis of (1) whether or not they referred to biographical and other social processes that were of special analytical interest in this study and (2) how they differed from each other in important analytical aspects. The idea was to strive for as much theoretical variation (Strauss, 1987) as possible.

From the very beginning of my research journey, I knew that I wanted to conduct more than one in-depth case study. The three single case studies explicated features that were specific to the single biographies but also provided initial insights into general phenomena (Riemann, 2018, 2019). By engaging in contrastive comparisons between these cases, and by additionally resorting to other interviews (in order to do justice to the theoretical variation in the data), I could gain some more analytical distance to develop an outline of a theoretical model (as Schütze calls it). This step entailed refining categories and some analytical foci that appeared fruitful for the comparative discussion of the whole data material, which was presented in the subsequent chapters.

One reader struggled to understand why I devoted so much time and space to a few cases while the majority of my interviews only became visible in small portions (if at all). He had the impression that he only got to know a few people very well but was at a loss as far as the other interviewees were concerned. Why did I conduct so many (58) interviews when most participants stayed in the shadow? Did I do anything worthwhile with these interviews at all? I was surprised by his reaction, as it is common practice in qualitative research to be selective about the use of empirical examples. That being said, I find his criticism helpful, as it gives me the chance, firstly, to recall some features of the analysis and, secondly, to reflect on the way I presented my findings.

1. The format of my presentation corresponds to the format of biographical studies in general, which are based on this specific methodology. A special feature of these studies are comprehensive and detailed single case analyses or 'portrait chapters' – analyses of very few cases which diverge from each other in important aspects in order to 'cover as much ground' as possible. Thereby they lend themselves to (later) contrastive comparisons whereby the process of generating a theoretical model begins. One aim of such single case studies is also to reveal something about the researcher's interpretive procedures, i.e., how s(he) understood the text by producing a (formal-substantive) structural description. My 'portrait chapter' about Adam Sanchez is not a simple retelling of his narrative in my own words but a careful sequential analysis. A basic assumption and legitimation for conducting such detailed single case analyses is that they produce (preliminary) general insights, such as the collective experience of being overwhelmed by the macro crisis during adolescence, the development of a biographical project, the processes of disillusionment, participation in a collective movement, the relevance of family support, the socially shared image of the English language as a door opener, attempts to survive under precarious circumstances in the receiving society, the development of European spaces or solidarity structures etc.

   Such extended single case analyses and their contrastive comparison serve an important function for grounded theorising: they reveal categories and analytical foci around which comparative chapters are organised. Now it is necessary to confront the categories which have emerged so far with 'the rest' or 'the bulk' of the data which had been collected – basically a process within the communicative scheme of argumentation. Do such categories 'stand the test' when new data come into play? In which way do they have to be differentiated? Which new ideas emerge? Just one example from my study: María Navarro, experienced a 'biographical rupture', a radical degradation and devaluation of her biography (as an academic librarian) during her work as a kitchen porter in a university setting. When confronting this category of 'biographical rupture' with new data it was possible to discover similar experiences in other interviews but also quite diverse experiences that I referred to as "taking pride in 'unskilled' skillsets". When illustrating such experiences and the underlying biographical conditions, I only referred to an excerpt from another interview (as a 'supporting document', so to speak). It would not have made sense if I had brought this interviewee's whole life history into play at this point. It was sufficient to refer to a biographical phase and experiences in the world of work. Of course, it is important that this is done without distorting the overall biographical context. I hope to have shown a little bit of how I worked with the 'other' data that did not become the basis of extended single case analyses or 'portrait chapters'.

2. When presenting my findings in the comparative chapters I always had to negotiate with myself how I could find a balance between my general propositions and the inclusion of empirical examples. I understand that someone who is unfamiliar with biographical research might be under the impression that this study revolves only around a handful of protagonists. That being said, I actually introduced 33 of my 58 interviewees by name. If I had made it my mission to include data extracts from every single informant in this sample, this book would not have been readable. Every page would have been plastered with quotes with no room for a proper analysis. This format would not have allowed for a detailed reconstruction of any biographical processes, which would have defied the purpose of this study.

While some life histories, such as those of Adam, María and Mateo, become visible in great detail, others appear only in the context of specific aspects of their biography. In the empirical chapters, I made an effort to include enough background information about each interviewee I quoted in order for readers to understand the specific aspect that is at the forefront of the discussion. For example, in my chapter on work experiences, I introduced a young woman who had moved to Scotland straight after graduating from university with a degree in social work. In Glasgow, Laura accepted a job as a cleaner in a hotel, an experience she described as deeply alienating. When writing up my findings, I carefully thought about the background information that would enable the reader to reconstruct the 'biographical rupture and devaluation' she experienced at the time. After careful deliberation, I decided that it was sufficient for the reader to know two aspects. Firstly, Laura had only just graduated from university, a sheltered environment she had enjoyed very much. It was particularly the transition from being a university student to becoming a cleaner in a foreign country that she experienced as a harsh break in her biography. Secondly, she deeply identified with the profession of social work, an academic achievement that was met with indifference at the hotel. Even though much of her past (e.g. her childhood) remains hidden in this abbreviated portrayal, it is possible to get a deeper sense of what her job as a cleaner meant against the backdrop of her previous achievements. Laura is simply one of many other informants in this study who I introduced in a brief – but nevertheless thoughtful and context-sensitive – manner. I would like to encourage readers unfamiliar with this form of analysis to pay attention to such details.

It would be wrong to assume that just because an interviewee's name did not appear in the presentation of my findings, his/her narrative was irrelevant in the analysis. When writing up my findings, I simply had to find a balance between different degrees of explicitness in order to avoid the risk of drowning in empirical examples. At different points in this book, I did refer to the informants in question in a more indirect manner. One example from my sub-chapter 'From studying to staying abroad':

> When speaking about how their Erasmus semester evolved into something long-term, several participants spoke of sympathetic mentors at their host university, who indicated that they recognised my informants' special talent and potential.

When referring to "several participants" I had various interviewees in mind without explicitly and individually introducing and quoting them.

The less visible part of my sample, furthermore, still informs the themes and categories I discussed in the empirical chapters. In order to illustrate this point, it is useful to revisit the case of Laura. If she had been the only person who had suffered from 'biographical rupture and devaluation' after accepting a menial job in the new country, I would not have included the topic in the presentation of my findings. Indeed, I came across similar experiences in many different narratives. When writing up my findings, I realised that it would have become repetitive and taken up unnecessary space to include data sequences of various informants to illustrate this one aspect of menial labour ('biographical rupture'). Laura's experiences at the hotel simply serve as an example of a phenomenon that also appeared in my wider (less visible) sample.

In the empirical chapters, I preferred somewhat longer interview excerpts in order to enable readers to critically assess my own interpretations (see my discussion of a longer argumentative sequence in chapter 7 on Brexit). I never intended to let single quotes "speak for themselves", and I always found it necessary to present my own analytical commentary. Some readers may find it strange that I sometimes referred to the same informants in different chapters of this book. The rationale behind using the same participant in different contexts is to enable careful readers to make connections between these pieces and form an image of this person's biography. One example is the case of Pablo, aged 52. I discussed his narrative firstly in the context of workplace harassment (cf. "On the experience of being othered") and secondly in the subchapter on working to maintain personal ties to Spain. Even though Pablo experienced intense bullying as a kitchen porter in London, he presented himself in an idealised light when speaking to his friends and family at home. Careful readers may gain a deeper understanding of how his 'filtered presentation of everyday life' diverged from what was actually happening when recalling his painful experiences at the cafe.

DATA OVERVIEW

The total sample consists of 58 autobiographical narrative interviews, and four follow-up interviews with three key informants (Diego, María, and Rocio). Twenty-seven of the participants had a migration history relating to Germany, where they were either currently based or had been prior to their return migration. One interviewee that I counted towards the German sample did not directly classify as a migrant. She was the mother of a young man who had worked in a town in Bavaria for six months before moving back to Spain.[10]

Respectively, 31 of my participants had a migration history relating to the United Kingdom. Eight of these 31 informants had returned to Spain at the time of our last interview. I interviewed two women (María and Rocio) in Bristol, and then once again after their return to Spain (during my fieldwork in the summer of 2017). In total, I interviewed 27 women and 31 men. Three informants were born in Latin America (Colombia, Chile, Brazil) but had moved to Spain at a young age. They had acquired Spanish citizenship, which enabled what has been referred to as 'onward migration' to a different EU member state (in this case Germany and the UK prior to Brexit) (Ramos, 2018). The majority of my informants were either single or had partners to whom they were not married. Only five out of the 57 informants had children.

Most interviews took place face-to-face in my interviewees' current city of residence (in Germany, the UK, or Spain). Prior to the interview, the participants were thoroughly informed about the process of the interview as well as its purpose. I gave them a consent form both in Spanish and in English, which informed them about the conditions. The participants were assured that all information that could lead to their identification would be masked. I changed not only their names, but – in many cases – also their real cities of residence. Instead of using quite technical pseudonyms such as "A-Town", I simply changed the names to different, yet comparable cities in the same country.

Interviewees Germany

No.	Name	Age	Education	Current occupation	Place of residence	Year of interview
1.	Ana	24	Physical Therapy (BA)	Au Pair	Cologne	2013
2.	Nicolas	40	Civil Engineering (MA)	Civil engineer	Aachen	2013
3.	Emilia	40	Archaeology (BA)	Unemployed/ Intensive German course	Aachen	2013
4.	Alma	23	Graphic Design (BA)	Graphic designer	Minden	2013
5.	Eva	23	Tourism (BA)	Internship in tourist office	Minden	2013
6.	Bruno	29	Mechanical Engineering (MA)	Mechanical engineer	Minden	2013
7.	Valeria	31	Business Administration (MA)	Intensive German course	Berlin	2014
8.	Tomas	24	Mathematics (BA)	Master student in mathematics at German university	Hamburg	2015
9.	Gabriela	25	Nursing (BA)	Nurse	Frankfurt	2015
10.	Daniela	27	Nursing (BA)	Nurse	Frankfurt	2015
11.	Martin	34	Mechanical Engineering (MA)	Mechanical engineer	Stuttgart	2015
12.	Irene	28	Nursing (BA)	Currently on maternity leave – before that she was working as a nurse	Offenbach	2015
13.	Camilla	25	Visual Communication (MA)	Illustrator	Berlin	2016
14	Pedro	22	High School; University drop out (fine arts)	Waiter in a cafe	Munich	2016
15.	Julian	25	Industrial Design	Master Student in Industrial Design at German University	Stuttgart	2016
16.	Mateo	32	Mechanical Engineering (MA)	Mechanical engineer	Berlin	2016
17.	Jose	23	Office Administration (Apprenticeship)	Cleaner at a hotel	Berlin	2016
18.	Fernanda	29	Biochemistry (PhD)	Administrator in a start-up company	Berlin	2016
19.	Sandra	25	Fashion Design (still enrolled in Spain)	Intensive German course	Berlin	2016

No.	Name	Age	Education	Current occupation	Place of residence	Year of interview
20.	Beatriz	28	Mechanical Engineering (enrolled in Germany)	Student in Mechanical Engineering at German University/ Office administrator	Berlin	2016
21.	Renata	45	Psychology (BA)	Currently unemployed	Potsdam	2016
22.	Clara	44	Film Studies (PhD)	Currently unemployed	Berlin	2016
23.	David	46	Mathematics (MA)	Currently unemployed	Berlin	2016

Returnees Germany

No.	Name	Age	Education	Former & current occupations	Former & current place of residence	Year of interview
24.	Guillermo	24	Early Childhood Education (BA)	Six-months internship in bi-lingual Kindergarten in Berlin; Currently pursuing master degree in Early Childhood Education in Spain.	Berlin, Seville	2017
25.	Alvaro	29	Business Administration (BA)	Worker at a carwash in Duisburg; Currently working as a Human Resource Manager for car manufacturer in Malaga	Duisburg, Malaga	2017
26.	Dolores	38	High School	Cleaner at a private company in Berlin; Cleaner at a hotel in Alicante	Berlin, Alicante	2017
27.	Martina	53	Geography (BA)	Mother of a returnee who worked in Germany		2015

10. Methodological Appendix

Interviewees United Kingdom

No.	Name	Age	Education	Current occupation	Place of residence	Year of interview
28.	Felipe	23	Physical Education (BA)	Au Pair	Bristol	2014
29.	María (2x)	33	Library Science (BA)	Kitchen porter at university	Bristol	2014, 2016
30.	Diego (2x)	30	Nursing (BA)	Nurse at public hospital	Bristol	2014, 2016
31.	Esteban	30	Archaeology (BA)	Kitchen porter at cafe	London	2014
32.	Matias	26	Physical Education (BA)	Kitchen porter in a restaurant, sports teacher	London	2014
33.	Rocio	22	English Literature (BA)	Au Pair	Bristol	2014
34.	Ignacio	36	Computer Sciences (BA)	Computer scientist at private company	Exeter	2014
35.	Oscar	29	Mechanic engineering (BA)	Currently unemployed	Cambridge	2014
36.	Rubén	29	Mechanic engineering (BA)	Factory worker	Bristol	2014
37.	Santiago	29	Office administration – apprenticeship	Night supervisor at hotel	London	2014
38.	Lucia	18	High school degree	Au Pair	Bristol	2014
39.	Sol	42	Human resource management (BA)	Childcare worker at a primary school	Cardiff	2014
40.	Antonio	31	Psychology (BA)	Care worker for children with cognitive disabilities	Cardiff	2016
41.	Daniel	40	Law and Finance (MA)	Project manager at multinational company	London	2017
42.	Laura	25	Social Work (BA)	Educator for people with cognitive impairments	Glasgow	2017
43.	Juan	42	Business Administration (BA)	Adviser at job centre	Aberdeen	2017
44.	Fabian	25	Chemistry (MA)	Factory supervisor at brewery	Glasgow	2017
45.	Magda	31	Civil Engineering (MA)	Civil engineer at a Scottish company	Glasgow	2017
46.	Liliana	38	Art History (BA)	Spanish language assistant at a high school	Glasgow	2017
47.	Pablo	52	Theatre Studies (BA)	Kitchen Porter at a restaurant	Glasgow	2017

No.	Name	Age	Education	Current occupation	Place of residence	Year of interview
48.	Sara	25	Journalism (BA)	Waitress at restaurant	Glasgow	2017
49.	Emilio	24	Mechanical Engineering (BA)	Gap year/ English course	Cambridge	2018
50.	Christiano	27	Business Administration (BA)	Master student at British University	Cambridge	2018
51.	Jorge	25	Office Administration – apprenticeship	Warehouse manager	Cambridge	2018
52.	Lorena	23	Business Administration & English (BA)	Controller at manufacturing company	Huntington	2018

Returnees United Kingdom

No.	Name	Age	Education	Former & current occupations	Former & current locations	Year of interview
53.	Nora	29	Business Administration (MA)	Employee at tourist company in Brighton; Project manager at international clothing company in Madrid	Brighton, Madrid	2017
54.	León	26	History (MA)	Erasmus student in Bristol, master student in St. Andrews; English teacher in Madrid	Bristol/ Edinburgh, Madrid	2017
55.	Adam	26	Audio-visual Studies (BA at private institute)	Hotel worker in Manchester; Master student in cinematography	Manchester, Madrid	2017
56.	Carmen	25	Statistics (BA)	Cleaner at a hotel in Brighton; Statistician at EU-financed employability project in Malaga	Brighton, Malaga	2017
57.	Manuel	23	Business Administration (BA)	Au Pair in Cambridge; Master student in Business Administration in Madrid	Cambridge, Madrid	2017

10. Methodological Appendix

No.	Name	Age	Education	Former & current occupations	Former & current locations	Year of interview
FU	María	34	Library Science (BA)	Kitchen Porter at university in Bristol, Receptionist at international company in Madrid	Bristol, Madrid	2017
FU	Rocio	25	English Literature (MA)	Au Pair in Bristol; English teacher at language school in Seville	Bristol, Seville	2017
58.	Ander	29	Law (MA)	Six months English course in Brighton; Business consultant in San Sebastian	Brighton, San Sebastian	2018

FU = Follow-up interview

CONSENT FORM

University of Cambridge, Department of Sociology

Consentimiento Informado

Título del Proyecto: Dejando España en tiempos difíciles: Experiencias de crisis, migración y nuevos comienzos

Nombre de la investigadora: Me-Linh Riemann

Como parte de un proyecto de investigación sobre la "nueva" migración desde España al Reino Unido (e Alemania) estoy realizando entrevistas biográficas. Se le pedirá preguntas sobre su historia de vida – incluyendo preguntas acerca de cómo su vida se desarrolló antes de la crisis económica en España, la forma en que usted experimentó la agitación financiera en su entorno personal, cómo la decisión de migrar desarrollo y qué tipo de experiencias que han hecho en el nuevo país. Esta investigación es parte de un proyecto de doctorado en sociología

La entrevista tomará aproximadamente 60 minutos.

Si está interesado en recibir más información sobre este proyecto, por favor escriba su dirección de correo electrónico en la hoja adicional o escribir un mensaje a mlhr2@cam.ac.uk

Por favor marque la casilla correspondiente
1. Confirmo que he entendido las instrucciones y que tengo la oportunidad de hacer preguntas.
2. Entiendo que mi participación es voluntaria y que estoy libre de retirarme en cualquier momento y sin necesidad de justificación.
3. Entiendo que mis respuestas serán anónimos y sólo se utiliza para la investigación académica.
4. Entiendo que la entrevista va a ser grabada.
5. Estoy de acuerdo en participar en este proyecto de investigación.

| Nombre del participante | Fecha | Firma |
| Nombre de la investigadora | Fecha | Firma |

NOTES

1. Introduction

1. I wrote this sentence before the horrendous invasion of Ukraine that started on 24 February, 2022. This event marks the end of the post-war order in Europe as we know it. There is no doubt that this is the beginning of a new – quite different – collective crisis.
2. According to Hedgecoe (2020), Germany is the European country with the most critical care beds per 100 000 inhabitants (namely 29.2 beds), whilst Portugal finishes last in an EU-wide comparison (4.2 beds).
3. At the time of writing, Spain has a vaccination rate of 80%, which is significantly higher than that of Germany (70.7%) or the United Kingdom (70.4%) (Statista, January 2022).
4. According to Holleran (2019, p. 467) the term was coined by Ortega Y Gasset following the consequences of the Spanish defeat in the Spanish-American War of 1898, but it was also used by many others, including Hemingway and members of his milieu in Paris after the First World War (Wohl, 1979). During the 2008 economic crisis, one could not escape the term "lost generation" when opening the newspapers or reading something about the fate of young people in Spain and other countries in Southern Europe.
5. In the 1980s and 1990s, Spain transitioned very rapidly from having one of the most rigid employment systems to one of the most flexible in Europe. For many years the Spanish labour market has therefore been highly divided into 'insiders' with permanent positions and 'outsiders' who either work under much more precarious conditions or do not work at all. The latter problem has been much more prevalent among young people, who entered the labour force at a less favourable point in time than their parents' generation (Golsch, 2003). The 1980s and early 1990s, furthermore, witnessed a significant increase in joblessness. This shift is especially visible in the youth unemployment rate, which rose from 14.1% in 1977 to 42% in 1996. By that time, more than a third of employment contracts had become temporary (Köhler, 2010). What changed in the mid-1990s is that Spain started to attract foreign investment flows that helped fuel an economic boom. It was a time period marked by easy access to capital and seemingly ever rising property

prices (Royo, 2014). Back then it was comparatively easy to get a job, even though the short-term nature of many work contracts did not allow for long-term planning (e.g. buying a house, family planning). At the time, Spain became Europe's highest recipient of immigration, attracting millions of people from Latin America and Africa but also central and eastern Europe (Fernández & Ortega, 2008). When the foreign investment flows suddenly subsided after the global financial crash of 2008, the real estate sector collapsed. What followed could be described as a chain reaction that exposed the fragility of Spain's previous economic success. Almost every industry was deeply affected by the deep recession, a process that led to countless bankruptcies, severe cutbacks, and large-scale lay-offs (Buendía & Molero-Simarro, 2018).

6. The OECD (2022) defines "youth unemployment rates" as "the number of unemployed 15- to 24-year-olds expressed as a percentage of the youth labour force. Unemployed people are those who report that they are without work, that they are available for work and that they have taken active steps to find work in the last four weeks." This excludes high school and university students, who are still in education and are therefore unavailable to work.

7. In the literature, the migration wave from southern Europe in the context of the 2008 economic crisis is commonly referred to as the 'new' south-north movement or mobility (Lafleur & Stanek, 2017). The emphasis is on 'new' to draw boundaries to previous migration waves from this region, including the 'guestworker' movement in the 1960s and 1970s. In this study, I put the term 'guestworker' or 'Gastarbeiter' in inverted commas, because I regard it as a euphemistic misnomer. A guest is usually not expected to work.

8. The situation of EU citizens in Britain has, of course, dramatically changed due to Brexit. At the time of writing, the Home Office is processing millions of applications for the so-called 'EU settled status'. It will take many months until reliable statistics will be made available to the public (O'Carroll, 2021).

9. There have been numerous historic examples of mass emigration waves from Spain, such as to the former colonies in Latin America from 1880 to 1914 (Sánchez-Alonso, 2000) and during the Spanish Civil War from 1936 to 1939 (Richards, 2006), or in form of the 'Gastarbeiter' movement in the 1960s and early 1970s (Oltmer et al., 2012). A major destination country for the migration was West Germany (unlike the UK).

10. The term 'economic exile' has a special connotation in the Spanish collective memory and often evokes associations with the Franco regime. Sometimes, young Spanish migrants take a critical stance toward such ascriptions as is visible in interviews with young Spaniards in London (Cortes, Moncó & Betrisey, 2015, pp. 48-50).

11. In 2013, the influential German magazine "Der Spiegel" dedicated one issue to the new arrivals from southern Europe, using the headline: "The new guest workers: Europe's young elite for Germany's economy". The authors' intentions behind choosing this title were twofold. Firstly, they drew parallels to the migratory routes of the 'guest worker' generation: a mass movement that has left its mark on the collective memory (cf. Glorius, 2016). After WW2, west Germany (along with France and Belgium) suffered from a severe labour shortage. The situation was exacerbated by the Eastern Bloc emigration restrictions and eventual erection of the inner-German border wall, which cut off the

cheap labour supply from the GDR. Employers had to look for workers elsewhere, which gave rise to large-scale recruitment programmes. Various sending nations participated in this 'guest worker' scheme including the PIGS states (i.e. Portugal, Italy, Greece, Spain), along with Turkey, Yugoslavia and some north African countries. The scale of the phenomenon was quite significant. After the recruitment programme stopped (mostly) by the mid-1970s in the context of the oil crisis, these migrants had often either gained permanent residence permits, become citizens or returned to their country of origin. Barbulescu (2017) argues that these 'guest workers' were in many ways the "pioneers of European free movement", as they established migratory routes between the south and the north as early as the late 1940s. The Spiegel authors were keen to point out that the 'new' arrivals differed from their predecessors in important aspects. The 'guest workers' were predominantly male and came from rural areas in Spain (Thränhardt, 2010) and elsewhere. Furthermore, their education level was mostly quite basic, as many had to leave school at a young age. In contrast to their predecessors, the 'new' arrivals from southern Europe constituted a much more diverse group. It included (mostly young) women and men from various socio-economic backgrounds who were trained in a range of occupations. What most of them share is a high level of education – something that the journalists alluded to by referring to them as "Europe's young elite". The Spiegel issue received mixed reviews in the Spanish community in Germany. Many people felt misrepresented by the title 'new guest workers', as they believed the historic analogy to be misleading. Whilst they did share the same nationality with their predecessors, the historic circumstances and educational profiles were very different. Some 'new' migrants also took issue with the media's focus on success stories, such as on the case of Spanish engineers in the south of Germany. Although some of the new arrivals had indeed found a well paid job in their field of expertise, many others worked in fields unrelated to their academic training.

2. Mapping the Field

1. Since then, the number of Poles in the UK has decreased slightly but is still estimated to be over 900,000 as of July 2020 (Statista, 2020).
2. It should be noted that Engbersen and Snel (2013, p. 35) take this term from the qualitative study of Eade, Drinkwater and Garapich (2006) on Polish migration to the UK, even though these authors do not use the term "habitus" (and other elements of Bourdieu's language) but "strategy": "They undertake a strategy of what we call *intentional unpredictability* – that is keeping options open, taking a 'wait-and-see approach' (….)." (pp. 68-69). See doc.ukdataservice.ac.uk/doc/6056/mrdoc/pdf/6056uguide.pdf.
3. See, e.g., articles in *Social Inclusion* 2019, *Vol 7* (4).
4. It might be helpful for readers who want to know more about the analytical procedures that I use to read this appendix before turning to my case studies and the following chapters.

3. Biographical Case Studies

1. I discussed Adam's and María's decision-making process to leave Spain elsewhere (Riemann, 2019). In the following case studies, I am citing myself whereever I discuss interview extracts that have appeared in the previous publication.
2. Concepts such as 'trajectories of suffering', 'biographical action scemes' and sub-categories such as 'biographical projects', 'action schemes of control' and 'action schemes of escape' have been developed in the sequential and comparative analysis of autobiographical narrative interviews (Schütze 1981, 1995, 2008). Interested readers are advised to read the methodological appendix of this study for more background information.
3. He decided against a formal English course, which was very expensive, and discovered a self-help initiative online, where Spanish and British people would meet in a cafe to practise each other's languages. He could, however, not find the cafe and decided not to pursue the project further.
4. Schütze (2014, p. 142) writes about codas at the end of narratives and their (possible) elaborations: "Such a coda is to be found at the end of every off-the-cuff narration of personal experiences (…). A coda ties the past time of the story events to the present time of actual narration, and it shows the outcomes of the narrated events and experiences for the narrator, his life, and present situation. Wherever the coda shows at least some elaboration, it is combined with an evaluation of the informant's social and biographical processes in their impact on his life course at length, and, too, on the collective 'we-units' at large, in which the informant is a member and which were at stake during the course of the events depicted." This is also visible at the end of Adam's biographical narrative, as he openly reflects on his personal journey and the structural conditions with which he is now faced.
5. What stands out in the beginning of María's narrative is the fact that she spoke very little about her childhood experience.
6. After completing an internship at a university library, she was once offered a temporary position as a librarian. Even though she enjoyed this type of work, she ultimately decided against it due to its unfavourable conditions.
7. Such self-interruptions and background constructions can occur in biographical narratives when informants express especially confusing and painful experiences, which they are still in the process of coming to terms with (Schütze, 2008, pp. 27-30; Riemann, 2018). I have included more information in the methodological appendix.
8. Other foci would have been possible, e.g., a specific focus on gender issues, generational belonging or Spanish citizens' experiences in different receiving societies (i.e. separating the chapters between my German and British sample). In this book, I focus on these themes whenever they become significant in the data but I chose not to develop entire chapters around them.
9. One example: The discovery of María's migration project as an 'action scheme of escape' from her intolerable situation in Madrid (i.e. family catastrophe, financial ruin) leads to the questions about whether there are also other kinds of trajectories of suffering (preceding migration projects) that can be detected in the rest of the data material.

4. Time to go?

1. This does not apply to the case of Daniel who was working as a project manager for a multinational firm in the UK. As I will discuss in more detail in my chapter on work experience, he belonged to what could be referred to as a 'transnational elite' of highly successful business people. For people in these circles, gaining international work experience appears to be a norm rather than an exception (Vorheyer (2016) on 'transnational mobiles').
2. Interestingly, Tomas continued his voluntary engagement for the movement after moving to Germany by co-founding an organisation that offered support for Spanish migrants abroad. In contrast to his engagement in Madrid, this new project required less time and focused more on providing practical support for people in need, which brought him visible relief.
3. 'Closed awareness context' is a concept that first appeared in Glaser's and Strauss's (1965) 'Awareness of Dying'. In their study, 'closed awareness context' referred to the situation where a patient is not being informed and does not know that he or she is dying. They differentiated between different awareness contexts: "open", "closed", "suspicion" and "mutual pretense". Hoffmann-Riem (1990) used the concept for her study on adoptive families.
4. Gentile (2014) defines 'milieuristas' as "people around 30 years old, with high skills and academic degrees who were surviving with precarious jobs and were earning a gross monthly salary not exceeding €1,000." (p. 126).
5. When speaking about their experiences with the economic crisis, several interviewees spoke about a certain 'time delay' between the financial collapse of 2008 and tangible repercussions in everyday life. In other words, they first started noticing the 'real life' effects of the crisis around 2010, which corresponds to Diego's experience at the hospital.

5. On Studying and Working Abroad

1. A few informants, however, criticised their co-nationals for underestimating their chances on the British or German labour market by "*not even trying*" to get a job in their field of expertise. That being said, many informants were under the impression that their cultural capital in the form of Spanish university degrees was devalued in the receiving society.
2. Against the backdrop of the economic crisis of 2008, unconventional forms of production, labour and non-financial rewards have gained much attention in Spain. Examples include ethical banks and eco-villages in Barcelona (Castells & Hlebik, 2017). It was surprising to observe how such alternative non-economic exchange networks span across borders, as they enabled individuals to move to a new country without having to take a job in the 'regular' economy.
3. The main reason why Juan could not sustain this alternative work arrangement long-term was the fact that he had accumulated debt in Spain due to the collapse of his company. He was under pressure to earn money, which is why he eventually took on a job as a kitchen porter in a restaurant.

4. Pablo's biographical narrative only reveals an impression of conversations he had at his workplace, or in other words how *he* had experienced them. Detailed communication patterns can be more easily reconstructed by using ethnographic fieldnotes or transcripts of everyday conversations.
5. During my fieldwork, I experienced a few situations where I felt a bit taken aback by my informants' use of the 'man/woman' tag (Hickey 2005). I remember quite vividly that another older male participant referred to me as 'woman' in the interview. One example: When I thanked him for taking part in my research project, he responded: *"You're welcome, woman!"*, a well-meaning expression that still made me cringe in the situation.
6. This is an important insight to keep in mind when discussing the topic of a new European solidarity emerging in resistance to Brexit (chapter 7).
7. Such initiatives, which can be found in many different countries across Europe, differ in their political and ideological affiliations (e.g. anarcho-syndicalism). These organisations frequently offer a wide spectrum of different activities, ranging from Marxist reading groups to very practical support such as legal advice (Roca & Martín-Díaz, 2017).
8. A few participants had jobs that fell somewhere in between the category of 'menial' and 'qualified' labour. While these informants did not practise their 'profession' yet, they worked in a related field. Laura had a university degree in social work and was working as an educator for people with disabilities at the time of our interview. Although this job was below her academic qualifications, it was still related to her academic training. She hoped that eventually the work experiences as an educator would help her find a position as a social worker. This pattern could be found in several other cases as well.
9. The 'joint' migration project of these two women resembled (to a certain extent) the patterns of earlier migration waves, such as the 'Gastarbeiter' or 'guest worker' movement of the 1960s/1970s. Back then, German employers would also travel to countries in southern Europe to recruit staff to work in the steel industry and coal mines. Sometimes, larger groups of migrants from specific villages would move to a German destination 'together'. That said, it is also important to point out that the contemporary recruitment of nurses from Spain is quite different as they are "headhunted" because of their special qualifications (cf. Godenau, 2017). Coincidently, the grandfather of Daniela's friend was a so-called 'Gastarbeiter' in Germany in the 1960s, who later returned to Spain.
10. The data suggests that the fear of miscommunication and putting patients at risk was temporary and my informants managed to overcome it relatively quickly. Furthermore, their employers both in Germany and the UK seemed experienced in training foreign staff and seemed to make sure that there were sufficient support structures in place to avoid escalations based on language barriers.
11. Interestingly, the topic of the economic crisis only came up when I asked him about his family. He described his younger brother as being 'ni ni' – a term with a negative connotation referring to young people who 'neither work nor study'. Daniel, however, believed his brother to be fully responsible for his lack of success as he described him as lazy and indecisive about his career path.

6. A Web of Social Relationships

1. In response to the economic crisis, private schools had switched to a bilingual system while public schools lacked the funding to employ new teachers (Sabaté-Dalmau, 2016).
2. The interview took place three months after his separation. Felipe was in deep pain at that moment, which was also visible in the textual structure of his narrative. He spontaneously interrupted his main storyline by inserting a background construction (revealing painful and chaotic experiences) in order to clarify how the couple's expectations and the reality of his migration experience diverged. I have explicated the detailed analysis of this case elsewhere (Riemann, 2018).
3. This type of filtered communication could also happen in reverse, as family members consciously chose not to inform migrants about problems at home.
4. The number of members in these Facebook groups should – however – not be regarded as a reliable indicator of how many Spanish people actually reside in the city. According to an expert informant (Ignacio) they often include e.g. people in Spain, who are currently contemplating migration and who use social media as a tool to collect information about possible destinations. Furthermore, some migrants only spend a very short amount of time in a city (a few weeks or months) before either moving back to Spain or to a third destination but they remain members of these social media groups.
5. There are, of course, other factors that have contributed to the rise of the Catalan independence movement. For a detailed analysis of the impact of the economic crisis on this mass movement see: Cuadros-Morato and Rodon (2019).
6. On Facebook, there are also a number of smaller groups specifically for Basque or Catalan people abroad (Oiarzerbal, 2012). These groups seemed much more selective in whom they admitted or did not admit as members of their online community. During my fieldwork I tried to join a platform for Catalans in London, but my request was rejected, as I did not speak Catalan (they put me through a little test).
7. My Catalan and Basque informants' tendency to bring up their sense of European identity also resembled to some extent the rhetoric of Scottish nationalists who oppose 'Brexit' (Arrighi, 2019).
8. The experiences of my informants seemed to differ from those of central and eastern European migrants, who more frequently planned to settle down in the receiving society for longer periods of time. They often expressed quite pessimistic views about what their futures would be like in countries such as Poland (cf. Jendrissek 2014, Gryzmala-Kazlowska 2017).
9. León's friends who he portrayed as suffering from autism and OCD serve as an example of such.
10. As indicated in previous chapters I also interviewed a few male au pairs. However, occupations that involve childrearing are still female dominated, which is something that several interviewees brought up in their narratives.

7. Established-Outsider Relations in Times of Brexit

1. As indicated in my fieldwork chapter, I incorporated my MPhil participants (2014) into my PhD sample. Some of these (early) interviewees may have left the UK for good before Brexit emerged as a topic in 2015. Some returnees I interviewed were deeply hurt by the outcome of the EU referendum even though they were no longer living in Britain by the time of the vote.
2. There are several publications that discuss the long-term social processes underlying the 'othering' of non-national EU citizens in the UK. In the past years, their presence in Britain has increasingly been presented as a social problem or crisis, which had a significant impact on the EU referendum of 2016 (Outhwaite, 2019; Favell & Barbulescu, 2018).
3. "The Established and the Outsiders" (Elias & Scotson, 1965) is a classic sociological text that emerged out of a local study on neighbourhood tensions in Winston Parva, a small town in the English Midlands, in the late 1950s and early 1960s. By studying the sharp social divisions between an 'old-established' group and a group of 'new residents' in this suburban community, they discovered social processes that were of universal significance.
4. This short narrative serves as a supportive document in a longer argumentative sequence in which he tries to undermine his opponent's position.
5. Such an instance of establishing a broader solidarity (or we-group) differs from practices of keeping distance from other groups of EU citizens in this context. In their study on how young Italian migrants reacted to Brexit, Mazzilli and King (2019) observed how some participants drew clear distinctions between themselves and central and eastern Europeans –there were tendencies to establish interethnic hierarchies and avoid stigma (Goffman, 1968a) by emphasising the essential differences between "us" and "them". Cortés Maisonave et al. (2019) also refer to tendencies of drawing a line between "us" and "them" (central and eastern Europeans) in their report about Spaniards in the Greater London area.
6. Diego mentioned how he had the idea to develop a recruitment programme between the UK and Spain with a former professor in Spain. Brexit had discouraged him from developing the idea further.
7. According to media reports (Noor, 2019), German hospitals have already started publishing job advertisements in English-Polish newspapers encouraging Polish nurses to 'come back home', emphasising better social benefits, the (geographic) proximity to Poland and the security of an EU member state.
8. In Glasgow, one participant mentioned how Scotland's First Minister Nicola Sturgeon sent out personalised letters to every registered EU citizen, assuring them her personal support.
9. It is important to point out that most of my participants were in their twenties and had only been in the UK for a short period of time. Their ties to the receiving society were not as deep as those of Europeans who had lived in Britain for many decades and who interpreted Brexit as a devaluation of their life's work (which is visible in the personal testimonies in Remigi, 2017).

8. An Uneasy Homecoming

1. Vathi (2017) writes: "One of the major 'sins' of the existing literature is its simplistic focus in terms of the types of migration that give rise to psychosocial issues. A division is observable between 'voluntary' migration, considered as psychosocially safe, and a concentration of research on forced migration and migrants' war-related traumas. (p. 3)"
2. Schütz (1945/1971) studied the homecoming experiences of American soldiers returning from WW2. While there are, of course, certain obstacles that are specific to people returning from war (cf. post-traumatic stress), Schütz aimed to discover insights that are applicable to other kinds of return migration.
3. In 1945, when Schütz first published the essay, it was common practice to use the masculine pronoun 'he' and 'his' whenever articulating an example of a more general phenomenon. I am aware that this language is outdated, as it violates gender sensitivities. It would be more appropriate to use 'they'/'their' or 'she/he'. That being said, I decided to use the original quote and to adjust the following sentence accordingly (using 'he') for the sake of making this paragraph coherent.
4. See also my discussion of 'A filtered presentation in everyday life' in chapter 6.
5. There have been several media reports about the so-called 'lost generation' of migrants returning 'home'. According to estimates, more than 80,000 Spanish migrants moved back to Spain (from various receiving societies in Europe and overseas) in 2018 alone (Lüdke & Zuber, 2019).
6. One year prior to the interview, Rocio had worked as a 'course leader' during a trip to England earning €800 a month. She was later promoted to manager, which is why she could draw contrasting comparisons between the two positions.

9. Conclusion

1. https://volvemos.org/
2. My special focus on some of my interviewees' experiences with Brexit as a dramatic turning point should not convey the impression that I have a distorted and uncritical view of what is happening in Germany (my other field site) and other European countries with regard to the endangerment of social rights of EU non-nationals. See, for the case of Belgium, Lafleur and Stanek 2017, and for Germany, e.g., https://www.dw.com/en/germany-limits-eu-citizens-access-to-benefits/a-36026606.
3. https://www.dw.com/de/spanier-als-deutsche-azubis-warum-mobipro-gescheitert-ist/a-40685728
4. For a comprehensive historical analysis of Spanish people's mistrust in political leaders, the military and the church see Preston's critically acclaimed book "A People Betrayed" (2020).
5. See Strauss (1993, pp. 97-106) and Betts et al. (2008) on the concept of 'biographical work'.
6. See case study of Mateo Lopez.
7. See also Vertovec's (2009, pp. 13-16) discussion on what is 'old' and what is 'new' about migrant transnationalism.

8. "Some migrants have no fixed aspirations or ideas about the future. Their options are open. They go to new destiantion countries without clear-cut aspirations of investing money in their home country or settling in the receiving country. This migratory habitus expresses the more individualistic ethos of unmarried labour migrants, who are less bounded by family obligations, borders and local labour markets than previous generations of migrants." (Engbersen & Snel, 2013, p. 35)
9. Given the enduring and unpredictable nature of this crisis, this label could be extended to 'class of 2021/2022'.
10. https://www.bbc.com/worklife/article/20200901-the-class-of-2020s-uncertain-present-and-future.
11. EU mobility is, of course, only one area that is deeply affected by Brexit. There are many other open questions, including whether peace in Northern Ireland is at risk, and the independence movement in Scotland is gathering momentum. At the moment, it is far from certain whether the United Kingdom will endure in the future.

10. Methodological Appendix

1. Even though instructive texts are available in English (see, e.g., Schütze 2008, 2014), special mention should also be made of the biographical studies of Polish sociologists that are based on this approach and have been published in English, e.g., a collection of studies on the biographies of Polish people who have experienced the radical systemic transformation after the breakdown of state socialism (edited by Kaja Kazmierska and Katarzyna Waniek, 2020). See also a collection of biographical studies on "The evolution of European identities" (edited by Robert Miller and Graham Day, 2012).
2. My reconstruction of these processes is partially based on a long biographical interview conducted by Kaja Kazmierska (University of Lodz) with Fritz Schütze (Kazmierska, 2014). See also the interview which Jakub Gałęziowski, a Polish oral historian, recently conducted with Fritz Schütze: Gałęziowski (2021).
3. See chapter 4 in my study. Schütze (1981, 1995) also spelled out the structure of such trajectories of suffering which he discovered in sequentially and comparatively analysing autobiographical narrative interviews. In the period in which he hit upon this phenomenon he closely cooperated with Anselm Strauss, who had also used the concept of 'trajectory' in his studies on dying conducted together with Barney Glaser (see especially Glaser & Strauss, 1968).
4. See Schütze (2008, pp. 26-36) for a discussion of the presentation markers of these structural processes and the language of their narrative presentation.
5. Also in everyday encounters, not just in narrative interviews.
6. A detailed discussion of this phenomenon can be found in Riemann (2018).
7. In reconstructing my field research, I will intentionally use the personal pronoun I in order to make this process (including my inner states and the difficulties which I had to deal with) as transparent as possible, i.e. to communicate what is involved in the work of doing research and under which conditions the data was collected. Such personal presentations are a common practice in qualitative publications.

8. I would like to point out that not all narratives were transcribed in full, as some interviews did not go very well (due to different reasons). Whenever I felt that a full transcription was not necessary, I wrote extensive field notes instead. Whilst I fully translated the biographical narratives of key informants, I also sequentially analysed quite a few interviews purely on the basis of the Spanish transcriptions. I then only translated specific data excerpts into English that I was considering for inclusion in the dissertation.
9. These public posts were made in Spanish.
10. Martina contacted me after reading a description of my research project online. She was deeply worried about her son, who got caught up in a trajectory of suffering (i.e. partly because of some traumatic experiences he had had in Germany). Martina did not expect any professional advice from me but appreciated being given the opportunity to narrate freely. This interview took place over Skype.

REFERENCES

Acea-López, L., del Mar Pastor-Bravo, M., Rubinat-Arnaldo, E., Bellon, F., Blanco-Blanco, J., Gea-Sanchez, M. & Briones-Vozmediano, E. (2021). Burnout and job satisfaction among nurses in three Spanish regions. *Journal of Nursing Management, 0*(0), 1-8.

Adler, L. & Ayala-Hurtado, E. (2021). *A Little Help from my Friends? Resolving Moral Tension between Meritocracy and Job-seeking Help* (Working Paper), presentation at SASE mini conference (2-5 July 2021).

Alberti, G. (2014). Mobility strategies, 'mobility differentials' and 'transnational exit': the experiences of precarious migrants in London's hospitality jobs. *Work, Employment and Society, 28*(6), 865-881.

Allport, G.W. (1942). *The use of personal documents in psychological science.* New York: Social Science Research Council.

Alpagu, F. (2019). "I am doing well in Austria." Biography, photography and migration memories of a 1970s guest worker. *Rassegna Italiana di Sociologia. 10*(1), 47-74.

Anderson, B. & Wilson, H. (2018). Everyday Brexits. *Area, 50*(2), 291-295.

Anderson, B. (2000). *Doing the dirty work?* London: Zed Books.

Apitzsch, U. & Siouti, I. (2007). *Biographical analysis as an interdisciplinary research perspective in the field of migration studies.* Frankfurt a. M.: Research Integration, Johann Wolfgang Goethe Universität and University of York.

Apitzsch, U., Bertaux, D., Delcroix, C. & Inowlocki, L. (2014). Introduction to the thematic issue on "Socialization, family, and gender in the context of migration". *Zeitschrift für Qualitative Forschung, 15*(1), 3-10.

Apitzsch, U., Inowlocki, L., Glaeser, J., Klingenberg, D., Pape, E. & Schwarz, C. H. (2019). Die Evaluation von Migrationspolitiken mittels Lebensgeschichten von Migrant*innen. Das deutsch-französische Projekt MIGREVAL. In N. Burzan (Ed.), Komplexe Dynamiken globaler und lokaler Entwicklungen. Verhandlungen des 39. Kongresses der Deutschen Gesellschaft für Soziologie in Göttingen 2018. http://publikationen.soziologie.de/index.php/kongressband_2018/article/view/1129/1337.

Arango, J. (2000). Becoming a Country of Immigration at the End of the Twentieth Century: The Case of Spain. In R. King, G. Lazaridis, & C. Tsardanidis (Eds.), *Eldorado or Fortress? Migration in Southern Europe* (pp. 253-276). London: Palgrave Macmillan.

Arce, M.E., Crespo, B. & Míguez-Álvarez, C. (2015). Higher Education Drop-Out in Spain – Particular Case of Universities in Galicia. *International Education Studies, 8*(5), 247-264.

Arrighi, J.T. (2019). 'The People, Year Zero': Secessionism and Citizenship in Scotland and Catalonia. *Ethnopolitics. 18*(3), 278-297.

Arundel, R. & Lennartz, C. (2017). Returning to the parental home: Boomerang moves of younger adults and the welfare regime context. *Journal of European Social Policy, 27*(3), 276-294.

Askins, K. (2016). Emotional citizenry: everyday geographies of befriending, belonging and intercultural encounter. *Transactions of the Institute of British Geographers, 41*(4), 515-527.

Ayala-Hurtado, E. (2021). Narrative Continuity/Rupture: Projected Professional Futures amid Pervasive Employment Precarity, *Work and Occupations, 0*(0), 1-36.

Bach, S. (2010). Managed migration? Nurse recruitment and the consequences of state policy. *Industrial Relations Journal, 41*(3), 249-266.

Bagnoli, A. (2003). Imagining the Lost Other: The Experience of Loss and the Process of Identity Construction in Young People. *Journal of Youth Studies, 6*(2), 203-217.

Bagnoli, A. (2007). Between outcast and outsider: constructing the identity of a foreigner. *European Societies, 9*(1), 23-44.

Bagnoli, A. (2009). On 'an introspective journey'. *European Societies, 11*(3), 325-345.

Baird, B. & McKenna, H. (2019). Brexit: the implications for health and social care. *The King's Fund.*

Ballaste-Isern, E. (2017). Espacios migrantes y nuevos movimientos sociales: el caso de Marea Granate. *Revista de Dialectología y Tradiciones Populares, 22*(1), 51-57.

Barbulescu, R. (2017). From International Migration to Freedom of Movement and Back? Southern Europeans Moving North in the Era of Retrenchment of

Freedom of Movement Rights. In J.-M. Lafleur & M. Stanek (Eds.) (2017). *South-North Migration of EU Citizens in Times of Crisis.* Springer Open.

Barley, N. (1989). *Native Land.* London: Penguin Books.

Bartram, D., Poros, M. V. & Monforte, P. (2014). *Key Concepts in Migration.* Los Angeles and London: Sage.

Bastia, T. (2011). Should I stay or should I go? Return migration in times of crisis. *Journal of International Development, 23*(1), 583-595.

Bauman, Z. (1999). *Liquid Modernity.* Cambridge: Polity Press.

Becker, H. S. (1966). Introduction to: C. R. Shaw (1966). *The Jack-Roller: A Delinquent Boy's Own Story* (pp. v-xviii). Chicago: University of Chicago Press.

Becker, H.S. (1998). *Tricks of the Trade.* Chicago: The University of Chicago Press.

Benito, B., Vicente, C. & Bastida, F. (2015). The Impact of the Housing Bubble on the Growth of Municipal Debt: Evidence from Spain. *Local Government Studies, 41*(6), 997-1016.

Benson, M. & O'Reilly, K. (2016). From lifestyle migration to lifestyle *in* migration: Categories, concepts and ways of thinking. *Migration Studies, 4*(1), 20-37.

Benson, M. & O'Reilly, K. (2009). Migration and the search for a better way of life: a critical exploration of lifestyle migration. *The Sociological Review, 57*(4), 608-625.

Bermudez, A. (2020). Remigration of "new" Spaniards since the economic crisis: the interplay between citizenship and precarity among Colombian-Spanish families moving to Northern Europe. *Ethnic and Racial Studies.* https://www.tandfonline.com/doi/abs/10.1080/01419870.2020.1738521?journalCode=rers20.

Bermudez, A. & Brey, E. (2017). Is Spain Becoming a Country of Emigration Again? Data Evidence and Public Responses. In J.-M. Lafleur & M. Stanek (Eds.) (2017). *South-North Migration of EU Citizens in Times of Crisis* (pp. 83-98). Springer Open.

Bermudez, A. & Oso, L. (2020). Recent trends in intra-EU mobilities: the articulation between migration, social protection, gender and citizenship systems. *Ethnic and Racial Studies, 43*(14).

Bertaux, D. (2016). *Le récit de vie.* Paris: Armand Colin. (4th edition).

Bertaux, D. (Ed.) (1981). *Biography and Society. The Life History Approach in the Social Sciences.* Beverly Hills and London: Sage.

Betts, S., Griffiths, A., Schütze, F. & Straus, P. (2008). Biographical Counselling: an Introduction. *European Studies on Inequalities and Social Cohesion, 1*(2), 5-58.

Bhambra, G.K. (2017). Locating Brexit in the pragmatics of race, citizenship and empire. In W. Outhwaite (Ed.), *Brexit: sociological responses* (pp. 91-99). London: Anthem Press.

Böckler, S., Gestmann, M. & Handke, T. (2018). *Neuzuwanderung in Duisburg-Marxloh: bulgarische und rumänische Zuwanderer und Alteingesessene im Ankunftsquartier.* Wiesbaden: Springer VS.

Bogdal, K.-M. (2011). *Europa erfindet die Zigeuner. Eine Geschichte von Faszination und Verachtung.* Berlin: Suhrkamp.

Bolognani, M. (2016). From myth of return to return fantasy: a psychosocial interpretation of migration imaginaries. *Identities, 23*(2), 193-209.

Booth, J. & Baert, P. (2018). *The Dark Side of Podemos? Carl Schmitt and Contemporary Progressive Populism.* London: Routledge Focus.

Botterill, K. & Burrell, K. (2020). (In)visibility, privilege and the performance of whiteness in Brexit Britain: Polish migrants in Britain's shifting migration regime. *Environment and Planning: Politics and Space, 37*(1), 23-28.

Botterill, K., McCollum, D. & Tyrell, N. (2018). Negotiating Brexit: Migrant spatialities and identities in a changing Europe. *Population, Space and Place, 25*(1), 1-4.

Bourdieu, P. (1984). *Distinction: A Social Critique of the Judgement of Taste.* Cambridge, MA: Harvard University Press.

Brücker, H., Hauptmann, A. & Vallizadeh, E. (2013). Zuwanderer aus Bulgarien und Rumänien: Arbeitsmigration oder Armutsmigration? *IAB Kurzbericht, 6/2013.* Nuremberg: Institute for Employment Research.

Buchan, J., Wismar, M., Glinos, I.A. & Bremner, J. (Eds.) (2014). *Health professional mobility in a changing Europe.* Observatory Studies Series, Vol. 32. European Observatory on Health Systems and Policies, World Health Organization.

Buendía, L. & Molero-Simarro, R. (2018). *The Political Economy of Contemporary Spain: From Miracle to Mirage.* London: Routledge.

Bulmer, M. (1984). *The Chicago School. Institutionalization, Diversity, and the Rise of Sociological Research.* Chicago: University of Chicago Press.

Bundesagentur für Arbeit (2022). *Personen nach Staatsangehörigkeiten*, https://statistik.arbeitsagentur.de/DE/Navigation/Statistiken/Themen-im-Fokus/Migration/Personen-nach-Staatsangehoerigkeiten/Personen-nach-Staatsangehoerigkeiten-Nav.html;jsessionid=E37170D79F9EA7BFF1A307D87D547EE2.

Burrell, K. (2009). *Polish Migration to the UK in the 'New' European Union after 2004.* London: Routledge.

Burrell, K. (Ed.) (2016). *Polish Migration to the UK in the 'New' European Union: After 2004.* London: Routledge.

Bygnes, S. (2017). Are They Leaving Because of the Crisis? The Sociological Significance of Anomie as a Motivation for Migration. *Sociology, 15*(1), 1-16.

Bygnes, S. & Erdal, M.B. (2017). Liquid migration, grounded lives: considerations about future mobility and settlement among Polish and Spanish migrants in Norway. *Journal of Ethnic and Migration Studies, 43*(1), 102-118.

Bygnes, S. & Flipo, A. (2017). Political motivations for intra-European migration. *Acta Sociologia, 60*(3), 199-212.

Cabrera, E.F. & Carretero, J.M. (2005). Human Resource Management in Spain: Are Cultural Barriers Preventing the Adoption of Global Practices? *Management Research, 3*(2), 149-160.

Cassain, L. (2016). Migration trajectories and return processes: An exploration of multi-generational family experiences between Spain and Argentina. *Transnational Social Review, 6*(1-2), 1-19.

Cassidy, K., Innocenti, P. & Bürkner, H. (2018). Brexit and new autochthonic politics of belonging. *Space and Polity, 22*(2), 188-204.

Castellani, S. & Roca, B. (2021). Bricolage in labor organizing practices: Spanish and Italian migrant activists in Berlin, *Journal of Industrial Relations, 0*(0), 1-24.

Castellani, S. (2018). 'Scivolando verso il basso: L'inserimento lavorativo dei nuovi migranti italiani e spagnoli in Germania durante la crisi economica. *Sociologia del lavoro, 149*(1), 77-93.

Castells, M. & Hlebik, S. (2017). Alternative Economic Practises in Barcelona: Surviving the Crisis, Reinventing Life. In Manuel Castells et al. (Eds.), *Another Economy is Possible: Cultures and Economy in a Time of Crisis* (pp. 160-186). Cambridge: Polity Press.

Castells, M. et al. (Eds.) (2017). *Another Economy is Possible: Culture and Economy in a Time of Crisis*. Cambridge: Polity Press.

Castells, M., Caraça, J. & Cardoso, G. (Eds.) (2012). *Aftermath. The Cultures of the Economic Crisis*. Oxford: Oxford University Press.

Chien, W. & Hassenzahl, M. (2017). Technology-Mediated Relationship Maintenance in Romantic Long-Distance Relationships: An Autoethnographical Research through Design. *Human–Computer Interaction, 1*(1), 1-48.

Cicourel, A. V. (1964). *Method and measurement in sociology*. Glencoe, IL: Free Press of Glencoe.

Clark, D. (2020). Polish population of the United Kingdom (UK) 2008-2019. https://www.statista.com/statistics/1061639/polish-population-in-united-kingdom/.

Clua i Fainé, M. & Sánchez García, J. (2017). Identidades en la migración. *Revista de Dialectología y Tradiciones Populares, 72*(1), 43-49.

Cobo-Duran, S. & Hernandez-Santaolalla, V. (2015). Esterotipos Regionales y Nacionales en Television: El Caso de Espanoles en el Mundo. In G. Valles &

R. Terceno (Eds.), *Contenidos y discurso communicativo audiovisual y textual* (pp. 159-178). Madrid: Terra Books.

Coletto, D. & Fullin, G. (2019). Before Landing: How Do New European Emigrants Prepare Their Departure and Imagine Their Destinations? *Social Inclusion, 7*(4), 39-48.

Conill, J., Castells, M., Cardenas, A. & Servan, L. (2012). Beyond the Crisis: The Emergence of Alternative Economic Practices. In M. Castells et al. (Eds.), *Aftermath. The Cultures of the Economic Crisis* (pp. 210-248). Oxford: Oxford University Press.

Corbin, J. & Strauss, A. (1988). *Unending Work and Care: Managing Chronic Illness at Home.* San Francisco: Jossey Bass.

Cortés Maisonave, A., Moncó Rebollo, B. & Barbosa Dos Santos Rodríguez, F. (2019). *Brexit, Relaciones de Género y Estrategias Transnacionales de Movilidad: Jóvenes Espanoles en Londres.* Madrid: Centro Reina Sofia sobre adolescencia y juventud.

Cortés, A., Moncó, B. & Betrisey, D. (2015). *Movilidad Transnacional de Jóvenes y Latinoamericanos: una comparación en contexto de crisis.* Madrid: Centro Reina Sofia sobre Adolescencia y Juventud.

Costa-Font, J., Jiménez Martin, S. & Viola, A. (2021). Fatal Underfunding? Explaining COVID-19 Mortality in Spanish Nursing Homes. *Journal of Aging and Health, 33*(7–8), 607–617.

Cox, R. & Narula, R. (2003). Playing Happy Families: rules and relationships in au pair employing households in London, England. *Gender, Place and Culture, 10*(4), 333-344.

Cuadras-Morató, X. & Rodon, T. (2019). The dog that didn't bark: on the effect of the Great Recession on the surge of secessionism. *Ethnic and Racial Studies, 42*(12), 2189-2208.

Cuzzocrea, V. (2019). Moratorium or waithood? Forms of time-taking and the changing shape of youth. *Time & Society, 28*(2), 567-586.

Davis, C. (2017). *Managing and imagining migration: The role of Facebook groups in the lives of "new" Italian migrants in Australia.* PhD dissertation, Faculty of Arts and Social Sciences, University of Sydney.

De La Calle, L. & Miley, J.T. (2008). Is there more assimilation in Catalonia than in the Basque Country? Analysing dynamics of assimilation in nationalist contexts. *European Journal of Political Research, 47*(6), 710-736.

Delcroix, C. (2013). *Ombres et lumières de la famille Nour.* Paris: Payot: Third expanded edition.

Department of Work and Pensions (2022). *National Insurance numbers allocated to adult overseas nationals to December 2021*, https://www.gov.uk/government/statistics/national-insurance-numbers-allocated-to-adult-overseas-nationals-to-march-2021/national-insurance-numbers-allocated-to-adult-overseas-nationals-to-december-2021.

Der Spiegel (2013). *Die neuen Gastarbeiter: Europas junge Elite für Deutschlands Wirtschaft*, No.9/ 25 February, 30-36.

Díaz Hernández, R. & Parreño Castellano, J.M. (2017). The recent emigration of young Spaniards: The emigrants' narrative versus the official and media perception. In B. Glorius & J. Dominguez-Mujica (Eds.), *European Mobility in Times of Crisis: The New Context of European South-North Migration* (pp. 245-266). Bielefeld: transcript.

Diaz-Parra, I. & Jover-Baez, J. (2016). Social movements in crisis? From 15-M movement to the electoral shift in Spain. *International Journal of Sociology and Social Policy, 36*(9/10), 680-694.

Dimitriadis, I., Fullin, G. & Fischer-Souan, M. (2019). Great Expectations? Young Southern Europeans Emigrating in Times of Crisis. *Mondi Migranti, 25*(1), 127-151.

Domecka, M. (2019). Biography, gender and migration. Reflexivity and transformation in migratory processes. *Rassegna Italiana di Sociologia, LX*(2), 357-383.

Domínguez-Mujica, J. & Díaz-Hernández, R. (2019). The Dilemma of Returning: the Liquid Migration of Skilled Spaniards 8 years down the Economic Crisis. *Canadian Studies for Population, 46*(1), 99-119.

Durkheim, E. (1897). *Le Suicide: étude des sociologie.* Paris: Alcan (English translation (1952)): *Suicide. A Study in Sociology.* London: Routledge and Kegan.

Ehata, R. & Seeleib-Kaiser, M. (2017). Benefit tourism and EU migrant citizens: Real world experiences. *Social Policy Review. 29*(1), 1-12.

Elias, N. & Scotson, J.L. (1965/1994). *The Established and the Outsiders.* London: SAGE.

Engbersen, G. & Snel, E. (2013). Liquid migration: dynamic and fluid patterns of post-accession migration flows. In B. Glorius, I. Grabowska-Lusinska, & A. Kuvik (Eds.), *Mobility in transition: migration patterns after EU enlargement* (pp. 21-40). Amsterdam: Amsterdam University Press.

Erikson, E.H. (1968). *Identity, Youth and Crisis.* New York: Norton.

Erikson, K.T. (1976). *Everything in its Path.* New York: Simon & Schuster.

Eurostat (2022). *Unemployment Statistics,* https://ec.europa.eu/eurostat/statistics-explained/index.php?title=Unemployment_statistics#Unemployment_in_the_EU_and_the_euro_area.

Favell, A. & Barbulescu, R. (2018). Brexit, 'Immigration' and Anti-Discrimination. In P. Diamond, P. Nedergaard & B. Rosamond (Eds.), *The Routledge Handbook of the Politics of Brexit* (pp. 118-133). London: Routledge.

Favell, A. & Nebe, T. (2009). Internal and external movers: East-West migration and the impact of EU enlargement. In A. Favell & E. Recchi (Eds). *Pioneers of European Integration: Citizenship and Mobility in the EU* (pp. 205-223). Celtenham: Edward Elgar.

Favell, A. & Recchi, E. (Eds.) (2009). *Pioneers of European Integration.* Celtenham: Edward Elgar.

Favell, A. (2008). *Eurostars and Eurocities: Free Movement and Mobility in an Integrating Europe.* Oxford: Blackwell.

Feaster, J. (2010). Expanding the Impression Management Model of Communication Channels: An Information Control Scale. *Journal of Computer-Mediated Communication, 16*(1), 115-138.

Feixa, C. & Rubio Ros, C. (2017). Narrativas culturales de la emigración juvenil a Europa. *Revista de Dialectologia y Tradiciones Populares, 22*(1), 9-22.

Fernández, C. & Ortega, C. (2008). Labor market assimilation of immigrants in Spain: employment at the expense of bad job-matches? *Spanish Economic Review, 10*(1), 83-107.

Fischer, W. & Rosenthal, G. (1997). Narrationsanalyse biographischer Selbstpräsentationen. In R. Hitzler & A. Honer (Eds.,), *Sozialwissenschaftliche Hermeneutik* (pp. 133-164). Opladen: Leske und Budrich.

Fox, J., Morosanu, L. & Szilassy, E. (2015). Denying Discrimination: Status, 'Race', and the Whitening of Britain's New Europeans. *Journal of Ethnic and Migration Studies, 41*(5), 729-748.

Frake, C. O. (1968). The Ethnographic Study of Cognitive Systems. In J. Fishman (Ed.), *Readings in the Sociology of Language* (pp. 73-85). The Hague: Mouton Publishers.

Galbany-Estragues, P. & Nelson, S. (2016). Migration of Spanish nurses 2009–2014. Underemployment and surplus production of Spanish nurses and mobility among Spanish registered nurses: A case study. *International Journal of Nursing Studies, 63*(1), 112-123.

Gałęziowski, J. (2021). "I never thought I could be seen as an oral historian" – Fritz Schütze about the autobiographical narrative interview and oral history in conversation with Jakub Gałęziowski. *Wrocławski Rocznik Historii Mówionej, Rocznik 11*, 238-260. https://wrhm.pl/wrhm/article/view/319.

Gallucci, S. (2013). Emotional Investments During the Year Abroad. A case study of a British ERASMUS student in Italy. *Apples – Journal of Applied Linguistics, 7*(2), 17-37.

Gentile, A. (2014). The Impacts of Employment Instability on Transitions to Adulthood: The *Mileuristas* Young Adults in Spain. In L. Antonucci, M. Hamilton & S. Roberts (Eds.), *Young People and Social Policy in Europe: Dealing with Risk, Inequality and Equality in Times of Crisis* (pp. 125-144). London: Palgrave Macmillan.

Giner-Monfort, J. & Huete, R. (2021). Uncertain sunset lives: British migrants facing Brexit in Spain. *European Urban and Regional Studies, 28*(1), 74-79.

Glaister, D. (2017, October 7). 'Hunt for Catalans' threat on London Spanish Facebook group page. *The Guardian.* https://www.theguardian.com/world/2017/oct/07/london-spanish-threaten-violent-catalan-hunt.

Glaser, B. & Strauss, A. (1968). *Time for Dying.* Chicago: Aldine.

Glaser, B. (1978). *Theoretical Sensitivity.* Mill Valley: The Sociology Press.

Glaser, B. & Strauss, A. (1965). *Awareness of Dying.* Chicago: Aldine.

Glaser, B. & Strauss, A. (1967). *The Discovery of Grounded Theory.* Chicago: Aldine.

Glorius, B. (2016). New "Guest Workers" from Spain? Exploring Migration to Germany in the Context of Economic and Societal Change. In J. Domínguez-Mujica (Ed.), *Global Change and Human Mobility* (pp. 225-247). Singapore: Springer.

Glorius, B. (2017). Study German to shape your future? Motives for foreign language acquisition among Spaniards. In B. Glorius & J. Dominguez-Mujica (Eds.), *European Mobility in Times of Crisis: The New Context of European South-North Migration* (pp. 105-131). Bielefeld: transcript.

Glorius, B. & Dominguez-Mujica, J. (Eds.) (2017). *European Mobility in Times of Crisis: The New Context of European South-North Migration.* Bielefeld: transcript.

Godenau. D. (2017). The role of intermediaries in Spanish emigration past and present: The New Context of South North Migration. In B. Glorius & J. Dominguez-Mujica (Eds.), *European Mobility in Times of Crisis: The New Context of European South-North Migration* (pp. 191-214). Bielefeld: transcript.

Goffman, E. (1968a). *Stigma. Notes on the management of spoiled identity.* New Orleans, LA: Pelican.

Goffman, E. (1968b). The Moral Career of the Mental Patient. In E. Goffman, *Asylums. Essays on the Social Situation of Mental Patients and other Inmates* (pp. 117-155). Harmondsworth: Penguin Books. (Original work published 1961)

Goffman, E. (1971). *The Presentation of self in everyday life.* London: Penguin Press.

Golsch, K. (2003). Employment flexibility in Spain and its impact on transitions to adulthood. *Work, Employment and Society, 17*(4), 691-718.

González Expósito, D. (2020). *Friendship and Social Life in Norway: An ethnographic study of Spanish migrants in Bergen*. Master Thesis, NLA University College.

González Ferrer, A. (2013). *La nueva emigración española. Lo que sabemos y lo que no*. Zoom Político 18. Fundación Alternativas.

González-Ferrer, A. & Moreno-Fuentes, F.J. (2017). Back to the Suitcases? Emigration during the Great Recession. *South European Society and Politics, 22*(4), 447-471.

Goodson, I., Antikainen, A., Sikes, P. & Andrews, M. (Eds.) (2017). *The Routledge International Handbook on Narrative and Life History*. London and New York: Routledge.

Gordano Peile, C. & Ros Hijar, A. (2016). Immigrants and mobile phone uses: Spanish-speaking young adults recently arrived in London. *Mobile Media and Communication, 4*(3), 405-423.

Gottschalk, L., Kluckhohn, C. & Angell, R. (1945). *The use of personal documents in history, anthropology and sociology*. New York: Social Science Research Council.

Gropas, R. & Bartolini, L. (2016). Southern European Highly Skilled Female Migrants in Male-Dominated Sectors in Times of Crisis: A Look into the IT and Engineering Sectors. In A. Triandafyllidou & I. Isaakyan (Eds.), *High Skill Migration and Recession: Gendered Perspectives* (pp. 160-192). London: Palgrave Macmillan.

Gryzmala-Kazlowska (2017). From connecting to social anchoring: adaption and 'settlement' of Polish migrants in the UK. *Journal of Ethnic and Migration Studies, 44*(2), 252-269.

Hall, K. & Hardill, I. (2016). Retirement migration, the 'other' story: caring for frail and elderly British citizens in Spain. *Aging & Society, 36*(1), 562-585.

Hedgecoe, G. (2020, March 28). In Spain, austerity legacy cripples coronavirus fight. *Politico*. https://www.politico.eu/article/in-spain-austerity-legacy-cripples-coronavirus-fight/.

Henley, J. (2020). British residents 'confused and alarmed' about post-Brexit future, *The Guardian*. https://www.theguardian.com/world/2020/mar/06/british-residents-in-spain-confused-and-alarmed-about-post-brexit-future.

Hickey, L. & Stewart, M. (Eds.) (2005). *Politeness in Europe*. Clevedon, UK: Multilingual Matters.

Hickey, L. (2000). Politeness in Translation between English and Spanish. *Target. International Journal of Translation Studies*. *12*(2), 229-240.

Hickey, L. (2005). Politeness in Spain: Thanks But No 'Thanks'. In L. Hickey & M. Stewart (Eds.), *Politeness in Europe* (pp. 317-330). Clevedon, UK: Multilingual Matters.

Himmelstine, C.L. & King, R. (2019). 'Healing Young Hearts': emotional and psychosocial dimensions of well-being among young adult Spanish migrants in the London region. *Nordic Journal of Migration Research, 9*(2), 161-177.

Hirschman, A. O. (1970). *Exit, Voice and Loyalty. Responses to Decline in Firms, Organizations and States.* Cambridge, MA: Harvard University Press.

Hoffmann-Riem, C. (1990). *The Adopted Child.* New Brunswick and London: Transaction.

Holleran, M. (2019). The 'lost generation' of the 2008 crisis: Generational conflict and memory in Spain. *Journal of Sociology, 55*(3), 463-477.

Home Office (2020). *The UK's points-based immigration system: policy statement*, https://www.gov.uk/government/publications/the-uks-points-based-immigration-system-policy-statement/the-uks-points-based-immigration-system-policy-statement.

Home Office (2021). *EU Settlement Scheme quarterly statistics, June 2021*, https://www.gov.uk/government/statistics/eu-settlement-scheme-quarterly-statistics-june-2021/eu-settlement-scheme-quarterly-statistics-june-2021.

House, J. (2005). Politeness in Germany: Politeness in Germany? In L. Hickey & M. Stewart (Eds.), *Politeness in Europe* (pp. 13-28). Clevedon, UK: Multilingual Matters.

Hsieh, Y.C., Apostolopoulos, Y., Hatzudis, K. & Sonmez, S. (2014). Occupational Exposures and Health Outcomes Among Latina Hotel Cleaners. *Hispanic Health Care International, 12*(1), 6-15.

Inowlocki, L. & Lutz, H. (2000). Hard Labour: The 'Biographical Work' of a Turkish Migrant Woman in Germany. *The European Journal of Women's Studies, 7*(3), 301-319.

Inowlocki, L. (2018). Internationalität der Biographieforschung: Herausforderungen und konstruktive Bedingungen. In H. Lutz, M. Schiebel & E. Tuider (Eds.), *Handbuch Biographieforschung* (pp. 697-707). Wiesbaden: Springer VS.

Irwin, S. & Nilson, A. (Eds.) (2018). *Transitions to Adulthood Through Recession: Youth and Inequality in a European Comparative Perspective.* Abingdon: Routledge.

Jaehrling, K. & Mehaut, P. (2012). 'Varieties of institutional avoidance': employers' strategies in low-waged service sector occupations in France and Germany. *Socio-Economic Review, 11*(4), 687-710.

Jahoda, M., Lazarsfeld, P. & Zeisel, H. (1933/1972). *Marienthal.* London: Tavistock.

Janta, H., Ladkin, A., Brown, L. & Lugosi, P. (2011). Employment Experiences of Polish Migrant Workers in the UK Hospitality Sector. *Tourism Management, 32*(5), 1006-1019.

Järvinen, M. & Room, R. (2017). *Youth Drinking Cultures: European Experiences.* London: Routledge.

Jendrissek, D. (2014). *Narratives of economic migration. The case of young, well-qualified Poles and Spaniards in the UK.* PhD dissertation, University of Southampton. https://www.researchgate.net/publication/299464694_Narratives_of_economic_migration_The_case_of_young_well-qualified_Poles_and_Spaniards_in_the_UK.

Jones, J. (2020). The uncertain present and future for recent graduates, *BBC*, https://www.bbc.com/worklife/article/20200901-the-class-of-2020s-uncertain-present-and-future.

Juhasz, A. & Mey, E. (2003). *Die zweite Generation. Etablierte oder Außenseiter? Biographien von Jugendlichen ausländischer Herkunft.* Opladen: Westdeutscher Verlag.

Kallmeyer, W. & Schütze, F. (1977). *Zur Konstitution von Kommunikationsschemata der Sachverhaltsdarstellung.* In D. Wegner (Ed.), *Gesprächsanalysen* (pp. 159-274). Hamburg: Buske.

Karakayali, J. (2010). *Transnational Haushalten. Biographische Interviews mit 'care workers' aus Osteuropa.* Berlin: Springer.

Kaźmierska, K. (2014). An Interview with Professor Fritz Schütze: Biography and Contribution to Interpretative Sociology. *Qualitative Sociology Review 10*(1), 284-359. http://www.qualitativesociologyreview.org/ENG/archive_eng.php.

Kaźmierska, K. & Waniek, K. (Eds.) (2020). *Telling the Great Change. The Process of the Systemic Transformation in Poland in Biographical Perspective.* Lódz: Wydawnictwo Uniwersytetu Lódzkiego

Keating, E. (2001). The Ethnography of Communication. In P. Atkinson et al. (Eds.), *Handbook of Ethnography* (pp. 285-301). London: Sage.

King, R. (2012). Sunset Migration. In Martiniello's & Rath's (eds.) *An Introduction to International Migration Studies: European Perspectives.* Amsterdam: Amsterdam University Press.

King, R. & Christou, A. (2014). Second-Generation "Return" to Greece: New Dynamics of Transnationalism and Integration. *International Migration*, *52*(6), 85-99.

King, R. & Pratsinakis, M. (2019). Special Issue Introduction: Exploring the Lived Experiences of Intra-EU Mobility in an Era of Complex Economic and Political Change. *International Migration, 58*(1), 5-14.

King, R. & Ruiz-Gelices, E. (2003). International Student Migration and the European 'Year Abroad': Effects on European Identity and Subsequent Migration Behaviour. *International Journal of Population Geography, 9*(1), 229-252.

King, R. & Williams, A.M. (2018). Editorial Introduction: New European Youth Mobilities. *Population, Space and Place, 24*(1), 1-9.

Köhler, H.-D. (2010). Spanien in Zeiten der globalen Wirtschaftskrise. *Politik und Zeitgeschichte, 36/37*(1), 7-13.

Kohli, M. & Robert, G. (Eds.) (1984). *Biographie und soziale Wirklichkeit. Neue Beiträge und Forschungsperspektiven.* Stuttgart: Metzler.

Kohli, M. (1986). The World We Forgot: A Historical Review of the Life Course. In: V. W. Marshall (Ed.), *Later Life: The Social Psychology of Aging.* Beverly Hills: Sage, 271-303.

Kohli, M. (Ed.) (1978). *Soziologie des Lebenslaufs.* Darmstadt and Neuwied: Luchterhand.

Komito, L. (2011). Social media and migration: Virtual community 2.0. *Journal of The American Society for Information Science and Technology, 62*(3), 232-244.

Komito, L. & Bates, J. (2009). Virtually local: social media and community among Polish nationals in Dublin. *Aslib Proceedings, 61*(3), 232-244.

Kraft, S. (2019). Welche Auswirkungen hat der Fachkräftemangel? *Pflegezeitschrift, 72*(6), 58-59.

Krzaklewska, E. (2013). Erasmus Students between Youth and Adulthood. Analysis of the Biographical Experience. In B. Feyen & E. Krzaklewska (Eds.), *The ERASMUS Phenomenon – Symbol of a New European Generation?* (pp. 79-96). Frankfurt am Main: Peter Lang.

Kuhlmann, E. & Jensen, T. (2015). Migration and integration of Spanish nurses in Germany: The need for multi-level governance. *European Journal of Public Health, 25*(3), 20-42.

Labov, W. & Waletzky, J. (1967). Narrative analysis: Oral versions of personal experience. In J. Helm (Ed.), *Essays on the Verbal and Visual Arts* (pp. 12-44). Seattle: University of Washington Press.

Lafleur, J.-M. & Stanek, M. (Eds.) (2017). *South-North Migration of EU Citizens in Times of Crisis.* Springer Open.

Lamont, M. & Molnár, V. (2002). The Study of Boundaries in the Social Sciences. *Annual Review of Sociology, 28*(1), 167-195.

Lamont, M. (1992). *Money, Morals, and Manners.* Chicago: University of Chicago Press.

Lever, J. & Milbourne, P. (2017). The Structural Invisibility of Outsiders: The Role of Migrant Labour in the Meat-Processing Industry. *Sociology, 51*(2), 306-322.

Lewis, O. (1961). *The Children of Sanchez.* New York: Vintage Books.

Lopez-Sala, A. (2017). The new emigration issue in the public and political debate in Spain. In B. Glorius & J. Dominguez-Mujica (Eds.), *European Mobility in*

Times of Crisis: The New Context of European South-North Migration (pp. 267-286). Bielefeld: transcript.

Lopez-Sala, A. (2019). You're not getting rid of us. Performing acts of citizenship in times of emigration. *Citizenship Studies, 23*(2), 97-114.

Lorenzo-Dus, N. & Bou-Franch, P. (2003). Gender and Politeness: Spanish and British Undergraduates' Perceptions of Appropriate Requests. In: J. Santaemilia (Ed.), *Género, lenguaje y traducción* (pp. 187-199). Valencia: Universitat de Valencia/Dirección General de la Mujer.

Luconi, S. (2003). Forging an Ethnic Identity: The Case of Italian Americans. *Revue francaise d'études américaines, 96*(2), 89-101.

Lüdke, S. & Zuber, H. (2019, September 14). Die verlorene Generation kehrt heim. *Der Spiegel*. https://www.spiegel.de/politik/ausland/spanien-und-portugal-wie-die-verlorene-generation-zurueckkehrt-a-1286328.html.

Lulle, A., King, R., Dvorakova, V. & Szkudlarek, A. (2018). Between disruptions and connections: "New" European Union migrants in the United Kingdom before and after the Brexit. *Population, Space and Place, 25*(1), 1-10.

Lulle, A., Morosanu, L. & King, R. (2018). And then came Brexit: Experiences and future plans of young EU migrants in the London region. *Population, Space, Place, 24*(1), 1-11.

Lulle, A., Janta, H. & Emillson, H. (2021). Introduction to the Special Issue: European youth migration, human capital outcomes, skills and competencies. *Journal of Ethnic and Migration Studies, 47*(8), 1725-1739.

Lutz, H. (2011). *The New Maids. Transnational Women and the Care Economy*. London: Zed Books.

Lutz, H., Schiebel, M. & Tuider, E. (Eds.) (2018). *Handbuch Biographieforschung*. Wiesbaden: Springer VS.

Mannheim, K. (1928). Das Problem der Generationen. *Kölner Vierteljahreshefte für Soziologie, 7,* 157-184. (English translation: The Problem of Generations. In K. Mannheim P. (1952), *Essays on the Sociology of Knowledge* (pp. 276-322). Edited by P. Kecskeméti. London and New York: Routledge and Kegan Paul).

Manzano-Garcia, G., Montanes, P. & Megias, J. (2017). Perception of economic crisis among Spanish nursing students: Its relation to burnout and engagement. *Nurse Education Today, 52*(1), 116-120.

Markovitz, Y., Boer, D. & van Dick, R. (2014). Economic crisis and the employee: The effects of economic crisis on employee job satisfaction, commitment, and self-regulation. *European Management Journal, 32*(3), 413-433.

Mas Giralt, R. (2017). Onward Migration as a Coping Strategy? Latin Americans moving from Spain to the UK Post-2008. *Population, Space and Place, 23*(1), 1-12.

Mazzilli, C. & King, R. (2019). "What have I done to deserve this?" Young Italian migrants in Britain narrate their reaction to Brexit and plans to the future. *Rivista Geografica Italiana, 125*(4), 507-523.

McCarthy, H.N.J. (2018). Spanish nationals' future plans in the context of Brexit. *Population, Space and Place, 25*(1), 1-14.

McDowell, L., Batnitzky, A. & Dyer, S. (2007). Division, Segmentation, and Interpellation: The Embodied Labors of Migrant Workers in a Greater London Hotel. *Economic Geography, 83*(1), 1-25.

McIlwaine, C. (2020). Feminized precarity among onward migrants in Europe: reflections from Latin Americans in London. *Ethnic and Racial Studies, 43*(14). DOI: 10.1080/01419870.2020.1738518.

McQuaid, R., Raeside, R., Eggdell, V. & Graham, H. (2014). Multiple scarring effects of youth unemployment in the UK (working paper).

Mead, G.H. (1934). *Mind, Self and Society.* Chicago: University of Chicago Press.

Meier, G. & Daniels, H. (2013). 'Just not being able to make friends': social interaction during the year abroad in modern foreign language degrees. *Research Papers in Education, 28*(2), 212-238.

Meinardus, P. (2017). Recruiting from Spain – a qualitative insight into Spanish-German labor migration projects. In B. Glorius & J. Dominguez-Mujica (Eds.), *European Mobility in Times of Crisis: The New Context of European South-North Migration* (pp. 215-241). Bielefeld: transcript.

Miller, R. & Day, G. (Eds.) (2012). *The Evolution of European Identities. Biographical Approaches.* Houndmills: Palgrave Macmillan.

Mills, C. W. (1940). Situated Actions and Vocabularies of Motive. *American Sociological Review, 5*(6), 904-13.

Mills, C.W. (1959). *The Sociological Imagination.* Oxford: Oxford University Press.

Minguez, A. M. (2016). Late Leaving of the Parental Home in Southern Europe: Lessons for Youth Policy. *Comparative Sociology, 15*(4), 485-507.

Mitchell, K. (2012). Student mobility and European identity: Erasmus study as a civic experience? *Journal of Contemporary European Research, 8*(4), 490-518.

Montero Lange, M. (2014). Innereuropäische Mobilität am Beispiel der neuen spanischen Arbeitsmigration nach Deutschland. In C. Pfeffer-Hoffmann (Ed.), *Arbeitsmigration nach Deutschland* (pp. 18-110). Berlin: Minor Kontor.

Morosanu, L. & Fox, J.E. (2013). 'No smoke without fire': Strategies of coping with stigmatized migrant identities. *Ethnicities, 13*(14), 438-456.

Morosanu, L., King, R., Lulle, A. & Pratsinakis, M. (2021). 'One improves here every day': the occupational and learning journeys of 'lower-skilled' European migrants in the London region. *Journal of Ethnic and Migration Studies, 47*(8), 1775-1792

Navarette-Moreno, L., Cuenca García, C., Diaz Chorne, L., Arcadio Flores-Vidal, P., Gentile, A. & Zúñiga Contreras, R. (2014). *La emigración de los jóvenes españoles en el contexto de la crisis. Análisis y datos de un fenómeno difícil de cuantificar.* Madrid: Observatorio de la Juventud en España.

Ní Laoire, C. (2008). 'Settling back'? A biographical and life-course perspective on Ireland's recent return migration. *Irish Geography, 41*(2), 195-210.

Ní Laoire, C. (2011). Narratives of 'Innocent Irish Childhoods': Return Migration and Intergenerational Family Dynamics. *Journal of Ethnic and Migration Studies, 37*(8), 1253-1271.

Noor, P. (2019, February 28). 'Better weather, better pay': German hospital looks to lure UK's Polish nurses. *The Guardian.* https://www.theguardian.com/world/2019/feb/28/better-weather-better-pay-german-hospital-looks-to-lure-uks-polish-nurses.

Nowicka, M. (2006). Mobile locations: construction of home in a group of mobile transnational professionals. *Global Networks, 7*(1), 69-86.

Nurse, L. & O'Neill, M. (2018). Biographical Research in the UK: Profiles and Perspectives. In H. Lutz, M. Schiebel & E. Tuider (Eds.), *Handbuch Biographieforschung* (pp. 709-720). Wiesbaden: Springer VS.

O'Carroll, L. (2019, September 23). Health cover for retired Britons in EU to last six months in no-deal Brexit. *The Guardian.* https://www.theguardian.com/politics/2019/sep/23/health-cover-for-retired-britons-in-eu-to-last-six-months-in-no-deal-brexit.

O'Carroll, L. (2019, Dec. 9). Campaigners attack Boris Johnson for EU nationals remarks. *The Guardian.* https://www.theguardian.com/world/2019/dec/09/campaigners-attack-boris-johnson-for-eu-nationals-remarks.

O'Carroll, L. (2021, May 10). EU citizens applying for settled status face legal limbo due to backlog. *The Guardian.* https://www.theguardian.com/politics/2021/may/10/eu-citizens-applying-for-settled-status-face-legal-limbo-due-to-backlog.

O'Carroll, L. & Gentleman, A. (2021, 28 June). 'The anxiety is palpable': EU citizens face looming settled status deadline. *The Guardian.* https://www.theguardian.com/politics/2021/jun/28/the-anxiety-is-palpable-eu-citizens-face-looming-settled-status-deadline.

OECD (2022). *Youth Unemployment Rate Definition.* https://data.oecd.org/unemp/youth-unemployment-rate.htm.

Oevermann, U. (2002). Klinische Soziologie auf der Basis der Methodologie der objektiven Hermeneutik – Manifest der objektiv hermeneutischen Sozialforschung. Institut für hermeneutische Sozial- und Kulturforschung (IHSK Frankfurt). https://www.ihsk.de/publikationen/Ulrich_Oevermann-Manifest_der_objektiv_hermeneutischen_Sozialforschung.pdf.

Office of National Statistics (2021). *Migration Statistics Quarterly Report*, https://www.ons.gov.uk/peoplepopulationandcommunity/populationandmigration/internationalmigration/bulletins/migrationstatisticsquarterlyreport/august2020.

Oiarzabal, P. (2012). Diaspora Basques and Online Social Networks: An Analysis of Users of Basque Institutional Diaspora Groups on Facebook. *Journal of Ethnic and Migration Studies*, *38*(9), 1469-1485.

Oliver, D. (2019). Nurses, degrees, and the workforce crisis. *British Medical Journal Online*, *365*(1), 1-2.

Olivieri, V. (2015). Sub-state nationalism in Spain: primers and triggers of identity politics in Catalonia and the Basque Country. *Ethnic and Racial Studies*, *38*(9), 1610-1626.

Oltmer, J., Kreienbrink, A. & Sanz-Diaz, C. (2012). *Das "Gastarbeiter"-System: Arbeitsmigration und ihre Folgen in der Bundesrepublik Deutschland und Westeuropa.* Munich: Oldenbourg Verlag.

O'Reilly, K. (2020). *Brexit and the British in Spain.* Project Report, Goldsmiths, University of London. http://research.gold.ac.uk/28223/.

Ortensi, L. & Barbiano di Belgioso, E. (2018). Moving on? Gender, education, and citizenship as key factors among short-term onward migration planners. *Population, Space and Place, 24*(5), 1-13.

Oso, L. (2020). Crossed mobilities: the "recent wave" of Spanish migration to France after the economic crisis. *Racial and Ethnic Studies*, *43*(14) DOI: 10.1080/01419870.2020.1738520.

Ousselin, E. (2009). Vers une banalisation des instances europeennes: L'Auberge Espagnole. *The French Review, 82*(4), 748-759.

Outhwaite, W. (2019). Migration Crisis and "Brexit". In C. Menjívar, M. Ruiz & I. Ness (Eds.), *The Oxford Handbook of Migration Crises* (pp. 93-109). Oxford: Oxford University Press.

Palmer, M. (1928). *Field Studies in Sociology. A Student's Manual.* Chicago: The University of Chicago Press.

Perks, R. & Thomson, A. (2016). *The Oral History Reader.* (3rd edition). London and New York: Routledge.

Perry, S.E. (2017). *Collecting Garbage: dirty work, clean jobs, proud people.* London and New York: Routledge. (Original work published 1978).

Pfeffer-Hoffmann, C. (Ed.) (2014). *Arbeitsmigration nach Deutschland.* Berlin: Minor Kontor.

Plummer, K. (1983). *Documents of Life. An Introduction to the Problems and Literature of a Humanistic Method.* London: George Allen & Unwin.

Plummer, K. (2001a). The Call of Life Stories in Ethnographic Research. In P. Atkinson, A. Coffey, S. Delamont, J. Lofland & L. Lofland (Eds.), *Handbook of Ethnography* (pp. 395-406). Los Angeles and London: Sage.

Plummer, K. (2001b). *Documents of Life 2. An Invitation to a Critical Humanism.* London, Thousand Oaks, New Delhi: Sage.

Ponzo, M. & Scoppa, V. (2009). The Use of Informal Networks in Italian Labor Markets: Efficiency or Favoritisms? *MPRA Paper.*

Pratsinakis, M., King, R., Himmelstine, C.L. & Mazzilli, C. (2019). A Crisis-Driven Migration? Aspirations and Experiences of Post-2008 South European Migrants in London. *International Migration, 58*(1), 15-30.

Preston, P. (2020). *A People Betrayed: A History of Corruption, Political Incompetence, and Social Division in Modern Spain.* Liveright Publishing Cooperation: New York and London.

Privitera, G. (2020). Coronavirus' lost generation [31.07.20]. *POLITICO.* Retrieved from: https://www.politico.eu/article/coronavirus-italy-lost-generation/ [access on 20.10.20].

Pumares, P. (2017). The changing migration projects of Spaniards in the UK. The case of Brighton. In B. Glorius, & J. Dominguez-Mujica (Eds.) (2017), *European Mobility in Times of Crisis: The New Context of European South-North Migration* (pp. 133-160). Bielefeld: transcript.

Quassoli, F. & Dimitriadis, I. (2019). "Here, There, in between, beyond…": Identity Negotiation and Sense of Belonging among Southern Europeans in the UK and Germany. *Social Inclusion, 7*(4), 60-70.

Quintana-Murci, E., Salvà-Mut, F. & Tugores, T. (2019). Making Spanish young women's transition to adulthood visible: a biographical analysis in times of crisis. *International Journal of Adolescence and Youth, Vol. 25*(1), 329-342. https://doi.org/10.1080/02673843.2019.1628080.

Ramos, C. (2018). Onward Migration from Spain to London in times of crisis: the importance of life-course junctures in secondary migrations. *Journal of Ethnic and Migration Studies, 44*(11), 1841-1857.

Recchi, E. (2015). *Mobile Europe. The Theory and Practice of Free Movement in the EU.* London: Palgrave Macmillan.

Remigi, E. (2017). *In Limbo: Brexit testimonies from EU citizens in the UK*. London: CreateSpace Independent Publishing Forum.
Richards, M. (2006). Between memory and history: Social relationships and ways of remembering the Spanish civil war. *International Journal of Iberian Studies, 19*(1), pp. 85-94.
Riemann, M.-L.H. (2013). *Leaving for Germany – A Qualitative Study on the Life Histories and Argumentative Patterns of Recent Spanish Labor Migrants*. Undergraduate Thesis at the University College Maastricht, the Netherlands.
Riemann, M.-L.H. (2014). *Life-histories in the Shadow of the European Crisis: A qualitative study on the biographical experiences of recent Spanish labour migrants in the UK*. MPhil dissertation at the Department of Sociology, University of Cambridge, UK.
Riemann, M-L.H. (2018). A moment of biographical analysis under the microscope: reading Felipe's autobiographical narrative. *Contemporary Social Science*, pp. 1-18.
Riemann, M.-L.H. (2019). Leaving Spain as a response to what? A biographical perspective on European migration processes in times of crisis. *Rassegna Italiana di Sociologia, LX*, 1, 75-99.
Riemann, M.-L.H. (2020). Leaving Spain: A Biographical Study on the Experiences of an Economic Crisis, Migration and New Beginnings. Doctoral Thesis completed at the Department of Sociology, University of Cambridge (November 2020).
Rio-Ruiz, M.A., Jimenez-Rodrigo, M.L. & Caro-Cabrera, M.J. (2015). The shifting financial aid system in Spanish University: grant recipients' experiences and strategies. *Critical Studies in Education, 56*(3), 332-350.
Roca, B. & Martin-Diaz, E. (2016). Solidarity Networks of Spanish Migrants in the UK and Germany: The emergence of Interstitial Trade Unionism. *Critical Sociology, 43*(7-8), 1197-1212.
Rodriguez-Arrastia, M., Ropero-Padilla, C., Fernández-Sola, C. & Portillo, M. (2021). Nursing emigration in the United Kingdom: A qualitative exploration of the Spanish nursing community, *Nursing Open, 8*(2), 675-687
Romanos, E. (2013). Collective learning processes within social movements: Some insights into the 15-M/Indignados movement. In C. Flesher Fominaya & L. Cox (Eds.), *Understanding European Movements: New social movements, global justice struggles, anti-austerity protests* (pp. 203-219). Abingdon: Routledge.
Rosenthal, G. & Bogner, A. (2017). *Biographies in the Global South: Life-histories embedded in Figurations and Discourses*. Frankfurt/New York: Campus.

Rosenthal, G. (2004). Biographical research. In C. Seale, G. Gobo, J. F. Gubrium, & D. Silverman (Eds.), *Qualitative research practice* (pp. 48-64). London: Sage.

Royo, S. (2014) Institutional Degeneration and the Economic Crisis in Spain, *American Behavioral Scientist, 58*(12), 1568-91.

Rubington, E. & Weinberg, M. S. (Eds.) (1968). *Deviance. The Interactionist Perspective.* New York: The Macmillan Company.

Rubio Ros, C. (2013). Londres, tierra prometida. La emigración de jóvenes titulados universitarios catalanes a Londres. *Revista de recerca i formació en antropologia. 18*(2), 158-174.

Rubio Ros, C. (2018). Barcelona calling: El retorno de la emigración juvenil. *Metamorfosis. Revista del Centro Reina Sofía sobre Adolescencia y Juventud. 8*(1), 103-111.

Rubio, C. (2017). Comiendo fuet en Londres: de la autoetnografía a la etnografía transnacional. *Revista de Dialectología y Tradiciones Populares, 72*(1), 29-36.

Rye, J.F. & Andrzejewska, J. (2010). The structural disempowerment of Eastern European migrant farm workers in Norwegian agriculture. *Journal of Rural Studies, 26*(1), 41-51.

Rzepnikowska, A. (2019). Racism and xenophobia experienced by Polish migrants in the UK before and after Brexit vote. *Journal of Ethnic and Migration Studies, 45*(1), 61-77.

Sabaté-Dalmau, M. (2016). The Englishisation of higher education in Catalonia: a critical sociolinguistic ethnographic approach to the students' perspectives. *Language, Culture and Curriculum, 29*(3), 263-285.

Salamon'ska, J. & Recchi, E. (2019). The social structure of transnational practices: Social transnationalism in an unsettled continent. In E. Recchi, & A. Favell (Eds.), *Everyday Europe: Social transnationalism in an unsettled continent* (pp. 61-86). Bristol: Policy Press.

Salazar, N. (2020). Labour migration and tourism mobilities: Time to bring sustainability into the debate, *Tourism Geographies*, DOI: 10.1080/14616688.2020.1801827

Salt, J. (2011). International Students and the Labour Market: Experience in the UK. In T. Modood & J. Salts (Eds.), *Global Migration, Ethnicity and Britishness* (pp. 132-149). London: Palgrave Macmillan.

Sánchez-Alonso, B. (2000). Those Who Left and Those Who Stayed behind: Explaining Emigration from the Regions of Spain, 1880-1914. *The Journal of Economic History, 60*(3), 730-755.

Sanchez-Gelabert, A., Figuera, M. & Elias, M. (2017). Working whilst studying in higher education: The impact of the economic crisis on academic and labour market success. *European Journal of Education, 52*(2), 232-245.

Satola, A. (2016). *Migration und irreguläre Pflegearbeit in Deutschland. Eine biographische Studie.* Fulda: ibidem.

Schlögel, K. (2019). *Das russische Berlin.* Berlin: Suhrkamp.

Scholten, P. & van Ostaijen, M. (2018). *Between Mobility and Migration: The Multi-Level Governance of Intra-European Movement.* Springer Open.

Schryro, K. (2018). Spanische Auszubildende in Regensburger Hotellerie- und Gastronomiebetrieben. Zur Bewertung des Förderprogramms MobiPro-EU aus Sicht der Betroffenen. *ForAP, 1*(1), 51-66

Schütz, A. (1945/1971). The Homecomer. In A. Schütz, *Collected Papers II, Studies in Social Theory* (pp. 106-119), edited by A. Brodersen. The Hague: Martinus Nijhoff.

Schütze, F. (1977). *Die Technik des narrativen Interviews in Interaktionsfeldstudien – dargestellt an einem Projekt zur Erforschung von kommunalen Machtstrukturen.* Arbeitsberichte und Forschungsmaterialien No. 1. Bielefeld: University of Bielefeld, Department of Sociology.

Schütze, F. (1981). Prozessstrukturen des Lebensablaufs. In J. Matthes, A. Pfeifenberger & M. Stosberg (Eds.), *Biographie in handlungswissenschaftlicher Perspektive* (pp. 67-156). Nuremberg: Verlag der Nürnberger Forschungsvereinigung.

Schütze, F. (1987). *Das narrative Interview in Interaktionsfeldstudien. Erzähltheoretische Grundlagen. Teil I: Merkmale von Alltagserzählungen und was wir mit ihrer Hilfe erkennen können.* Studienbrief, Fernuniversität Hagen.

Schütze, F. (1992). Pressure and Guilt: War Experiences of a Young German Soldier and their Biographical Implications. *International Sociology, Vol. 7,* 2 (June): 187–208, and 3 (September): 347-367.

Schütze, F. (1995). Verlaufskurven des Erleidens als Forschungsgegenstand der interpretativen Soziologie. In H.-H. Krüger & W. Marotzki (Eds.), *Erziehungswissenschaftliche Biographieforschung* (pp. 116-157). Wiesbaden: Leske and Budrich.

Schütze, F. (2008). Biography Analysis on the Empirical Base of Autobiographical Narratives: How to Analyse Autobiographical Narrative Interviews. *European Studies on Inequalities and Social Cohesion,* 1/2 (Part I): 153-242, and 3/4 (Part II): 5-77.

Schütze, F. (2014). Autobiographical Accounts of War Experiences. An Outline for the Analysis of Topically Focused Autobiographical Texts – Using the Example of the "Robert Rasmus" Account in Studs Terkel's Book, "The Good War." *Qualitative Sociology Review 10*(1), 224-283. http://www.qualitativesociologyreview.org/ENG/Volume28/QSR_10_1_Schutze.pdf.

Schütze, F. & Schröder-Wildhagen, A. (2012). European Mental Space and its Biographical Relevance. In R. Miller & G. Day (Eds.), *The Evolution of European Identities* (pp. 255-278). Houndmills: Palgrave Macmillan.

Schwartz, R. & Halegoua, G. (2014). The spatial self: Location-based identity performance on social media. *New Media & Society, 17*(10), 1643-1660.

Serra, B. (2014). *Sobradamente preparado para limpiar váteres en Londres: la voz esperanzada de una juventud dispuesta a ganar la batalla del futuro.* Barcelona: Peninsula Atalaya.

Shaw, R. C. (1966). *The Jack-Roller: A Delinquent Boy's Own Story.* Chicago: University of Chicago Press. (Original work published 1930)

Sime, D., Moskal, M. & Tyrrell, N. (2020). Going Back, Staying Put, Moving On: Brexit and the Future Imaginaries of Central and Eastern European Young People in Britain. *Central and Eastern European Migration Review,* DOI:10.17467/ceemr.2020.03.

Sinatti, G. (2008). The Polish Peasant Revisited. Thomas and Znaniecki's Classic in the Light of Contemporary Transnational Migration Theory. *Sociologica, Italian journal of sociology on line, Vol. 2.* Doi: 10.2383/27725.

Singerman, D. (2007). *The Economic Imperatives of Marriage: Emerging Practices and Identities Among Youth in the Middle East.* Middle East Youth Initiative Working Paper No. 6. https://ssrn.com/abstract=1087433.

Siouti, I. (2013). *Transnationale Biographien*, Bielefeld: Transcript.

Siouti, I. (2017). Biography as a theoretical and methodological key concept in transnational migration studies. In I. Goodson et al. (Eds.), *The Routledge International Handbook on Narrative and Life History* (pp. 179-189). London and New York: Routledge.

Siouti, I. (2019). New Migrations from Greece to Germany in Times of the Financial Crisis: Biographical Research Perspectives. In J.A. Panagiotopoulou, L. Rosen, C. Kirsch & A. Chatzidaki (Eds.), *'New' Migration of Families from Greece to Europe and Canada* (pp. 57-72). Wiesbaden: Springer VS.

Sironi, M. (2018). Economic Conditions of Young Adults Before and After the Great Recession. *Journal of Family and Economic Issues, 39*(1), 103-116.

Standing, G. (2011). *The Precariat: A Dangerous New Class.* London: Bloomsbury Academic.

Statista (2022). *Coronavirus (COVID-19) deaths worldwide per one million population as of December 31, 2021, by country.* https://www.statista.com/statistics/1104709/coronavirus-deaths-worldwide-per-million-inhabitants/.

Statista (2022). *Youth unemployment rate in EU member states as of December 2021.* https://www.statista.com/statistics/266228/youth-unemployment-rate-in-eu-countries/.

Statista (2022). *Number of Covid-19 vaccine doses administered in Europe as of December 14th, 2021 by country.* https://www.statista.com/statistics/1196071/covid-19-vaccination-rate-in-europe-by-country/.

Statistisches Bundesamt (Germany) (2021). *Bevölkerung und Erwerbstätigkeit: Ausländische Bevölkerung. Ergebnisse des Ausländerzentralregisters.* https://www.destatis.de/DE/Themen/Gesellschaft-Umwelt/Bevoelkerung/Migration-Integration/Publikationen/Downloads-Migration/auslaend-bevoelkerung-2010200187004.pdf?__blob=publicationFile.

Strandh, M., Winefield, A., Nillson, K. & Hammarstrom, A. (2014). Unemployment and mental health scarring during the life course. *European Journal of Public Health, 24*(3), 440-445.

Strauss, A. (1987). *Qualitative Analysis for Social Scientists.* Cambridge: Cambridge University Press.

Strauss, A. L. (1993). *Continual Permutations of Action.* NY: Aldine de Gruyter.

Stubberud, E. (2015). 'It's Not Much': Affective (Boundary) Work in the Au Pair Scheme. In R. Cox (Ed.), *Au Pairs' Lives in Global Context: Sisters or Servants?* (pp. 121-135). London: Palgrave Macmillan.

Szczepanski, J. (1962). Die biographische Methode. In R. König (Ed.), *Handbuch der empirischen Sozialforschung.* Vol. 1 (pp. 551-569). Stuttgart: Enke.

Tamesberger, D. & Bacher, J. (2020). COVID-19 Crisis: How to Avoid a 'Lost Generation', *Intereconomics, 55*(1), 232–238

Thomas, W.I. & Znaniecki, F. (1918-1920). *The Polish Peasant in Europe and America.* Boston: Richard G. Badger – The Gorham Press. https://archive.org/details/cu31924082469507/page/n193/mode/2up.

Thompson, P. (1978). *The Voice of the Past. Oral History.* Oxford: Oxford University Press. (1st edition).

Thompson, P. & Bornat, J. (2017). *The Voice of the Past. Oral History.* Oxford: Oxford University Press. (4th edition).

Thomson, A. (2007). Four Paradigm Transformations in Oral History, *The Oral History Review, 34*(1), 49-70.

Thränhardt, D. (2010). Spanische Arbeitswanderer in West-, Mittel- und Nordeuropa seit dem Ende des Zweiten Weltkriegs. In K.J. Bade et al. (Eds.), *Enyklopädie Migration in Europa. Vom 17. Jahrhundert bis zur Gegenwart* (pp. 992-997). Paderborn and Munich: Schöningh and Fink.

Tiburcio Jiménez, T. (2017). Berlin. Wie bitte? An Exploration of the Construction of Online Platforms for the Mutual Support of Young Spanish Immigrants in Berlin. In U. U. Fromming, S. Kohn, S. Fox & M. Terry (Eds.), *Digital Environments. Ethnographic Perspectives Across Global Online and Offline Spaces* (pp. 171-193). Bielefeld: transcript.

Tintori, G. & Romei, V. (2017). Emigration from Italy after the Crisis: The Shortcomings of the Brain Drain Narrative. In J.-M. Lafleur & M. Stanek (Eds.). *South-North Migration of EU Citizens in Times of Crisis*. Springer Open.

Treaty on European Union (1992). Luxembourg: Office for Official Publications of the European Communities. https://europa.eu/european-union/sites/europaeu/files/docs/body/treaty_on_european_union_en.pdf.

Tremlett, G. & O'Carroll, L. (2021, May 13). EU citizens arriving in UK being locked up and expelled. *The Guardian*. https://www.theguardian.com/politics/2021/may/13/eu-citizens-arriving-in-uk-being-locked-up-and-expelled.

Tremmlett, G. & O'Carroll, L. (2021, 13 May). EU citizens arriving in UK being locked up and expelled. *The Guardian*. https://www.theguardian.com/politics/2021/may/13/eu-citizens-arriving-in-uk-being-locked-up-and-expelled.

Tyrrell, N., Sime, D., Kelly, C. & McMellon, C. (2018). Belonging in Brexit Britain: Central and Eastern European 1.5 generation young people's experiences. *Population, Space and Place, 25*(1), 1-10.

Urbanos-Garrido, R.M. & Lopez-Valcarcel, B.G. (2015). The influence of the economic crisis on the association between unemployment and health: an empirical analysis for Spain. *The European Journal of Health Economics, 16*(2), 175-184.

van Eckert, S., Gaydis, U. & Martin, C.R. (2011). Embitterment among German academic and non-academic nurses. *The Journal of Mental Health Training, Education and Practice, 6*(2), 104-112.

van Mol, C. (2014). Erasmus Student Mobility as a Gateway to the International Labour Market? In J. Gerhards, S. Hans & S. Carlson (Eds.), *Globalisierung, Bildung und grenzüberschreitende Mobilität* (pp. 295-314). Wiesbaden: Springer VS.

van Mol, C. & Michelsen, J. (2014). The Reconstruction of a Social Network Abroad. An Analysis of the Interaction Patterns of Erasmus Students. *Mobilities, 10*(3), 423-444.

Vathi, Z. & King, R. (Eds.) (2017). *Return Migration and Psychological Wellbeing: Discourses, Policy-Making and Outcomes for Migrants and their Families*. London: Routledge.

Vathi, Z. (2017). The interface between return migration and psychosocial wellbeing (Introduction). In Z. Vathi & R. King (Eds.), *Return Migration and Psychological Wellbeing: Discourses, Policy-Making and Outcomes for Migrants and their Families*. London: Routledge.

Vertovec, S. (2009). *Transnationalism*. Milton Park: Routledge.

Vertovec, S. (2013). Circular migration. In E. Ness (Ed.), *The Encyclopedia of Global Human Migration*. Hoboken, NJ: Wiley-Blackwell. https://doi.org/10.1002/9781444351071.wbeghm135.

Vijande Rodríguez, R. & Ruiz Yepes, G. (2018). The impact of the host-country language on international adjustment: Spanish engineers in Germany. *Lengua y migración/ Language and Migration, 10*(1), 79-108.

Vilar-Sanchez, K. (2020). Lexical Contact Phenomena Among Spanish Migrants in Cologne. In A. Lynch (Ed.), *The Routledge Handbook of Spanish in the Global City* (pp. 387-405). Milton Park: Routledge.

Visa Barbosa, M., Soto Merola, J. & Rubio Ros, C. (2016). Information treatment of young Spanish emigrants in television news programmes and videos produced by emigrants (2009-2015). *Revista Latina de Comunicación Social, 71*, 1036-1047.

Vogt, K. (2017). The timing of a time out: the gap year in life course context. *Journal of Education and Work, 31*(1), 47-58.

Voivozeanu, A. (2019). Precarious Posted Migration: The Case of Romanian Construction and Meat-Industry Workers in Germany. *Central and Eastern European Migration Review, 8*(2), 85-99.

Vono de Vilhena, D. & Vidal-Coso, E. (2012). The impact of informal networks on labour mobility: Immigrants' first job in Spain. *Migration Letters, 9*(3), 237-247.

Vorheyer, C. (2016). "Transnational mobiles" – Erkenntnisse zu einer (fast) übersehenen Migrationsgruppe. *Österreichische Zeitschrift für Soziologie, 41*(2), 55-79.

Waniek, K. (2012). *Polish Immigrants to Germany. Biographical analysis of narrative interviews with young Polish people who left for Germany between 1989 and 1999*. Lódz: Wydawnictwo Uniwersytetu Lódzkiego.

Waniek, K. (2019). Emigration of Wladek Wisniewski as an escape – a reinterpretation of *The Polish Peasant in Europe and America* volume 3 in the light of the autobiographical narrative interview method. *Przeglad Socjologiczny. Vol. LXVIII* (4), 49-73.

Wassermann, M., Fujishiro, K. & Hoppe, A.K. (2017). The effect of perceived overqualification on job satisfaction and career satisfaction among immigrants: Does host national identity matter? *International Journal of Intercultural Relations, 61*(1), 77-87.

Wengraf, T. (2001). *Qualitative Research Interviewing: Biographic Narratives and Semi-structured Methods.* Sage: London.

Wohl, R. (1979). *The Generation of 1914.* Cambridge, MA: Harvard University Press.

Wood, A. (2020). *Despotism on Demand.* Ithaca and London: Cornell University Press

Wood, A. & Burchell, B. (2014). Zero hour contracts as a source of job insecurity amongst low-paid hourly workers. *ILM Research Report, University of Cambridge.* https://ora.ox.ac.uk/objects/uuid:f115e386-543b-4608-b818-0f3c1dcd4dc4.

World Health Organization (WHO) (2022). *WHO Coronavirus (COVID-19) Dashboard.* https://covid19.who.int.

Worm, A. (2019). *Fluchtmigration. Eine biographietheoretische und figurationssoziologische Studie zu lebensgeschichtlichen Verläufen von Geflüchteten aus Syrien.* https://ediss.uni-goettingen.de/handle/11858/001735-0000-002E-E5DC-F.

Yahirun, J. (2012). Take Me "Home": Return Migration among Germany's Older Immigrants. *International Migration, 52*(4), 231-254.

Yu, K.H. (2019). Negotiating 'otherness' as skilled migrants. *Journal of Industrial Relations, 61*(2), 198-224.

INDEX

Acquiring foreign language skills, 131-132
Alternative economic practices, 140-141, 283 note 2
Argumentation in narrative interviews (extended sequences), 73-74, 105-107, 193-199
Au pair work, 137-140
Awareness context of suspicion, 126, 200

Background constructions, 95-96, 126-127, 152-153, 282 note 7
Basque, self-identification as, 176-177
Becker, Howard S., 52-53
Being othered, 145-149
Biographical action schemes of escape, 80-81
Biographical action schemes of taking control, 61-62, 96-98
Biographical analysis, features and steps of, 54, 236-238, 254-256
Biographical case studies, 57-109, 191-199
Biographical perspective on the 'new' Spanish migration, 21-24, 49-55
Biographical projects, 59-60, 76-77
Biographical rupture, 142-145
Biographical significance of menial labour, 152-154
Biographical work, 266
Brexit, 46-47, 66-67, 74, 89, 189-205, 242-243, 280 note 8

Catalonian, self-identification as, 94, 102, 173, 174-176
CEE citizens' migration, 32-35
Chicago School of Sociology, 55, 238, 245-247
Class distinctions among Spanish migrants, 173-174
Closed awareness context, 126, 283 note 3
Codas at the end of narratives, 73-74, 282 note 4
Collective disenchantment, 201
Collective mood of demoralisation, 116-119
Collective movement, 60-61, 114-115
Communication technology, 166-168, 216-217
(Contemplating) returning (in the literature on the 'new' Spanish migration), 47-49
Covid-19, 13-14, 16, 241-242
Creative metamorphosis, 88, 252

del Corral, Marina, see: Spanish public controversy

'Economic exile', 280 note 10, see: Spanish public controversy
Elias and Scotson, 194, 196-197, 286 note 3
Epistemic force of extempore storytelling, 252-253
Erasmus program (attractions of participating), 112-116

Established-outsider relations, 189-205
Ethnomethodological conversational analysis, 255
EU mobility, phases of, 28-38
European spaces, 63-65
Exchange programmes as pathways into a long-term stay in the receiving society, 133-136

Family obligations, 79, 103, 211-213
Filtered presentation of everyday life, 168-170
Finding participants online, 262-263

'Gastarbeiter' ('guest workers'), 280 note 9, 280-281 note 11, 284 note 9
Gender, 185-187
Generational experiences, 116-117, 119-124, 184-185, 240-241
Goffman, E., 21, 168
Grounded Theory, 23, 55, 236, 227, 255, 267

Health-related problems among migrants, 149-150
History of biographical research, 245-249
History of the research approach, 249-252
'How' vs. 'why' questions, 52-54

Intercultural miscommunication, 147-149
Institutional expectation patterns of the life-course, 79, 252, 211-213
Intra-group tensions in the Spanish community, 173-177

'Juventud sin futuro', see: Spanish public controversy

King, Russell, 28-32, 40, 133, 205, 207-208, 2014, 2020

Lay theorising on 'cultural differences', 179-184

Liquid migration, 202, 239-240, 281 note 2, 288 note 8
Living abroad (in the literature on the 'new' Spanish migration), 41-46
'Lost generation', 14, 117, 279 note 4

Maastricht Treaty, 28-31
Marienthal study, 59, 118-119, 122
'Maroon Wave', see: Spanish public controversy
Mead, George H., 135
Migration statistics, 18
Mills, C. Wright, 24, 52-53
Mini jobs, 142
Motives of migration (in the literature on the 'new' Spanish migration), 38-40

Narrative constraints, 250-251
Narrative interviewing, 250, 253-254, 264-266
Narrative preamble, 57
National tensions among migrants from Spain, 174-177
'New' migration from Spain (statistical estimates: 17-19; in the academic literature: 38-49)
Nursing, 155-158, 191-199

Politeness, 180-183
Precarity, 116-119, 120, 141-145, 149-155
Preparing for the departure (in the literature on the 'new' Spanish migration), 40-41
Presenting analytical findings, 268-271
Professional recognition, 128-131
Resistance at the workplace, 150-152
Return migration, 207-226

Schemes of communication (narration, argumentation, description), 51-55
Schütz, Alfred, 25, 215-217, 287 notes 2 and 3
Schütze, Fritz, 22-23, 249-256
Skilled labour, 155-161
Social media, 170-173, 285 notes 4 and 6

South-North mobility, 35-37, 280 note 7
Spaces of transition, 178-179
Spanish public controversy on the causes of the 'new' migration, 19-21
'Spirit of adventure', see: Spanish public controversy
Strauss, Anselm 23, 55, 236, 227, 255, 267
Structural processes of the life course (institutional expectation patterns, biographical action schemes, trajectories of suffering and losing control, creative metamorphoses), 251-252, 282 note 2

Theoretical sampling, 255, 262
Trajectories of suffering and losing control, 69-70, 78-79, 96, 122-128, 213-214, 252, 288 note 3
Transnational mobiles, 160-161
Transnationalism, 19, 30, 238-239

UK Points-Based Immigration System, 203-204
Unemployment in Spain, 14-16, 59, 279-280 note, 280 note 6
Unskilled labour, 141-155
'Unskilled' skillsets, 154-155

Vocabularies of motive, 52
Voluntary work, 86-87, 161-163, 283 note 2

Waithood, 121, 123, 220
Work experiences in the receiving society, 65-66, 82-83, 85-86, 137-163

Zero-hour contracts, 82-83, 85-86, 141-142

www.ingramcontent.com/pod-product-compliance
Ingram Content Group UK Ltd.
Pitfield, Milton Keynes, MK11 3LW, UK
UKHW021847140426
5217IPUK00022B/1635